Unquenchable Love

Unquenchable Love

Gender, Sexuality, and Theology in Conversation

René Erwich *and*
Almatine Leene

CASCADE *Books* • Eugene, Oregon

UNQUENCHABLE LOVE
Gender, Sexuality, and Theology in Conversation

Cascade Books
An Imprint of Wipf and Stock Publishers
199 W. 8ᵗʰ Ave., Suite 3
Eugene, OR 97401

www.wipfandstock.com

PAPERBACK ISBN: 978-1-6667-7824-3
HARDCOVER ISBN: 978-1-6667-7825-0
EBOOK ISBN: 978-1-6667-7826-7

Cataloguing-in-Publication data:

Names: Erwich, René, author. | Leene, Almatine, author.

Title: Unquenchable love : gender, sexuality, and theology in conversation / René Erwich and Almatine Leene.

Description: Eugene, OR : Cascade Books, 2024 | Includes bibliographical references and index.

Identifiers: ISBN 978-1-6667-7824-3 (paperback) | ISBN 978-1-6667-7825-0 (hardcover) | ISBN 978-1-6667-7826-7 (ebook)

Subjects: LCSH: Sex—Religious aspects—Christianity. | Homosexuality—Religious aspects—Christianity. | Gender identity—Religious aspects—Christianity. | Gender nonconformity—Religious aspects—Christianity.

Classification: BT708 .E80 2024 (paperback) | BT708 .E80 (ebook)

VERSION NUMBER 07/23/24

This book is for Christiaan, Marieke, Areanne, and Rozemarijn Erwich who are everything to me and with whom I could share the relevance of this book in many conversations.

This book is for Sebastiaan, Gideon, and Johanan Bester, because I hope they experience in the future a world that knows more space for open, vulnerable, and informed conversations about sexuality, gender, and theology.

Contents

Preface

Place me like a seal over your heart,
like a seal on your arm;
for love is as strong as death,
its jealousy unyielding as the grave.
It burns like blazing fire,
like a mighty flame.
Many waters cannot quench love;
rivers cannot sweep it away.
If one were to give
all the wealth of one's house for love,
it would be utterly scorned.[1]

THIS BOOK IS TITLED *Unquenchable Love: Gender, Sexuality, and Theology in Conversation*. The title is reminiscent of that ever-fascinating biblical text, Song of Songs, which can be safely called an erotic book. There are many layers that we can discern in Song of Songs, but this beautiful love poetry brings the height, depth, width, and length of love, passion, and desire to the reader's attention in a special way. The beloved (she) calls on her "opposite" to carry her in two places: inside and outside, in the heart and on the arm (or around her neck). She experiences a profound love that is emotionally, but also physically, bound and grounded, anchored even. And together, in the combination of the seal and the imprint in the heart, in the dedication and in the physical wearing, their desire becomes

1. Song 8:6–7 (NIV). Throughout this book, unless otherwise stated, we use the NIV translation.

tangible. Love is like a fire and finds its source in God. Love consumes everything, occupies everything. In fact, you can only surrender to it. So it is with God, too. God is like a fire.[2] Love burns away anything selfish, even fear. It is an unquenchable fire, against which and in which almost nothing can stand. Not even the primal forces of the sea can extinguish it.

Are these words too much, especially at the beginning of a book that also pays attention to the shadowy sides of human sexuality and its brokenness? We could have chosen other texts, yet it is these verses in Song of Songs that make clear what our point of orientation is: anyone who wants to say something meaningful about gender and sexuality (from a Christian perspective) would do well to start with the relationship between God's love for people and the love between people. For all that is beautiful, but also for all the shadows and brokenness of human sexuality, it helps to reflect on the fire that never dies. That fire that is very closely related to God. The current discussions about gender and sexuality, the struggle to find appropriate theological language for the discussion, and the search for connections between sexuality and theology, are attempts to unravel something of that much greater mystery: love itself, the fire of God. At the same time, it is not helpful to rationalize the mystery of love away completely, and that is the starting point of this book.

Conversations about sexuality require thinking space, because before you know it, we are only talking in a moralistic way. If there are discussions at all, in Christian circles, they often focus directly on the physical act of sex, or the perceived boundaries of sexuality, and use cautionary language. In our experience, these conversations are often limited and not particularly in-depth while, in the last century, a lot has changed about how we understand gender and sexuality, and many new scientific insights have been gained. This creates new questions about gender and sexuality, and new practices and perspectives. We think it is important to discuss these different insights. For this reason, we have chosen to interpret the current social context, provide a historical overview, discuss scientific approaches, and share theological insights as our book unfolds. We hope this exploration will clarify—or at least put into proper perspective—the much larger fire, desire, and passion.

2. Deut 4:24; Heb 12:29; Isa 31:9.

What This Book Is and Is Not About

The fact that we characterize this book primarily as an exploration, hoping there will be room for conversation, also implies that we are not going to prescribe what we think should happen; we try to avoid that as much as possible. Of course, we have our own norms and values, and we will not shy away from them further along in the book, but it is not our aim to turn this book into an ethical discourse. Neither of us are ethicists, but we are theologians, admittedly a systemic theologian (Almatine) and a practical theologian (René), so if you are looking for an ethical framework, you will have to go and look elsewhere. We certainly refer to authors and scholarly experts who have something to say about sexual ethics, and it would be foolish not to do so. Consider, for example, Hans De Knijff's still monumental work, *Venus aan de leiband. Europa's erotische cultuur en christelijke sexuele ethiek* [*Venus on a Leash: Europe's Erotic Culture and Christian Sexual Ethics*].[3] Additionally, this does not mean that we will not occasionally give suggestions on what we think might be desirable, but what we mainly want to do is map the terrain and make it possible to navigate this complicated landscape a little easier. In that sense, we prefer to be guides. This book is not aimed at expressing a preference for a particular form of living together, nor is it some kind of apology for marriage. While we both are happily married to our respective spouses, and we both have a positive view of marriage—based on our own theological views of it and in relationship to our ecclesial traditions—this book is not meant to be an apology for a "traditional" Christian view of marriage as such. We see the benefits of Christian marriage in our society but, at the same time, that does not answer all of our challenges—as we will see. If every now and then it turns out that we are stepping into typical pitfalls, it is not because of our generous group of readers, who have offered advice and wise counsel and followed along with us, but because we have decided otherwise for ourselves (and probably for obvious reasons).

As we wrote above, we want to provide space for this theme of love in all its diversity, and with the aim of bringing some order to the existing confusion. We actually hope that what we do here, and in the following chapters, will help people to think through their ministry practices and perspectives, in which a tension between sexuality and theology is visible. So then, a first-aid manual, which instructs us on what to do, how to respond, and how to prevent further harm, this book is not. It is,

3. De Knijff, *Venus aan de leiband*.

however, a very serious attempt to connect a concept that is close to all of our hearts with science, theology, and faith. For us, these are not domains to be kept apart as if they were siloed. We live here and now as people of faith who are, as a colleague once so eloquently put it, "stumbling in the light." Much can go wrong in how we think about and deal with issues around sexuality: with young people, between the young and the old, in churches and religious groups, and in relationships between people of any gender or sexuality. At the end of the day, we are just people on the journey together, finding support with each other and with God. So, this book is primarily an exploration of essential issues to do with sex and theology, and the interconnections between the two.

In Christian Theological Perspective

As far as possible, we position ourselves and our subject matter within a Christian theological tradition and perspective. This is a conscious choice that has to do with our audience. We realize that this may be a narrow perspective, and some of our audience may not recognize themselves in arguments about sexuality, especially ones in which Christian and theological values are regularly included. Nonetheless, we chose this because we believe that there is value in theological reflection on human sexuality, gender, and desire from an explicitly Christian perspective, even though this may be a minority perspective, and which is, therefore, not shared by everyone. We think a dialogue that incorporates values from the Christian tradition can be meaningful even when many people would not necessarily embrace those values. The fact remains (as we will continue exploring in chapter 2) that insofar as we can speak of a history of sexuality, it shares a lot of common ground with Christian norms and values. Looking to this history also shows us that there is an ambivalence or an ambiguity when it comes to faith and sexuality. One broad example from our own study of the history of sexuality is that we discovered if we look carefully at the relationship between church, faith, and theology on the one hand, and sexuality and erotica on the other, it turns out that things have not always gone so badly between those two partners. Sure, much has gone wrong in the history of the relationship between church and sex, but we also learned that it wasn't all doom and gloom either. We think this is an important fact, because it can adjust the often-negative perceptions of the relationship between faith and sex. Human sexuality, in its many manifestations, sways with the waves of culture and society, in every century and everywhere, really. Simply acknowledging this helps to put things in a little perspective, even when new challenges or one-sidedness is lurking today. And it helps to escape the impression that faith and sex are each other's mortal enemies, relating to each other like water and fire. So, we place our story in a Christian perspective and show that we can, perhaps, see very different vistas with one set of theological lenses on than with another.

Who Are We Writing This For?

Initially, we were thinking of a specific target audience of broadly evangelical Christians who want to know more about gender, sexuality, and relationships. Within this, we thought to focus on churches and Christian groups that are willing to wrestle with the complexity of human sexuality and relationships, mainly because they constantly encounter this lived complexity. However, we recognize that people from all walks of life, people of different faiths, or those with no faith, may also wish to read this book. Though sections of it may feel foreign, this book is for them too. Of course, we also write for leaders in church and in society, for example pastors, ministers, and other community leaders who want to read a little more about theological backgrounds to and perspectives on gender and sexuality, and hopefully it can help them to carry these perspectives—this dialogue—into all kinds of circles and groups. It is with these kinds of conversations in mind that we decided to end each chapter with a number of questions for discussion and reflection.

Sources and Framework

In this book, we use a number of sources that have been informative and inspiring for us in different ways. Current literature from different perspectives informs our various chapters. In each chapter, we limit ourselves to the most accessible sources in psychological, theological, and medical research and, where we feel it is necessary, we will sometimes choose to present a brief excursion into a specific theory that helps us to move forward in our thinking. Our starting point in presenting research and theories is that these sources are, in principle, equal conversation partners, contributing to the conversation from different backgrounds and perspectives. And also where it is necessary, we will weigh the evidence of these contributions theologically and show to what extent they are decisive in our view.

Approach and Structure

A complex subject like sexuality makes us want to be careful in our approach. We believe that the basic principles of Richard Osmer's "Four Tasks" model can serve us well in this regard.[4] Osmer, an American practical theologian, focuses mainly on how to shape the development of reflective practices around church and faith. Throughout his book, he refers to practices that can be studied and improved by performing four practical-theological tasks. Each task actually consists of a number of smaller tasks that we need to perform in order to eventually develop a new practice. Each task can be introduced by posing a specific key question, which can then be answered using smaller and larger research tasks. The four tasks function as a kind of circle that we can process and work through.

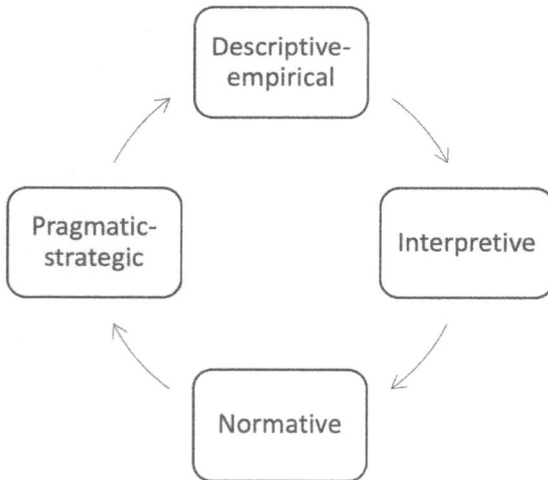

In the schematic figure above, we could move back and forth through the tasks in multiple directions. Though the various chapters in this book mostly deal with one task, that does not exclude input from other tasks. Reality is always more complex and capricious than can be captured in a model. Nevertheless, we think the model does support our goal: to create

4. Osmer, *Practical Theology,* Introduction.

space for further thinking about dealing with gender and sexuality in faith communities, and to discern well between a number of different concepts, and these different tasks, in our communal discussions. Here, we briefly summarize these four tasks and then refer to the chapters in which the various tasks are discussed. In each of the following chapters, we briefly refer back to this approach.

Task	Key question	Activity	Where in this book?
Empirical-descriptive	*What is going on?*	Examine and discern how themes play a role in church and society	Chapter 1 and partially chapter 6
Interpretive	*Why is this going on?*	Use various (scientific) lenses to understand gender and sexuality	Chapters 2 and 3
Normative	*What should be (ideally) going on?*	Apply theological reflection to develop a framework	Chapters 4 and 5, partially chapter 6
Pragmatic-strategic	*What will we do differently in practice?*	How can complex themes be discussed in practice?	Chapter 7

Table 1—Osmer's Four Tasks in this book

In chapter 1, "Introduction: Thinking Space?," we start with an exploration of gender and sexuality in society. In doing so, we also present a brief overview of developments in Christian circles. Furthermore, we give extensive attention to various terms, such as eroticism, intimacy, gender, and sexuality, as well as to intersexuality, transgender, and many other terms. How should we understand these concepts and how do they relate to each other? By using different models, we hope to bring some clarity to the complexity of gender and sexuality. It is our main focus in this chapter to describe this complexity. We do so partly also in chapter 6, but the discussion of the complexity there is mainly with a view to further theological reflection.

In chapter 2, "Gender and Sexuality: A Look into History," we take a look at what could be called the history of sexuality in a nutshell. This serves not only as a cultural-historical overview, but we also take a closer look at the various views on the relationship between faith, religion, and sexuality. We discuss the fragile relationship between the church and sex and, especially, the roots of this fragility. Of great importance, in our opinion, is the role that various core texts from the Bible play in these debates, although we will go into this more specifically in chapter 4. In the next section, we review various themes relating to views on sexuality in antiquity. We continue to trace these themes through the history of the early church, after which we keep tracing them through the Middle Ages. The aim of this brief historical exploration is to develop a sensitivity for a number of themes. We then move on to the worthwhile developments of the Reformation, followed by highlighting salient aspects of the modern era and more recent views in a concluding section. History is thus presented as an important lens through which we search for a better understanding of what is going on today.

Chapter 3, "Gender, Sexuality, and Modern Science," addresses gender and sexuality in relation to recent and emerging scientific insights. Here we look for the various scientific lenses through which we can study gender and sexuality, while keeping as our starting point the central notion that this is foremost and always about people. And we answer questions such as: What theoretical perspectives do different sciences adopt? How do they approach the complex nature of human gender and sexuality? We believe there are good lessons to be learned from these various new scientific insights. We thus continue our second task, which we started in chapter 1, of working to define and understand these concepts and bring clarity to the complexity. We elaborate on the concepts around gender that we introduced in chapter 1 and work on clarifying the terms "gender essentialism" and "gender constructivism." Biological and genetic insights are discussed, along with the role gender variations play. We then describe variations in gender identity and related sexual orientations and expressions. Psychology and neuroscience also receive attention, and we focus on a key question: how do psychology and neuroscience look at human sexuality and gender? Moreover, we show how the phenomenon of human sexuality is approached from anthropological and sociological perspectives. In the final section, we again take stock of where we have landed so far and provide our conclusions for the chapter.

In chapter 4, "Gender and Sexuality in the Bible," we will discuss crucial biblical themes that define the relationship between God, faith, and sexuality. In doing so, we initially zoom in on the ways in which we read the Bible when it comes to sexuality. What perspectives can we discern? We demonstrate how the lenses we use to read the Bible immediately impact our conclusions when discussing sexuality. In a follow-up section, we look at the existing diversity and the bigger picture, particularly in relation to the attention given to the so-called creation order in many discussions. A large number of themes are discussed throughout this chapter. We discuss the visible gender hierarchy in the Hebrew Bible, concepts such as endogamy and exogamy and, of course, the views on gender in the New Testament. Related to these arguments are other topics we discuss, such as divorce, adultery, prostitution, sexual pleasure, purity, and promiscuity. While presenting these themes, we do not avoid questions around homosexuality and homoerotic relationships. We conclude the chapter by focusing on the role a biblical theology can play in supporting a new and transformative perspective. The reading lens we choose in this chapter (i.e., desire as a core concept) constitutes a perspective that we consider of great value in approaching ideals around gender and sexuality. This chapter forms the prelude to a more theological sequel in chapter 5.

In chapter 5, "'Desire' as a Theological Framework for Gender and Sexuality," we initially summarize where we find ourselves after the journey of discovery in the previous chapters. This is a necessary exercise in order to develop a more personal theological vision on sexuality. We do this, once again, in all modesty and contend that it is important to make the connections between a number of key themes, one of which receives extra attention: the connection we see between desire, sexuality, and physicality. We then reframe this into our theological approach, with a more normative perspective on the concept of desire. After introducing this perspective on desire, we address four different paths for theological reflection, and we then choose to combine this with a transformative approach into a trinitarian perspective. We conclude the chapter with a reflection on (sexual) desire as embodied grace. With this, we offer a provisional theological and normative framework for gender and sexuality.

In chapter 6, "Hot Issues," current practices, and continuing complex themes, are central to our discussions, but not without always linking them back to chapter 5 with a brief theological reflection. Throughout this chapter, the following concepts are discussed: polyamory, purity and virginity, issues of sexuality around illness and disability, and sexuality and power and violence, but we also devote space to thinking through the issues of pornography, prostitution, and finally sexual abuse, rape, and incest. Of course, the latter topics require much more time and space than are available to us, but at the same time, we did not want to shy away from these difficult topics or leave them unnamed.

Finally, in chapter 7, "Unquenchable Love: Looking Back and What to Do Next?," we do what the title promises: we take a look back at the ground we've covered and we look forward. What has our journey yielded so far and is it meaningful? What is the harvest? Where do our contributions stand out the most and where do they help the conversation and the people we write about in the book's introduction? And what requires further attention—more than can be provided in the scope of this book and its context of creating a thinking space? In short, we pause, and acknowledge that new challenges will undoubtedly surface. And with these challenges in our hearts and minds, we formulate a number of options for getting started with this book and its themes, and with that we also complete the process Osmer sets out in his "Four Tasks" model (see above).

About Us

Life is full of surprises, twists, and turns. When we started this project in 2016, we had no idea when it would be completed. René's interest in the connections between gender, sexuality, and theology came from the challenges he encountered in the church and in his pastoral practice. He served for many years as a pastor and also later as a lecturer in theology and professor of practical theology. He regularly met with people who became stuck when it came to questions around the relationship between their faith and sexuality, and he certainly also met with people who had questions around gender and identity. These questions were precious and touching but unfortunately, the church seemed insufficiently able to deal with them. Above all, he saw a lot of confusion and embarrassment and quite often rejection and abuse. For Almatine, her experience was no different. In her role as pastor, teacher, and chair of Safe Church, she regularly discussed and drew attention to the issues of gender and sexuality in various ways. So, once we started the conversation, early in 2016, to write this book together, we quickly became excited about the possibilities. Almatine was working from South Africa, and René was at that time in the Netherlands, and we regularly shared texts and talked about our views on crucial parts of the discussion. This book therefore bears quite a few traces of our conversations.

When René emigrated to Australia, where a new task awaited him, we continued the dialogue and in 2019 we even gave a seminar together in Melbourne. In the time that followed, Almatine decided to move back to the Netherlands with her family to make a fresh start as a local church pastor. And then there was the COVID pandemic and all our plans were cruelly disrupted. We had a plan to present the results of our joint work in Stellenbosch. We almost got there, but René had to travel back to Melbourne just before the conference started because the international borders were to be closed. When Almatine moved back to the Netherlands, a busy year awaited her, including her appointment as theologian of the year, and we decided that René would try to finish the book. So, although we shared a lot of conversation and much of the work together, René did a lot of the writing on his own in the final phases, especially in chapters 3, 4, 5, and 6. And, in the end, we managed to finish it together. Finally, a word of thanks to our coreaders, professor Mariecke van den Berg and professor Peter Ben Smit, is in order. They were willing to provide feedback on some of the crucial chapters, and we also thank professor Ruard R. Ganzevoort for his input on a much earlier conceptual stage of the book.[5] A final and special word of thanks is for our initial editor of the English text of this book: Erin M. Hutton. Without her input and wisdom, this book would never have been published.

It is our sincere hope that this book may contribute to many conversations and that these conversations will be conducted from a place of deep respect for each other's views on faith and life, whatever they may look like.

Professor René Erwich and Dr. Almatine Leene
September 2023

---

5. Prof. Dr. C. A. M. van den Berg is professor of feminism and Christianity at the Radboud Universiteit in Nijmegen (The Netherlands). Prof. Dr. Peter Ben Smit is professor of contextual Bible interpretation at the Vrije Universiteit in Amsterdam. Prof. Dr. Ruard R. Ganzevoort was professor of practical theology and dean of the faculty of religion and theology at the Vrije Universiteit in Amsterdam.

1 ——————————————————————

Introduction

Thinking Space?

Confusion about Eros

IT WAS THE BEGINNING of 2022 when more than ten million Dutch people watched the YouTube broadcast of the popular documentary *BOOS*, in which people who had been sexually harassed on the set of the television program *The Voice* spoke up about what they had experienced. John de Mol, who was the longtime director of the program, was given the opportunity to respond. Several people filed charges against well-known Dutch performers Marco Borsato and Ali B, who were members of the jury during the program, as well as against pianist Jeroen Rietbergen. This led to many reactions on various (social) media, and the program was put on hold. Reference was made to the #MeToo movement, which originated in 2006 with Tarana Burke but started trending again in 2017 when actress Alyssa Milano caused a worldwide Twitter storm by posting an appeal to women to come forward if they had been victims of sexual violence and abuse. The result was an explosion of #MeToo posts, which attracted a lot of attention, especially in Hollywood. In a very short time, it became clear once again how far-reaching and widespread the problem of inappropriate sexual behavior and sexual harassment really is. However, the good news is that the silence around sexual violence and abuse was broken and we can only hope that this is the case once and for all. Exactly three years before the revelations of what had been happening on

The Voice of Holland, the public's attention was captured by the Nashville Declaration.[1] Two hundred and fifty men, including a large number of local church ministers, signed this declaration, which stated that sexuality is reserved for marriage between a man and a woman. For a short time, the declaration occupied the collective consciousness of the Netherlands and seemingly everyone had something to say about it. Prime minister Mark Rutte gave his opinion, the leader of the Reformed political party Kees van der Staaij had to defend himself as one of the signatories, and the document was soon called a gay hate manifesto. In the weeks that followed, the reactions to the document confirmed how differently people think about sexuality in Christian circles. In this first chapter, we want to explore the *confusion* around sexuality we observe in Christian circles and beyond, because writing a book about sexuality is closely related to the context in which we live. As indicated in our preface, we will seek to answer the core question "What is going on?" with the aim of focusing on the role sexuality plays in church and society. We then clarify various concepts such as eroticism, sexuality, and intimacy. And finally, we outline what we intend to cover throughout this book when it comes to considering the connection between theology and sexuality.

Eros in Christian Circles

Christianity and sexuality have a difficult history together.[2] Sexuality used to be quite taboo in Christian circles, but this is now changing considerably. It even seems to be enjoying a kind of revival. In 2013, the opinion magazine *De Nieuwe Koers* gave ample space to the theme of sexuality, albeit with some diffidence.[3] In particular, the relationship between love and lust proves a tricky topic when it comes up for discussion. In one of the articles, called the "passion coach," former pastor Marc Angenent asks for space for passion and pleasure and, in fact, calls on Christians to reclaim sex as a good gift of God from the clutches of pornography and one-dimensional eroticism. Guidance and education for young people is included in the magazine too.

---

1. The poor Dutch translation of the original text published by the Council on Biblical Manhood and Womanhood in Nashville, Tennessee.

2. Brown, *God and Grace of Body*, 35–37.

3. *Nieuwe Koers* 2 (2013).

It was this target group—young people—that Esther Kaper had in mind with her book *Hot Issues*.[4] She was looking for a more positive approach to sexuality in the hopes of reducing the often-cramped teaching on sexuality young people receive. Several editions of the book followed, and more titles by other authors with a similar approach appeared, such as *In gesprek over sex, Tussen de lakens* and *PUUR! In balans—Je lust & je leven,* and *Ik wil heel dicht bij je zijn*.[5] On the internet, the Christian erotica website intimitijd.nl has been available since 2012. The website reports: "Our mission is to make sexuality a subject of discussion for Christians in the Netherlands. Sex is made to be enjoyed." On that site you will find "a selection of quality products that can be used to give a new impulse to the intimate time together."[6] The fact that things have changed in recent years is also apparent when the author of the bestseller *I Kissed Dating Goodbye*, Joshua Harris, returns to the book in 2016 saying he regrets writing it and the publisher also admits that, in retrospect, he should not have published it. In the infamous book, the author advises against kissing before marriage, or even dating before marriage, and paints a picture of women who are patient and sexually passive.[7]

That the attention given to sexuality has been placed in a more positive light can also be seen in the stimulating essay by theologian and publicist Frank Bosman, with the significant title *God Loves Sex*. On the one hand, Bosman calls attention to the sex pessimism from which, according to him, the Christian tradition seems to suffer: physicality, femininity, and sexuality "are not automatically approached positively." He presented this view in an interesting online lecture for the University of the Netherlands.[8] On the other hand, he also asks for room for the shadowy side of the experience of sexuality in society: "The Christian tradition is not completely deluded when it points out the dark sides . . ."[9]

Publications warning against these dark sides are everywhere. For example, the American authors Steve Arterburn and Fred Stoeker wrote a book entitled *Every Young Man's Battle: Strategies for Victory in the*

---

4. Kaper, *Hot Issues*.

5. Borger, *In gesprek over seks*; Leman, *Tussen de lakens*; van de Pol-Drent, *Puur!*; Drost-de Wit, *Ik wil heel dicht bij je zijn*.

6. https://intimitijd.nl, translated by the authors.

7. Harris, *I Kissed Dating Goodbye*.

8. Bosman, "Waarom doen christenen."

9. Bosman, "Waarom doen christenen"; translated by the authors.

Real World of Sexual Temptation.[10] The book points out the struggle of young men to survive in a hypersexual culture. And they are not alone in pointing this out. In the US, so-called *purity balls* have been organized in evangelical circles for some years now. After a long period of preparation, young women make the promise of virginity (until marriage) and the fathers of these young women in turn promise to protect their daughters so that they will remain virgins until their marriage. The rituals associated with this, such as the exchange of *purity rings*, are significant. It is worthwhile to take note of these purity balls.[11]

It is safe to say that there is great embarrassment in dealing with the subject of sexuality in various corners of the Christian world. It is clear that the subject is often reduced to ethical questions about what is allowed and what is not, and what is good and what is not. This is also evident from a survey conducted in 2020 by *BEAM*, the youth branch of the Dutch Evangelical Broadcasting Company. A survey completed by 1,700 young people between the ages of twelve and twenty-five shows that almost half of the researched population find it difficult to make personal choices about sex and that there are very different opinions about sex before marriage. It seems that while there is an enormous opportunity to start a conversation around sexuality, it is still taboo, uncomfortable, and misunderstood.

Of course, all of the above examples are not unrelated to developments that have taken place in the West in recent years. While the sexual revolution in the 1960s brought about major changes in how we deal with sexuality, things do not necessarily seem to have become any easier. In his fascinating reflection *How to Think More about Sex,* the well-known philosopher Alain de Botton expresses the great discomfort that characterizes the social approach to sexuality. He characterizes the history of how we deal with sexuality as a path from ignorance and guilt to freedom. He concludes, however, that we have not succeeded sufficiently in feeling truly free. De Botton writes:

> Tame it though we may try, sex has a recurring tendency to wreak havoc across our lives: it leads us to destroy our relationships, threatens our productivity, and compels us to stay up too late in nightclubs talking to people whom we don't like, but

---

10. Arterburn and Stoeker, *Every Young Man's Battle.*

11. See "Purity Balls" and "My Life Inside." Another documentary shows clearly what the questionable sides are of this practice; compare "Virgin Daughters." Also see Gregoire et al., *Great Sex Rescue.*

whose exposed midriffs we nevertheless strongly wish to touch. Sex remains in absurd, and perhaps irreconcilable, conflict with some of our highest commitments and values. . . . We should accept that sex is inherently rather weird instead of blaming ourselves for not responding in more normal ways to its confusing impulses. This is not to say that we cannot take steps to grow wiser about sex. We should simply realize that we will never entirely surmount the difficulties it throws our way. Our best hope should be for a respectful accommodation with an anarchic and reckless power.[12]

Whether liberal or conservative, religious or secular, sexuality by its very nature continues to unleash both constructive and destructive forces on us all. But does de Botton's resigned and almost defeatist approach have it covered? On the contrary, for it could lead to a situation where we no longer have to deal with our incapacity or confusion when it comes to sex. In any case, we would no longer have to pay attention to these problems, because things are the way they are, and we have to make the best of it. This is precisely why a solid theological reflection on sexuality is so necessary. But how can we do that in a constructive way? Before we can answer that question, we need to discuss what exactly we mean by these various concepts.

Definitions, Concepts, and Terminology

This book deals with various interrelated concepts. Therefore, we think it is good to pause here and discuss what we mean by terms like eroticism, sexuality, gender, and intimacy, and how these concepts relate to each other.

Eros and Sex

Driving on the motorway near Cape Town (when we wrote this chapter, Almatine was still living in South Africa), you come across a building called "Eros school." On enquiry, it turns out that it is a school for the care and guidance of the disabled, and the name "Eros" is an abbreviation. Perhaps it is not the best abbreviation, since the Greek word refers to the ancient Greek god of love and sexual desire. The word "erotic" is derived from this word (for more details see chapter 5). At the very least,

---

12. De Botton, *How to Think*, 5–6.

the name "Eros" for a school causes some confusion. However, confusion about eroticism is much greater than the name of this school suggests. The perceptions of and ideas about what eroticism is, is of course determined by culture and time. A random scientist would give a different description to, say, a photographer, or the director of an erotic film. According to the Merriam-Webster dictionary, eroticism refers to an erotic theme or quality, a state of sexual arousal, or an insistent sexual impulse or desire. In any case, it is not always clear what is included and what is not. How, for example, does eroticism relate to sexuality and intimacy? Sophie de Wijn, author of, among other books, *Verkering na je zestigste* [Dating after your sixtieth], says: "Sexuality is the engine of life. Eroticism is the fuel on which that engine runs, and intimacy is the station where the fuel can be obtained."[13] This makes a clear distinction, but it does not tell us exactly what the engine looks like or what kind of fuel we are talking about.

The term "sexuality" should not be confused with the term "sex," which generally refers to a more biological term often used to indicate whether someone is genetically a man or a woman.[14] In common parlance, the term "sex" often refers to "having sex," which, as research shows, can also have a wide range of meanings and is not just limited to sexual intercourse.[15] The fact that a definition is not so easy to give, is at least partially because in Europe and in many other parts of the world, too, it is still taboo to talk about eroticism and sexuality, and yet at the same time we find unashamed referrals to sex in very many places.

At first glance, the latter certainly seems to be the case in the Netherlands. This is best illustrated in the world-famous *Red Light District* (De Wallen), a neighborhood in Amsterdam where an average of seven hundred scantily clad women wait for their next client behind approximately four hundred windows. Because the Netherlands is one of the few countries in the world where prostitution has been legalized, this district has become an attraction for millions of tourists every year. By the way, you don't have to travel to Amsterdam to experience this reality. A simple visit to almost any bookstore makes it possible to come into contact with an endless variety of magazines and books promoting erotica. In October

13. De Wijn, *Verkering na je zestigste*, 23.

14. In this book we frequently refer to the standard work of Lehmiller, *Psychology of Human Sexuality*.

15. We also frequently refer to Carroll, *Sexuality Now*; and Thatcher, *God, Sex, and Gender*.

2015, *Linda* magazine featured the "girls of pleasure" in a winking and lighthearted way. Linda de Mol herself appears on the cover in suspenders, with a suggestive red light in the background. The magazine does not romanticize the sex industry and offers plenty of space for the dark side of prostitution. Of course, it is not the case that a themed special issue is necessary to discuss sexuality, because it pops up in every edition of the monthly magazine.

The same applies to many other magazines. Everything from television to car magazines use terms and illustrations that refer to desire and erotica. Sex sells. It's even used in the advertising of ice cream. Still, the scope of books and magazines is small compared to that of the internet. EDC Internet Ltd., an erotica wholesaler, has a turnover of EUR 10 million per year. Over 12 percent of all internet pages are dedicated to pornography and every second some thirty thousand internet users watch it. And we are not even talking about dating and relationship sites.

The internet has caused a revolution with regard to sexuality. A study by Rutgers and Soa Aids Nederland, entitled *Sex Under Age 25*, shows that social media and the internet have caused a shift in the starting age for sexual experiences. In an article in national newspaper *NRC Next*, researchers report a surprising fact: despite the proliferation of many dating apps and the incidence of "sexting," young people have started having sex later in their lives than five years ago. "In 2012, half of the young people in the Netherlands had had sexual intercourse by the age of 17.1, compared to 18.6 now. Also, young people have engaged in other sexual activity, such as oral sex, at least a year later."[16] These new results are probably at odds with the widespread opinion that young people are "sexually indiscriminate" and engage in all kinds of experimentation without restraint. Eros has long ceased to be direct physical contact between people because the ubiquity of the internet means eros may be experienced at a distance. *"Sex is everywhere,"* wrote Brenot and Coryn in the comic book *The Story of Sex* in 2016, and they have a point.[17] By the way, the comic book is delightfully disarming, because it manages to approach such a complex theme with humor.

---

16. Borrel, "Jongeren beginnen later met seks"; translated by the authors.
17. Brenot and Coryn, *Story of Sex*.

Changes in Culture and Society with Regard to Sexuality

Indeed, sex is everywhere. Is adaptation, like de Botton suggests, to this complex force enough? Is the sexual revolution really complete and is everything back in balance? Love, sex, and romance remain risky topics and their impact on relationships is perhaps greater than ever before. You don't have to be a pessimist to think that broad cultural experimentation with sex has led to some problems.[18] We see a trail of relational debris, and often with consequences, for example, for children who witness the relationship breakdowns. This is not necessarily about marriage break-down as an isolated phenomenon. It is part of the bigger question of the impact from the fact that sex is everywhere and affecting individuals and groups. Is this a kind of cultural deformity? To answer this question, Jonathan Grant, pastor of a large Anglican church in Auckland, New Zea-land, takes the formative power of a person's cultural context as his start-ing point. Referring to Charles Taylor's book *Modern Social Imaginaries*, he concludes that the secular understanding and practice of sexuality is deeply rooted in the social life of Christians.[19] People's self-images are so deeply imbued with secular notions that they are no longer equipped to live devotedly, particularly in relation to their sexuality. Grant contends that the church is myopic: it does point out the importance of the Bible, but it has insufficient insight into the impact the dominant culture and its values have on people, especially when it comes to themes concerning identity and sexuality. Grant thus claims there is a disconnect between culture and faith. If we understand him correctly, the reflection of bibli-cal values and norms does not sufficiently influence secular values and norms. People suffer from an expressive individualism: the expression and experience of one's own values and norms are in the foreground, with their main concern being romantic and authentic. Sexuality, then, is par-ticularly suited to the actualizing and developing of the self.[20] Emotional intuition, according to Grant, then serves as a person's moral compass, and the waning of sexual desires and feelings is a sign to end a relation-ship and begin a new one.

Grant sees four profound moral changes occurring that have to do with sexuality, especially among young people: first, the rise of sexuality as something intrinsically good and almost separate from relationships,

18. Bosman, *God houdt van seks*; and Grant, *Divine Sex*.

19. Grant, *Divine Sex*, 21–31.

20. Grant, *Divine Sex*, 30–31.

but also, second, the seemingly new ideal in which men and women have sex as equal partners and in all kinds of gender roles (see chapter 3). Third, he sees the widespread idea that sexuality belongs to a liberation from authority, and fourth, a kind of moral shift where sexuality is now one of the most crucial parts of personal identity.[21] This latter notion seems to have an almost paradoxical effect in practice because, on the one hand, there is talk of this ideal, and on the other hand, young people experience great difficulty with really connecting in intimate relationships.[22] Grant is inspired by the research of anthropologist Helen Fisher, who describes romantic love (and especially the emphasis on authenticity) as an addiction.[23] Fisher argues that there are three phases to romantic love: obsession during early romantic love, sexual intimacy, and deep personal connection. MRI studies carried out by Fisher showed that the first phase (falling in love) mainly occurs in the "engine" of our brain, which takes care of our basic needs. This "obsession" stage has much the same effect on our brain "engine" as cocaine! Fisher calls this the *infatuation drug*: falling in love becomes something like ecstasy. This phase, however, is short-lived. The second phase is the experience of *bonding* in a sexual sense. In this phase there is strong sexual attraction and a physiological reaction to sex, during which neurotransmitters such as dopamine and oxytocin ensure a deep emotional bond. According to Fisher, this also explains why there is no such thing as "ordinary sex" without emotion.[24] The third and final phase is that of a deep relational connection and security that can be felt with a long-term partner.

There is undoubtedly much that can be said for Grant's description of romantic love, but we may wonder whether many of today's problems can be solved with the remedy he recommends for it. We have found that further analysis of Grant's view of authenticity is necessary because it is too generalized. We think Grant goes too far when he states that our modern culture's emphasis on romantic love has become the moral background against which everything relating to human sexuality and relationships is viewed.[25] Moreover, Christian authenticity is presented too quickly as the remedy, and we find ourselves left asking: what exactly

21. Grant, *Divine Sex*, 37.

22. Grant, *Divine Sex*, 38.

23. Grant, *Divine Sex*, 39–42; Grant refers to the research of Fisher in Fisher et al., "Romantic Love," 361.

24. Grant, *Divine Sex*, 40.

25. Grant, *Divine Sex*, 47.

does (his vision of) Christian authenticity look like and does it not also involve the presence of cultural values? This approach does not seem whole or right to us. Hence, in chapter 3, we will discuss this in more detail when we look at the greatly increasing number of medical and biological facts and discoveries, from various scientific disciplines, that we must work to understand to formulate a theology of sexuality.

Grant sees a broad social movement in which sexuality has become separated from relationships and marriage, and sees this as proof that sex is primarily regarded as a consumer product.[26] Sex has become part of the entertainment industry, with an emphasis only on short-term connections between people. People live their lives in fragments and compartments, and the entertainment industry plays on this. Grant adds to this the major influence of social media and digital technology, which he contends makes a certain kind of connection possible between people, but not with a community.[27] There is indeed evidence of this "hyper-connection" and he rightly asks questions about what this entails and, especially, what this means for human sexuality (see chapter 6 for more discussion of this).

It is clear that the nature of relationships is changing, and so are the ways in which people enter into relationships. Online dating is standard and there seems to be, ironic as it may sound, great confidence in what the underlying algorithms can do to select the right partner. Grant claims that research shows 80 percent of people who date online give disinformation in their personal profiles.[28] If that is true, it is a very worrying percentage. Be that as it may, Grant is certainly not positive about the general social trends around relationships and sexuality. He believes that the combined effect of a cultural emphasis on authenticity and postmodern thinking has created a tendency toward hypersexuality. The result is a hypersexual self: sexuality divorced from who people really are, sex as a kind of natural hunger or sex as "fast food," sex as something to make us happy—but meaningless sex leaving feelings of emptiness, and porn as the ultimate sexual educator.[29]

26. Grant, *Divine Sex*, 80.
27. Grant, *Divine Sex*, 85–91.
28. Grant, *Divine Sex*, 91.
29. Grant, *Divine Sex*, 96–100.

Gender and Sexuality

When we talk about sexuality, the concept of gender comes up automatically. If you think about it for a moment, you may soon come to the conclusion that sex and gender are not just about the biological side of things. We know that people are more than their biological "make-up," no one will deny that. At the start of January 2017, a thematic issue of *National Geographic* appeared with the title "Man/Woman: Identity in a Changing World." The issue called attention to the major changes in how we talk about and understand gender identity. What about the traditional man-woman split? Does it still exist? What influence do changing ideas about gender have on the experience of being a man or a woman and on the practice and perception of sexuality? The studies presented ranged from the influence of classic Disney cartoons on the self-perception of boys and girls, to explorations of gender dysphoria and incongruence (when a person's gender identity is different to the sex they were assigned at birth). We may also be familiar with Caster Semenya's story, the South African athlete who has been a world champion several times. Semenya is an intersex woman assigned female at birth. She was asked to undergo sex verification testing, physiologically has more than three times the amount of testosterone than the average woman, and very publicly experienced racism and sexism. In the Netherlands, there are approximately eighty thousand people born with an anatomy that does not conform to the expected norms for male and female bodies. Margriet van Heesch completed a PhD on the study of sex variations. In her thesis, she draws attention to the various stories and experiences of people who are intersex. For example, Liselot:

> Liselot was four years old when she had her first operation. It was in the mid-1970s. She does not remember the operation well, but she does remember being told later that it had "something to do with groin ruptures, some things were sewn up and taken out." She also remembers being told when she was about ten years old that she did not have a uterus. Later, she would have to take pills to make her breasts grow. "If it's that easy," she had responded, "then give me a penis." She thought: "If there were pills for breasts, there must be pills for penises too." Or, perhaps, "these things could be glued on," she had thought. Her parents had mentioned her wishes to a concerned doctor, but as "something like that would only work partly," he advised against it. Her plans to play basketball and ride a moped were

also thwarted. She later learned that the doctors had advised her parents to raise her "unequivocally as a girl."[30]

Van Heesch was particularly interested in the absence of stories of Dutch people with gender variation, so she went on to investigate this in her studies. As it turns out, there are many stories of people who discovered they are intersex, and that there are many gender variations other than "male" and "female." This casts a different light on what is generally considered to be the male and female binary and adds to the complexity of our discussions. Much of the perceived difficulty in conversations and debates about human sexuality can be traced back to a lack of clarity about what we mean when we use terms like masculine and feminine and male and female.

The South African report "Diversity in Human Sexuality"[31] illustrates the different layers of what is referred to as the gender spectrum. But to what extent does this help us to clarify the use of such terms, in a debate that is already complex and multilayered. To begin with, the image below provides clear divisions between the categories of gender identity, gender expression, biological sex, and sexual orientation. These clarifications will certainly help us to do justice to each of these concepts, but also to people and the way in which they experience and express their gender and sexuality.

At first look, these classifications provide more clarity about the different concepts we are dealing with. But in fact, this approach is still based on a binary understanding in which extremes play a normative role: man versus woman, male versus female, heterosexual versus homosexual, etc. The more fluid nature of gender and sexuality (more complex, with more and different gender identities and sexual orientations) is not reflected in this.

---

30. Van Heesch, *Ze wisten niet of ik een jongen of een meisje was* [They did not know whether I was a boy or a girl], 9. Chapter 3 takes a more in-depth look at this study.

31. "Diversity in Human Sexuality." Compare the detailed report of the Academy of Science of South Africa.

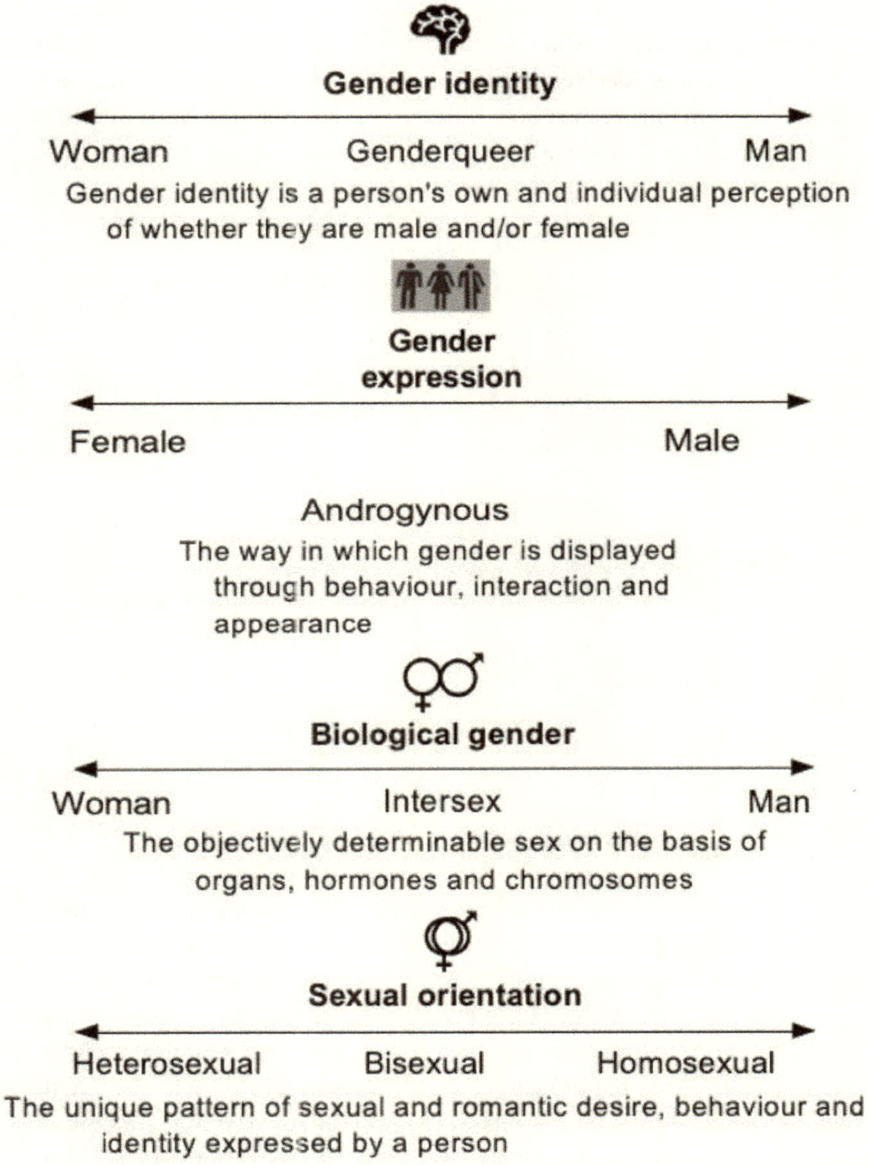

Gender identity

Woman　　　　　Genderqueer　　　　　Man

Gender identity is a person's own and individual perception
of whether they are male and/or female

**Gender
expression**

Female　　　　　　　　　　　　　　Male

Androgynous

The way in which gender is displayed
through behaviour, interaction and
appearance

Biological gender

Woman　　　　　Intersex　　　　　Man

The objectively determinable sex on the basis of
organs, hormones and chromosomes

Sexual orientation

Heterosexual　　　Bisexual　　　Homosexual

The unique pattern of sexual and romantic desire, behaviour and
identity expressed by a person

Figure 1. Source: "Diversity in Human Sexuality," 17.

Sam Killermann's popular publication is interesting and useful for us in this context.[32] Killermann, who describes himself as a multidisciplinary artist and comedian, wants his book to contribute to social justice in society. His *genderbread person* is very popular on the internet.[33] Although it remains unclear how Killermann came up with his model, it is a fun, simple, and accessible way to help us understand gender.

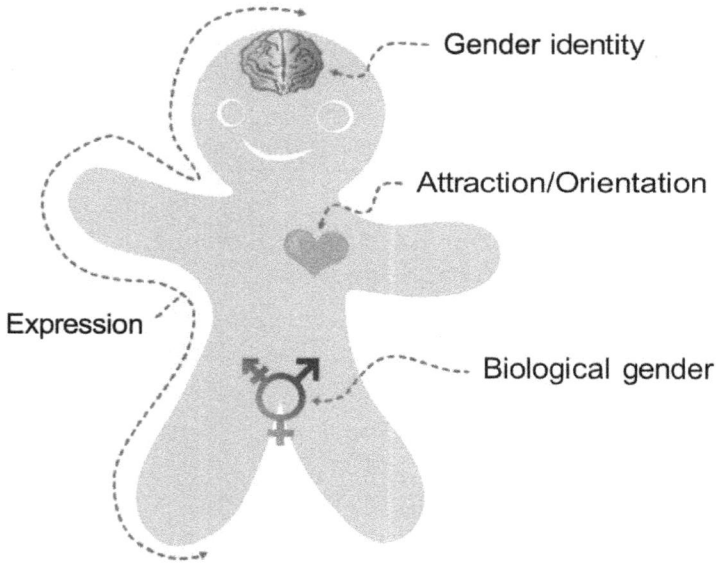

Figure 2. Source: Killermann, "Genderbread Person."

Killermann explains that he is convinced that people do not position themselves along a scale (as depicted in Figure 2) for the different layers or dimensions of their identity, but that they can perhaps be positioned through the different layers. He even goes a step further by stating that gender identity, gender expression, (biological sex or biological) gender, and sexual (and romantic) attraction are independent of each other. With his approach, Killermann wants to draw attention to what the literature calls binary thinking about male and female. Binary thinking refers to the existence of only two genders, male and female, whereby everyone can be classified in one of these two categories without exception. This

32. Killermann, *Guide to Gender.*
33. Killermann, "Genderbread Person."

binary thinking can also be found in the wider debate on sexuality. It not only defines what is male/masculine and female/feminine, but also determines what role expectations (behavior, including sexuality and the experience of it) are culturally attached to it and who can or may attract whom. Killermann sees gender identity (see illustration) primarily in the way in which we interpret our own "chemical make-up" (hormone levels, etc.) inside. It also has to do with the social roles people take on as men or women, or somewhere in between the two.

Gender expression refers to the way people show gender (in society, sometimes based on traditional roles), by the way they act, dress, and enter into relationships. There is a middle position, which Killermann and others refer to as androgynous (a person who expresses or presents their gender in a way that cannot be clearly distinguished), which is an ambiguous mix of the two opposite poles. Biological sex refers to the objectively observable biological and genetical make-up of a person, with regard to internal and external sex organs and chromosomes. On the corresponding spectrum, an intersex position is indicated as well as male and female, because intermediate situations do exist. For example, someone can be born with a penis (which is visible externally), but with a functional female internal reproductive system at the same time.

Finally, the genderbread person shows a spectrum associated with sexuality and sexual orientation (and attraction). In the classical sense, this is indicated by the terms "heterosexual" for people who feel attracted to the opposite sex, and "homosexual" for people who feel attracted to the same (their own) sex. Sexual orientation then has to do with who we feel attracted to physically, emotionally, and spiritually, based on our own gender position. Again then, according to Killermann, this is a continuum on which bisexual (and other) orientations are possible.

Killermann's proposal is thought-provoking. His approach, as portrayed above, opens up the discussion to other ways of looking at gender and sexuality. It is a theory that is widely embraced, such as by the Rutgers Foundation. However, the genderbread person has also been heavily criticized. Tineke van der Waal, for instance, discusses what she suspects is the reasoning behind it.[34] In a newspaper article, van der Waal immediately refers to the thoughts behind the genderbread person as "gender ideology." With an appeal to the Canadian neuroscientist and sexologist Debra Soh, she rejects the approach, claiming it is not based on facts. It is a myth, says van der Waal, that there are more than two genders. It is a

---

34. Van der Waal, "Kinderen krijgen les in nieuwe genderideeën."

myth, she says, that sexual orientation and gender identity are separate. Van der Waal opts for a strictly biological approach and, according to her, gender is strictly biologically determined. She contends that we should take a sober look at the occurrence of gender dysphoria. According to van der Waal, gender dysphoria often occurs in children, who may grow out of it. The fact that there are girlish boys and boyish girls is not a problem and it does not mean that they are transgender. Van der Waal does not seek to talk to other (neuro)scientists, but concludes that there is no biological-scientific basis for gender diversity. She believes that gender dysphoria is actually a psychiatric condition, often, she says, diagnosed as a disorder on the autism spectrum.

We cannot escape the impression that the heteronormative perspective taken here blocks all chances for an open discussion, and it does not do justice to, for example, people who are intersex. Moreover, it is bad practice that all kinds of other work and opinions present in (neuro) science, the medical community, and broader social discourses have not been heard. Van der Waal's conclusions, therefore, are dangerous, because they easily lead to the stigmatization of people who really do suffer from gender dysphoria. We think it is good practice to take Killermann's explanation seriously, if only because these broader spectrums apply to so many people. Of course, the nexus of gender and human sexuality we are at is complex, but that is not a good argument for avoiding the complexity altogether or avoiding the discussion as a whole.

Turning to another publication, we encounter once again a resistance to what is being called "gender ideology." According to Reverend C. P. de Boer, gender ideology dominates debate in church and society, especially the belief in "God as Father in a world dominated by men."[35] The problem with this view of "gender ideology" is that it does not do justice to the broader context in which scientists usually speak about sex and gender. "Gender ideology" manifests itself primarily where the traditional male-female relationship is not embraced, or where people present themselves as nonbinary or genderqueer, for example. From a scientific point of view, the study of gender ideology mainly focuses on describing the cross-cultural similarities and differences in the vision of what male, female, and other identities are. This view can therefore focus on a binary understanding of gender (as in the two newspaper articles mentioned above with an appeal to biographical data), but also on a much more

35. Boer, "Genderideologie."

flexible understanding of gender (with a stronger appeal to gender as something that develops and is formed culturally). In the two articles mentioned, "gender ideology" is mainly seen as a threat, and discussions about scientific insights (including historical ones) were dismissed as irrelevant. We will return to these scientific insights and to Debra Soh's views in chapter 3.

In this book, we use a number of key terms that will come up again and again. In the table below, we have listed these terms and provided them with a short explanation.

Concept	Description
Gender	A psychosocial term that refers to the psychological, cultural, and social characteristics we think belong to men and women.
Gender identity	A person's own and individual perception of whether they are male and/or female.
Gender roles	A set of cultural norms and values that determine how people of a specific gender should behave.
Gender role conformity	Refers to the extent to which gender expression conforms to the prescribed cultural values and norms for a particular gender.
Gender stereotyping	Generalized beliefs about the qualities and characteristics of men and women.
Gender expression	The way gender is displayed through behavior, interaction, and appearance.
Gender diversity	Variations in gender expression, which can be found in the historically imposed binary thinking about man and woman.
Binary thinking	(With regard to sexuality is) oppositional thinking about gender, sex, male, and female.
Gender dysphoria	An experience of "mismatch" between one's physical sex and gender identity.
Genderqueer	The umbrella term for gender identities that are not exclusively male or female (bigender, trigender, polygender, etc.).
Biological gender or biological sex	The "objectively" determinable sex based on organs, hormones, and chromosomes.
Sexual orientation	The unique pattern of sexual and romantic desire, behavior and identity that a person expresses.
Heteronormativity	Refers to a privileged position associated with heterosexuality, which is based on the normative assumption that there are only two genders, that gender (as assigned at birth) always determines (biological) sexual orientation, and that only sexual attraction between these two opposing genders should be considered normal.

Concept	Description
LGBTQI	An abbreviation referring to lesbian, gay, bisexual, transgender, and intersex. The first three (LGB) are used to refer to the sexual orientation/identity of persons, the T stands for a specific gender identity, and the I for a biological variant. In much literature, these are clustered together because of experiences of exclusion and discrimination. Much literature now speaks of LGBTQ, referring to other queer identities (cf. above).
Intersex	The term that refers to a variety of genetic, physiological, and anatomical characteristics that do not correspond to the predominant and typical definitions of male and female.
Transgender	The term for people who have a gender identity that differs from the sex that was assigned at birth; the experienced gender identity does not coincide with the birth sex.

Table 2—Terminology—gender and sexuality

Later in this book, we will zoom in on the meaning of these concepts and return to the definitions described above where necessary.

Theological Reflection on Sexuality

In the last part of this first chapter, we are already anticipating what is to come: a more substantive look at history, which ultimately serves as a prelude to a number of theological reflections. The latter is certainly not a matter of course. According to Elizabeth Stuart, reflection and theorizing about sexuality from a theological perspective is a fairly new phenomenon.[36] Stuart notes that a certain fatigue is felt in discussions; think for example of the many fierce debates about homosexuality. This can be caused by the fact that there is a lot of emotion involved and the arguments are often already presumed to be known.

Anyone who wants to think about sexuality from a theological perspective would do well to say something about the various sources from which this happens and to be aware of the emotions involved. Our starting point is the need to consider our own experience, the traditions in which we stand, science, and also the Bible, with each other. In doing so, we are aware that we bring our own prejudices and assumptions with us, but we want to try to clarify them honestly as much as possible (see the foreword). It is a risky adventure we have embarked on, but we feel that

36. Stuart, "Theological Study of Sexuality," 18–31.

we should not shy away from the challenge, because of the importance that sexuality has in society and especially for Christian communities. Theology is above all a "logic of hope" that aims to contribute to a life of wisdom. It is about discerning and understanding people's pain, hope, suffering, and joy, and the art of connecting this to the reality of God and God's love.[37] By definition, it must be a theology that initiates into *the kingdom of the impossible.*[38] From this perspective, we want to relate the Bible, experience, history, and science to each other, in order to create a mental space in which we can shape our view of sexuality. For us, it is clear that a careful discussion of gender and sexuality requires a new way of thinking. This involves raising some very difficult issues and we need to be prepared to think about them honestly, even if this is sometimes against our grain. In this sense, we ourselves have experienced many a surprise, for example when we were confronted with a completely different possible reading of groups of biblical texts, or when neurological insights disrupted our own thinking about gender. In the remainder of this chapter, we will give the reader a few previews of this, to be discussed in more detail later on. But before delving a little deeper into history in the next chapter, we will briefly discuss the historical context of the "two-sex theory" as it strongly manifests itself today. It is also important to note that we do not claim to have the last word on a theology of sexuality. We present our framework here in a very provisional form.

For a long time, the standard view has been that there are only two genders: male and female. In the context of society, and certainly within religious and church frameworks, people seem content with this two-sex theory. And with a reference to Genesis 1:27 (NIV)—"So God created mankind in his own image, in the image of God he created them; male and female he created them"—it is not surprising that we find there are also two sexes; it all seems quite clear. But could it be more complex than this? And is there, perhaps, room for the idea that there are more than two distinct sexes? In antiquity, the idea was that there were not two sexes, but only one sex, and that sex was called "man."[39] We will return to this in detail in chapter 4, when we look at specific biblical texts; here is just a short excursion. In any case, anyone who looks at this verse cannot

37. Erwich, "Practical Theology," 40.

38. Halík, *Nacht van de biechtvader*, 34.

39. This was the dominant view in antiquity. See Thatcher, *God, Sex, and Gender*; and Thatcher, *Redeeming Gender*.

fail to notice that the male perspective is the starting point, if not only in the many songs and liturgies of the Christian tradition.

In fact, this is a form of sexism, the favoring of one sex over another, and it has had—and is still having—a profound impact. There was a "one-sex theory" very much present in antiquity. The Greek physician Galen (129–216 BC) believed that men and women had the same sex organs, with the difference being that women had them on the inside and men had them on the outside. According to him, the female scrotum was hidden on the inside. For Aristotle (384–22 BC), it was quite clear that the father was responsible for the form of the conceived child and the mother for its "content." She, after all, provided the child with *materia*, content, in the womb—this is still reflected in the Latin word for mother, *mater*. The male—and deemed more perfect—sperm was the carrier of the life-soul, and the hotter the ejaculation, the greater the chance that the new world citizen would be a man. Female menstrual blood was seen as responsible for the child's content during pregnancy. Pregnant women did not menstruate because they needed the blood to nourish the developing child in the womb. The purpose of sex was to have children, the female orgasm was not necessary, and in many cases was even thought to be better avoided.[40] Men were *hot*, women were *cool*. The male heat was a symbol of strength, and the female coolness of softness of weakness.

This short historical excursion (see chapter 2 for more context) already gives a very different picture and different nuance to how we think about gender and sexuality, and often we are not aware of this history. This approach helps us to look behind the scenes of our own modern conceptions of the two "opposite" sexes, which tend to place everyone at one end or the other of the continuum. There appeared to be a single spectrum from male to female, which was strongly related to power, virtue, status, and, last but not least, temperature! And if there is only one sex, any discussion about the equality of the sexes is *a priori* nonsensical, because there are not two sexes, there is only one sex. Being a man or a woman is then primarily an achievement related to the social and cultural influences one is subjected to. However, there were no guarantees. Whoever behaved unmanly at any time could lose his "manhood" in a social sense.[41] In times of new emphasis on what is and is not "masculine" and "feminine," this provides new insights.

40. Laqueur, *Making Sex*, 35–37.
41. Conway, *Behold the Man*, 15–34.

If you look at history, as we just briefly did, but also at all the scientific discoveries that are being made in our time, you could get quite confused. What, then, is a responsible way to deal with sexuality and how do we define concepts like "masculinity" and "femininity" from a theological point of view, while taking scientific insights seriously? We cannot understand sexuality if we do not take its various aspects into account. Human sexuality refers to a fundamental part of the personality, through which and in which we experience our own connectedness with ourselves, others, the world, and God. In the context of all this complexity, Adrian Thatcher offers us an appealing and useful definition of sexuality:

> Sexuality especially involves the powers or capacities to form deep and lasting bonds, to give and receive pleasure, and to conceive and bear children. Sexuality can be integral to the desire to commit oneself to life with another, to touch and be touched, and to love and be loved. Such powers are complex and ambiguous. They can be used well or badly. They can bring astonishing joy and delight. Such powers can serve God and serve the neighbor. They also can hurt self or hurt the neighbor. Sexuality finds expression at the extreme ends of human experience: in love, care, and security, or lust, cold indifference, and exploitation. Sexuality consists of a rich and diverse combination of relational, emotional, and physical interactions and possibilities. It surely does not consist solely of erotic desire.[42]

This broader definition does justice to our intentions, because we want to place human sexuality, with its ambiguous character, in a broader—and subsequently also mainly theological—framework, without wanting to design an ethic. When thinking about sexuality, Christians are often tempted to determine what is and is not allowed, that is, where the boundaries are. But in doing so, they almost always immediately choose a starting point that also determines the outcome. Usually, that is marriage. We think this is too limited. Thinking about sexuality requires an approach that does justice to the breadth and complexity of the whole phenomenon we call sexuality. This cannot be done without properly and clearly defining the concepts we are talking about. We cannot do this without taking an honest look at the cultural fluctuations that affect how we think about human sexuality. As we shall see, the ripples of time have an enormous influence on what we shall call the "sexuality script," i.e., the

---

42. Evangelical Lutheran Church in America, "Social Statement on Human Sexuality," quoted in Thatcher, *God, Sex, and Gender*, 202.

body of normative principles that determines our behavior and what we see as good and bad in it. Especially for Christian communities of faith, this approach seems to be helpful in discerning what is really important, in the church and especially in pastoral counselling of people who have questions about sexuality. At the same time, we do not want to avoid the various difficult concepts and theories. The fact is that many churches struggle to work through issues with homosexuality, and have many questions about gender and people who are transgender. How can we best contend with the increased sexualization in society, in what has been called a kind of sexual marketplace (cf., our discussion of Grant above)?

The approach that we choose in this book is one in which theology, faith, and science are always closely related to each other, as we have out-lined above. This requires room for thought and openness to other views, because the seeming ease with which all kinds of scientific discoveries are used, in all areas of life, does not seem to apply to the domain of sexuality and relationships, and that can feel alienating. What is the significance of much of the research into forms of expression of sexuality? Do medi-cal and psychological science have anything to offer us here, or does it not suit us, because we might have to adjust our views? In short, we ask for maximum (mental) space to get the conversation going properly and going well. Our starting point is that religion, God, faith, theology, and sexuality (in no particular order) are interrelated.

In a beautiful essay entitled "The Body's Grace," former Anglican archbishop Rowan Williams provides the direction in which we want to go.[43] Williams tells his story by means of another story: Paul Scott's *Raj Quartet*. In this novel series, the main characters experience the tragic side of human sexuality. Scott's protagonist, Sarah, discovers love and sexuality. She notices (in addition to all the disappointment) how much her body is the cause of happiness for herself and for the one she loves. Williams typifies this experience as a form of grace: knowing yourself as desirable and meaningful. And so it is with the whole history of creation, incarnation, and our incorporation into the body of Christ, according to Williams. This whole history of creation tells us again and again that God desires us. We are made so that we will find, over and over again, that we may "grow into" the same triune God who loves us. For Williams, this fact is fundamental when it comes to human relationships: there is an analogy between God's desire to love us, to be desired by God, and the

43. Williams, "Body's Grace," 309–21.

desire of people to actually desire each other, love each other, and be a reason for joy for each other. Williams wants to connect this theological rationale with human sexuality. In a sexual relationship, Williams says, there is a sense in which I am no longer in charge of who I am. Every real experience of desire puts me in the position of not being able to satisfy my own needs without distorting them. Right now, in this experience, there is an enormous helplessness of my own self. If I want to be the cause of joy with my body, then I have to be there for the other with my body, so that I can be perceived, accepted, nourished. When I am focused on the joy and desire of the other, my surrender becomes loving. Longing for my joy means longing for the joy of the one for whom I long. In such a surrender lies grace, the grace of the body. In this way, Williams gives human sexuality, and the desire that goes with it, a theological basis: God and sex are connected, with desire as the basic motive. This will be discussed in more detail later, when we look at gender and sexuality through a specific lens and place it in a theological framework.

Questions for Discussion

- To what extent do you recognize the confusion around gender and sexuality that we wrote about at the beginning of this chapter?

- The quote from Alain de Botton (when writing about sex) points out the importance of "a respectful accommodation with an anarchic and reckless power." Do you think this is possible?

- To what extent does Jonathan Grant's analysis of "the hypersexual self" have meaning for your own thinking about gender and sexuality?

- In this chapter, we introduce a number of key concepts about gender, gender identity, sexuality, and so on. To what extent are these concepts new to you?

- Killermann's "genderbread person" is a simple illustration of a complex theme. What does the image, and the emphasis on a much more flexible and mobile understanding of gender and sexuality, evoke in you?

2

Gender and Sexuality

A Look into History

Introduction

THINKING ABOUT SEXUALITY AND gender in the twenty-first century is not an isolated event, but requires historical reflection for at least three reasons. First, we can understand the present better if we have knowledge of the past. The way we think about sexuality in our century is not something that has come out of the blue, it has been shaped by what was said, written, and lived in the centuries before. Christians are often inclined to focus only on the Bible and we tend to avoid church history. But it is an illusion to think that what we read in the Bible is not related to a historical interpretive framework, and one that can be directly applied to our contemporary context. There are theological questions to be asked here, but they will be discussed in another chapter. We live our own history and cannot escape it, and nor should we want to. Of course, it should also be noted that history cannot be described objectively or completely. It is always subjective: we read and see history through the dual lenses of our own time and culture.

A second reason for the importance of historical reflection is that history shows there have been very different views on gender, sexuality, and marriage. By knowing this, we can be more informed and speak into complex situations with more accuracy. The idea that things are radically different in the twenty-first century than they were in all the centuries before is incorrect. History can surprise and unsettle us, especially when it comes to sexuality.[1]

A third reason for the importance of historical reflection is that historiography is not only meant to describe, but also to be learned from. It is not necessarily the case that there has been such a progression in thinking about sexuality that we can dismiss history as old-fashioned or outdated. It would be arrogant to think that in all respects we have more knowledge and resources than people in the past. Learning from history means that we can and must be critical of our own time. History helps us not to make current thinking the measure and end of everything.

This chapter cannot give a complete overview of history; that is impossible. But one thing at least will become clear from this chapter, and that is that through the ages people have thought very differently about eroticism, physicality, and gender. This puts sexuality, and how we think about it in our time, in a broader perspective. We also hope to make clear what influence Christianity has had on thinking about and experiencing sexuality, and how the sexual morals and customs of Hellenistic culture have shaped Christian thinking. The question we must first ask, however, is whether sexuality has a history at all. That question may sound strange, but it needs to be asked, because it is a key debate among scholars, and because we must determine what we mean when we are talking about sex and sexuality throughout history. After that, we will go on an excursion through antiquity, early church history, the Middle Ages, the Reformation, and modern times. We continue on the search, outlined in our introduction, for insight into the various ways in which we can view gender and human sexuality. And along the way, we ask ourselves what lessons history can teach us to better understand sexuality. At the end of this chapter, we will draw some conclusions and ask some questions for reflection.

History and Sexuality: Virgin Territory

For a long time, there was little interest in the history of sexuality. According to the American historian Vern Bullough, sex was "virgin territory" in history.[2] Michel Foucault believed that sexuality was a modern invention; the discussion and naming of sexuality did not occur before

1. Garton, *Histories of Sexuality*, ix.
2. Weeks, *What is Sexual History?*, 13.

modern times.[3] Since the beginning of the nineteenth century, scholarly attention to the history of sexuality has increased enormously. And the question has arisen as to whether there is, in fact, a history of sexuality in general. David Halperin believes that sex has no history.[4] It is a fact, a biological function of a body, which lies outside of culture and history. Sexuality, however, does have a history, because it is influenced by culture. It is important to differentiate that sex has no history, because this then means that it is a natural fact and part of our humanity; it is universal, regardless of time and culture. However, people react to sex differently and have developed different rules over the centuries, and there is much to be said and reflected on. Yet sex and sexuality are not separate. It is therefore important to define sex and sexuality properly, and it turns out that scientists use different definitions, which makes for different readings of history. At the same time, what we define as sexuality is a historical construct in which different conceptions of gender, biology, eroticism, and desire come together, but do not merge into one unified concept of "sexuality."

It should come as no surprise then, that historians have a wide variety of views on the relationship between history and sexuality. On the one hand, historians argue that sexuality is an invention (see above), a medicalized theory of human behavior, which came into being at the end of the nineteenth century. On the other hand, scholars have also argued that sex and sexuality have influenced all parts of history.[5] For example, Justin Lehmiller, a social psychologist, writes that the study of sexuality dates to the time of the early Greek philosophers, who wrote and theorized about various topics related to sexuality.[6]

Yet the scientific study of sexuality, as we know it today, is very young. It began around the turn of the twentieth century, when several physicians, psychiatrists, and early sexologists, such as Heinrich Kaan and Richard von Krafft-Ebing, published on sexual behavior. These publications show, among other things, a shift from sexual deviations as moral shortcomings, to the view that they were medical and mental issues. The year 1906 is generally considered to be the birth of sexology, at least in the Netherlands. In 1907, German scientist Iwan Bloch published his book *Das Sexualleben unserer Zeit* (Sex in Our Times). He

3. Halperin, "Is There a History of Sexuality?," 257–74.
4. Halperin, "Is There a History of Sexuality?," 257–74.
5. Toulalan and Fisher, *Routledge History of Sex*, 2.
6. Lehmiller, *Psychology of Human Sexuality*, 29.

introduced and described the concept of "sexology" as: "If we are to do justice to the wide-ranging importance of love in the lives of everyone, of society and of the evolution of human civilization, then this special field of research must be regarded as a component of the general study of humanity."[7] Sexology, according to his view, is a synthesis of several other sciences, including general biology, anthropology, ethnology, psychology and philosophy, the history of literature, and the global history of our civilization. Given this broad scope, in this chapter, we will keep our focus to a description of history.

Sexuality in Ancient Times

When we use the term antiquity, we are referring to the period that began around 500 BC and ended around 400 AD, when the Greco-Roman Empire had lost almost all of its power. Of course, there was plenty of human history before this point, but this time period is where many lines of argument converge. Moreover, antiquity was the time period in which Christianity was born. In this section, we will mainly deal with the period before the beginning of the Christian era, taking a look at Greek and Roman societal structures and some of the philosophical thinking at that time. Greek philosophers influenced early Christian thinking on sexuality and therefore it is important to discuss them. Furthermore, we will pay attention to the connections between sexuality and the gods. We cannot harmonize Greek and Roman culture entirely; there were too many differences which prevent that. For example, the Romans were more ambivalent toward sodomy than the Athenians, and women in Rome generally had a higher civil status than women in Athens.[8] But, of course, there were also many similarities and quite a few of them will be discussed here.

Status and Power

Greco-Roman society consisted of many layers into which people were divided, based on status and power. It was only possible for a select group of men to be included in the social stratum reserved for the most

7. Bloch, *Sexualleben unserer Zeit*, 3–7.
8. Garton, *Histories of Sexuality*, 31.

powerful. They were the elite. Women and slaves (who made up approximately a quarter of society) were seen as inferior and had no rights.

Their norms regarding sexuality were related to this division of society. For men with power and status, there were basically no norms. There were rules for dealing with younger boys (that is, concerning pederasty), but the norms mainly applied to women. They were not allowed to cheat and certainly not to divorce. We know little about what women thought in antiquity, because most sources were written by men. However, what men wrote about women gives us at least some idea. It shows that women were thought to be good for fertility; they were expected to have children and raise them. The preference was for a son. All women were expected to marry (around the age of fourteen) and, in principle, the same applied to men (around the age of thirty), although they had much more freedom within marriage. Sexuality for them, contrary to what was expected of women, was not limited to marriage. Marriage was very important in antiquity, however. If you postponed a wedding, you risked being fined.

Women were divided into different categories, as befitted the stratified society of the time. There was the younger, sexually immature girl in one category and the virgin who was marriageable (between her twelfth and fourteenth year of life) in another category. These two groups were watched over by a male guardian, often the brother or father. There were two other categories: the married, sexually active woman and mother or the woman who was no longer fertile. Here, too, women had to be watched and, in most cases, this was done by the husband. Men saw women as sex-crazed creatures who needed to be under the guardianship of a man. So, it is not surprising that they were legally considered incapable of acting. Women were rarely seen in the streets—men did the shopping—and men and women often lived separately. Among the poorer population, you could see women working because it was necessary. In Sparta, one of the most important city-states of ancient Greece, women generally played a larger role in society because they had to produce good soldiers. Therefore, they often had some money or a piece of land.

Among the Romans, different forms of marriage were possible, based on class. Until 445 BC, legal marriage was only possible for the nobility of society, the patricians. Marriage through the layers of class was not possible. For plebeians, there was another form of civil marriage where, unlike in the case of the patricians, the legal effect of the wife passing to the family of the husband was absent. This changed after 445 BC.

Besides these types, another form of marriage was possible. A law written around 45 BC stated that the relationship between a man and a woman who lived together for a year was a marriage under civil law. If they did not want this, for example, because they did not want the woman to be completely subject to the husband, then they had to stay away from each other for three nights a year.[9] In the period immediately preceding the Christian era, women played a greater role in Roman society than in Greek society. Although a woman was not allowed to hold public office, she did have a central position as *mater familias*.

Halperin points out that in classical Athens, sex was part of a hierarchical and political structure.[10] Sex was reserved for the elite and was not seen as a reciprocal encounter between two or more people, but as something that took place between two different kinds of people, where the one with more power had control over the body of the one without power. The person higher in the hierarchy took the initiative and was entitled to pleasure. Male citizens were allowed to have sex with people of a lower social and political status: women of any age; free men of any age after puberty, but who were not yet old enough to be considered citizens; and foreigners and slaves of both sexes.[11] Sex was not so much about the other person's sex as it was about status. Sex, like war, was a domain where you represented your social status. The central theme of Greco-Roman sexual culture was activity versus passivity and not, for example, homosexuality versus heterosexuality. Being penetrated meant that you submitted to the authority of the other person. Sanctions would apply if a man had sex with someone of the same status. Same-sex relations in antiquity were no reason to renounce heterosexual marriage or procreation. Greek homosexuality, therefore, cannot be compared with modern-day homosexuality.[12]

Philosophers on Sexuality

For the philosopher Plato (427–347 BC), the word "eros" meant sexual lust, but also the philosophical desire for truth. Plato said that we must choose between the two kinds of knowledge of eros: the philosophically intellectual (the rational) and the physical, carnal knowledge, and that

---

9. Halperin, "Is There a History of Sexuality?," 10.
10. Halperin, "Is There a History of Sexuality?," 10–21.
11. Halperin, "Is There a History of Sexuality?," 12.
12. Garton, *Histories of Sexuality*, 31.

these are incompatible. That the two are incompatible is particularly evident in Plato's famous story of the shadows in the cave. In it, Plato states that people are, as it were, stuck in a cave and see all things as shadows on a wall. You talk about what you see—houses, chairs, beds, etc.—but these are in fact only shadows. Only after death your is soul free from your body and only then can your soul really see. In short, the body is a prison for the soul. Only when man is freed from it can he see how things really are. This story illustrates that the body was less important to Plato and that he made a clear distinction between body and soul. Sex was a physical, bodily act, and therefore less important.

Another well-known story, about the "polka-dot people," also shows something of Plato's view of sexuality. It can be found in his *Symposium*.[13] In it, seven guests sitting around a table tell stories about love. One of the guests, the comedy writer Aristophanes, tells us that people were originally spherical and had two sexual organs. These people were androgynous. The word refers to a fusion of the Greek words *aner* (man) and *gyn* (woman). Some people had two male sexual organs, others two female ones, and still others one of each. So, from that point of view, there were three genders. They also had four arms and legs and two faces each. The idea of the spheres is illustrated by two human backs against each other. Zeus, the Greek supreme god, at some point split people up and since then every human being has been searching for their original half. This story seems to make room for homosexual relationships and shows how the relationship between the different sexes should be, namely that they seek each other out so that they can become reunited and one again.

The philosopher Aristotle (348–22 BC) wrote, besides many philosophical works, a biological book entitled *De generatione et corruptione*.[14] In it, Aristotle elaborates his views on pleasure. He writes the following: "The pleasure experienced during coitus is because not only semen, but also air is expelled."[15] According to Aristotle, sexual pleasure is not restricted to men: "Some people think that a woman produces semen during coitus because she sometimes experiences as much pleasure as a man and at the same time secretes fluid with him." There is no connection between her pleasure and pregnancy: "It happens that a woman does not

---

13. Waterfield, *Plato*.

14. Aristotle's *De generatione et corruptione*, translated with notes by C. J. F. Williams. The quote is from the Dutch translation in Ferwerda, *Aristoteles*.

15. Ferwerda, *Aristoteles*, 23–28; translated by the authors.

become pregnant even if her pleasure is no less than that of the man and the man and woman are on an equal footing."[16]

Aristotle sought an answer to the question of why male sperm was necessary for pregnancy if women also produced sperm. According to him, the man provided the soul of the embryo, because his seed was more powerful (cf. chapter 1). Aristotle developed this theory further by defining natural and unnatural sexual practices. The female contribution to procreation was merely that of a greenhouse in which the valuable male seed did its work. Masturbation was forbidden, according to him, because then one committed murder; it was against nature, since the valuable male seed was lost.

Even though women were only meant for procreation, this did not mean that birth control was out of the question. Although, some philosophers felt that as many children as possible should be born. For example, Aristotle advised women to rub their wombs with olive oil to prevent pregnancy. And Aristotle and Plato believed that it was better for parents to have only one child. Influenced by Plato and Aristotle, Greek and Roman philosophers held that a man who allowed himself to be led by "passions" was unfit to lead. The strongest ones chose abstinence.[17]

In antiquity, the focus was not about two opposite genders, because all bodies were thought to have male and female aspects, although they remained opposite characteristics. However, one was more perfect than the other. There was also a hierarchy in which men from the higher social strata were at the top of the societal ladder and women at the bottom. They were *less* masculine, which is different from not being masculine at all. Aristotle wrote that woman was a deformed man. By the way, there is much discussion about the exact meaning of these statements because they (like all statements) have to be read in their specific context.[18] It was believed that the genitals of a male were on the outside and the female's genitals on the inside. The ovaries were seen as testicles, the uterus as scrotum, the labia as foreskin, and the vagina as penis. The male body was seen as more perfect, as active because it produces sperm, and as warm, while the female body was seen as passive and cold. It was believed that women also had male sperm and vice versa; however, the male sperm was more powerful. So male and female are principles, not sexes.[19] The differ-

16. Ferwerda, *Aristoteles*. 23–28; translated by the authors.

17. Bos, *2000 Jaar Nederlanders en hun sexualiteit*, 972.

18. Mayhem, *Female in Aristotle's Biology*.

19. Swancutt, "Disease of Effemination," 193–234.

ence is only gradual. Thomas Laqueur calls this idea the *one-sex theory*: there is one sex and that is male.[20] It was not until around the 1800s that this idea changed. We will come back to this later.

Gods and Sexuality

The above discussion of Plato and Aristotle already shows that there was a strong connection between people and the gods in antiquity. We think it is interesting to elaborate on this a bit more. According to Dutch theologian Hans de Knijff, this approach from antiquity can be described as *naturalism*.[21] By this, he meant that there was a strong connection with the earth and that the gods, in their sexual appetites and relationships, were also described anthropomorphically (as if they were people). Christianity, he said, broke with this naturalism. In the next section we will discuss to what extent this was indeed the case.

Dutch cultural historian Jacob Slavenburg shows how sexuality and religion were connected in antiquity.[22] There were many stories in which gods had sexual contact with each other and in which gods had sexual intercourse with people. In antiquity, fertility was linked to women, so that meant the "highest" deity was represented as a woman: the virgin mother. This meant that male gods were relegated to second place. These female gods often became pregnant unfertilized. There was also a practice of holy marriage (*hieros gamos*), which was usually a short-term, strictly sexual relationship with gods. The sexual ritual involved two people (priests/priestesses) playing the role of gods, and in this way sexuality and the gods were closely linked. Gods could manifest themselves in priests and priestesses, in holy "temple prostitutes," and in kings and queens. Through sexual unification, gods could connect with humans and humans could also experience the *hieros gamos* among themselves. These sexual rituals were nearly always about fertility, but later also about wholeness. And apart from the sexual aspect, the *hieros gamos* has a strong spiritual character, because the participants' perceptions of being closer to the gods at that time was much stronger.

Sexuality was thus already interwoven with religion in antiquity, and the aforementioned structures of society were already quite well

20. Laqueur, *Making Sex.*
21. De Knijff, *Venus aan de leiband*, 22.
22. Slavenburg, *Vrijen met God*, 1–20.

established. It was in this context that Christianity was born. It is therefore not surprising that the thoughts and structures of antiquity have influenced Christianity.

Early Church History

In our chapter about the Bible and sexuality, we will take a deeper dive into what Judaism, Jesus, Paul, and other writers said and/or wrote about sexuality. Here, it suffices to state that Jesus did not say much about sexuality at all. In fact, he does not say a word about homosexuality, although he was critical of polygamy. And concerning adultery: Jesus acquits the accused woman (in John 8) and, earlier in the same Gospel, speaks to a Samaritan woman (in John 4) who had several relationships. In the synoptic Gospels, Jesus also responds to a remark about marrying in the hereafter, explaining there is no marriage in the resurrection to come (Matt 22:30; Mark 12:22–25; Luke 20:34–36), and speaks to the hemorrhaging woman (Matt 9:20–22; Mark 5:25–34; Luke 8:43–48).

It was Paul especially (see chapter 4), who had a great influence on Christian thinking about sexuality. This was related, among other things, to the city of Corinth, where he visited several times. In Paul's thinking, the soon-to-be-expected return of Christ probably plays a major role. Paul is also not unequivocal about women and sexuality, and he seems to contradict himself. That makes it difficult for us to pinpoint what he might have meant. On the one hand, he gives women authority, and he states that a woman has authority over the body of her husband, and that is—at least—remarkable. On the other hand, he seems to silence women in worship. This same paradox applies to marriage and celibacy. On the one hand, Paul encourages people to marry and, on the other hand, to remain celibate. This remarkable contradiction would remain visible for much longer, and maybe that is one of the reasons why the Greek philosophers had a great influence on the thoughts of theologians in the first centuries of the church's history.

In general, it can be said that sexuality was seen by the church fathers as something negative, and yet this is too one-sided a view. According to theologian and ethicist Stanley Grenz, the church of the first few centuries AD placed sexuality in the context of morality, and sexuality was, in principle, good.[23] However, Grenz's view is probably too positive. This

---

23. Grenz, *Sexual Ethics.*

argument could be made for Paul's thoughts, but in the first few centuries after Christ, the idea that the body was subordinate to the spirit was quite dominant. In gnosticism, the body was seen as inherently evil and, as a reaction to this, Paul emphasizes the goodness of the body. We find the theological basis for this in the incarnation of Christ. It is possible that in Paul's time there was a fairly holistic approach to the body. But gradually, under the influence of Greek philosophy, gnosticism, and dualistic thinking, the view arose that the body was less important. Thinking in terms of "nature" is a Greek idea, but it permeates Christianity. Which leads us to suspect there was no complete break with "naturalism," as De Knijff suggested.[24] It was only at the end of the Middle Ages that people raised their voices in favor of the naturalness of sexuality, and regarding it as positive.[25]

Celibacy and Virginity

In ancient times, abstaining from sexuality was seen as an important task. Soon—in the first centuries of church history—this applied to Christians and was also made compulsory for clergy. By 303 AD it was demanded that bishops, priests, and deacons, as well as clergymen serving at the altar, should abstain from conjugal intercourse and stop begetting children. So, celibacy was not quite yet compulsory. At the Council of Elvira in 306 AD, it was decided that higher clergymen (the pope, deacons, and bishops) should abstain from sex. Children cost money and material things attracted them to the world. So, priests could marry, but had to live chaste lives. This practice was valid until the end of the sixth century. Besides these practical reasons, there were other arguments that were used to defend celibacy. The priest Hieronymus (circa 347–420) believed that Mary's husband, Joseph, had remained a virgin and, based on the Gospel of James, which was popular in early church history, he believed that the virginity of Mary had also been preserved.

In any case, for most of the church fathers, celibacy stood above marriage. Hieronymus compared the body to a dark forest full of roaring wild beasts. He was the main inspiration for Augustine (354–439), who prayed: "Give me chastity and self-control." And he added: ". . . but not at

---

24. De Knijff, *Venus aan de Leiband*, 89.

25. Pleij, *Oefeningen in genot*, 137–40, 386–98.

once."[26] He had preferred to satisfy his desires. Until his conversion, he had a concubine, about whom, he says in his *Confessions,* that this was "a union based on lust," and with her he had a son. During his time in Milan, he was to marry a woman of higher rank but, in the meantime, he kept a mistress. After his conversion at the age of thirty-two, he abstained from sex. According to Augustine, holiness meant being able to control yourself. Lust and passion were diametrically opposed. For example, Augustine believed that after the fall, God punished Adam and Eve with uncontrolled lust (the opposite of healthy passion). And, because the fall began with lust, that made sexuality a terrible sin. He was adamant it was specifically Eve who lured Adam into the trap of sexual temptation. So, he even refers to Jesus's commandment to love your enemies when it comes to loving your wife. For Augustine, sex is something to be ashamed of.

It needs to be said, however, that Augustine was not as negative as some of the other church fathers. He believed that sexuality existed before the fall, in contrast to, for example, the church father Origen (184–253), who castrated himself. He later regretted this. Origen believed people were androgynous before the fall and that sexuality therefore played no role at that time. The problem, according to Augustine, was that after the fall, human sexuality was controlled by unreasonable passions and a violated free will. People could control their genitals before the fall and not afterwards. Genitalia that erected itself without permission was evidence of rebellion against God!

The influence of Plato and Aristotle on Augustine, Origen, and other church fathers can hardly be overestimated. The idea that lust is sinful, and something you should be ashamed of, was linked by Christians to the doctrine of sin. Salvation is first and foremost about the soul, not about the body. Christians therefore also appropriated the idea of self-control over the body from the Greeks. This lifestyle is called encratism. It is a form of radical asceticism (living in abstinence) and refers to early Christian religious groups—called encratites—who rejected marriage and any physical enrichment. Regarding marriage, Clement of Alexandria (150–215) believed that the only moral reason for sex was to produce children; sexual intercourse for other reasons is against nature. Again, the idea that Jesus would soon return had great influence, especially at the beginning of church history. After all, if having children was less important, then marriage populated the earth, and virginity the heavens, and heaven was

---

26. Augustine, *Confessions,* book 8, chapter VII, 17.

the main priority for many people. Self-castration was therefore desirable. Moreover, it was a slap in the face to the devil, who was denied access to what was thought to be the main entrance to the male body.[27]

Of course, there are other interpretations from this period. Historian Robin Lane-Fox is critical of the image of an early church which maintained a strict marriage morality.[28] According to him, the whole of Greco-Roman society was dominated by feelings of honor and shame when it came to sexual behavior. It was therefore not a kind of Sodom and Gomorrah. Literary scholar John Winkler confirms this view.[29] According to him, the emphasis was on health, masculinity, and citizenship when it came to sexuality. The writings from the time often described "macho" behavior, but that does not mean that this was the practice. Homosexual relations (and marriages) were legal in the first two hundred years of state religion and the church was very tolerant.[30] Nevertheless, Christians were certainly conspicuous for their celibacy. The imperial court physician Galenus (140–99), for example, wrote of Christians: "Their contempt for death is visible to us every day, as is the fact that they abstain from sexual intercourse. For among them are not only men, but also women, who abstain from intercourse all their lives."[31] From here, we will now consider the relationship specifically between men and women in more detail.

The Third Sex

Women played a major role in early church history. But, culturally, their femininity was still a problem. They were seen as failures, as imperfect men. According to theologian April DeConick, this tragic situation for women did not so much originate in a certain interpretation of the Bible, by theology, or even social structures, but finds its cause more in the female body itself.[32] The male body was understood to be the norm, and the female body was not wanted. Tertullian asked women to cover their bodies, including their faces (with a veil), and to make themselves

27. Pleij, *Oefeningen in genot*, 33.

28. Fox, *Pagans and Christians*, 309–10, 332, 340.

29. Compare Winkler, *Constraints of Desire*.

30. Carroll, *Sexuality Now*, 12.

31. Bos, *2000 Jaar Nederlanders en hun sexualiteit*, 972.

32. DeConick, *Holy Misogyny*, 117.

as unattractive as possible. He believed that a woman's natural beauty should be ignored and hidden under clothing. If a man saw this beauty he could end up in hell. This focus created a kind of framework that defined everything from gender roles to the sexual act itself.

Also, for this time period, it is not easy to say much about the position of women in the early church, because the sources were written by men. But, of course, this does tell us at least something about the position of women. That gender roles were not as important as the transcendence of sexuality all together was shown by the existence of a group of female virgins who lived in the desert. Sexual abstinence offered people with a low status (women, the poor, and the uneducated) the opportunity to become a hero. According to Clement, these virgins had overcome their sexuality and could therefore hold male positions in the church. They were no longer seen as women, but as members of a third gender. Many virgins left their homes and went to live in the desert as independent women. They suffered from hunger so that their breasts disappeared, and they did not menstruate, so that they began to look like men. Many pilgrims therefore thought they were dealing with men.[33]

In 403 AD Jerome (circa 342–420) wrote a letter to Laeta, a mother who wanted to dedicate her young daughter to the church. In his letter, one can read what Laeta had to do to preserve her daughter's virginity so that her body could become a temple of God. She should never see herself naked and she was not allowed to receive compliments from any man. Therefore, she always had to be accompanied by her mother.[34] The idea that women were actually failed men, a thought present in antiquity, can thus be found in early church history. The bishop of Emesa, Nemesius, stated in the fourth century AD that the female genitals were inside the body and not outside.[35] This idea was to endure for centuries to come.

Middle Ages

The Middle Ages covers a long period of time, from the year 500 to 1500 AD. In fact, in the Middle Ages we see the climax of early Christian thinking. It is not so much a question over new points of view on sexuality, but rather of more church influence on society and therefore more control

33. DeConick, *Holy Miscgyny*, 117.
34. DeConick, *Holy Miscgyny*, 119–20.
35. Laqueur, *Making Sex*, 4.

over people's sexuality. Most of the sources we have come from church circles; their authors were of high bourgeois origin and their readers often belonged to the higher spiritual class as well. Of course, most of the population were not priests but farmers, for example, and we know little about how the rules of the church were received by them. In any case, it is likely that these written texts had a fairly limited social reach and it is highly likely that people thought very differently about sexuality and that they did not always comply with the requirements of the church. Even if only because these requirements were impossible![36] No archives were kept tracking how many people got married. That only started in the time of the Reformation. Nevertheless, there are some things we can say about the way people thought about sexuality in the Middle Ages.

The vision of the church fathers had ensured that marriage, for a long time, was despised in the Middle Ages. From the ninth century, this became less and less the case, and the clergy became interested in marrying the laity. It was less about the marriage ceremony, and more about the question of who could marry whom and when they could have sex. The church had a firm grip on what people were and were not allowed to do. For example, it was forbidden to have sex during Lent and Advent, in the Easter and Pentecost weeks, on Saint's days, and on Sundays, Wednesdays, Fridays, and Saturdays. If you could find a day on which it was allowed, then completely undressing was forbidden, as well as tongue kissing, oral sex, caressing, and sexual positions other than the missionary position.[37] Sex within marriage was, in principle, only for the purpose of procreation. Humans should follow the example of animals in this respect. Seed was not to be wasted, because potential life was hidden within it. Prostitution was sometimes necessary, because one did not want a man's seed to be wasted and, therefore, it was usually tolerated. Marriage as a sacrament was not so much a means of grace as much as an extinguishing agent for burning desire. The early medieval church was, according to Dutch historian and sociologist David Bos, obsessed with the danger of incest up to the fourth degree of kinship.[38] In 813 AD, the church had forbidden marriages with fourth-degree cousins and, in the eleventh century, they tried to extend this to the seventh degree. This made it difficult for people in small communities to marry. Many kings and aristocrats did not much care about these bans because they wanted

36. Pleij, *Oefeningen in genot*, 141–43.
37. Bos, *2000 Jaar Nederlanders en hun sexualiteit*, 979.
38. Bos, *2000 Jaar Nederlanders en hun sexualiteit*, 9.

to marry someone of noble birth. Only when one was dissatisfied with the marriage did the rule come in handy as a dissolution clause. Around 1100 AD, the first Christian wedding rituals appeared in France, but even then, the church did not play a very active role in the marriage ceremony, and it certainly had not played much of a role before that.

Celibacy

At the Synod in Mainz in 1075 AD, Pope Gregory VII (1021–1085) decreed that from then on celibacy also applied to priests and deacons. They were not allowed to marry or have sex. If the priest or deacon was already married, an exception could be made. If they did not remain celibate, they could expect severe punishment. Masturbation was also considered a repulsive sin. Over time, the rules became stricter and in 1123 AD celibacy became obligatory for ordinary priests too. However, this did not quite work out in practice. Many priests were married, and it was not until 1139 AD that there was a general ban on married men becoming priests. From then on, the wives of priests were called whores.[39] Gradually, marriage had become an ecclesiastical matter and therefore it became impossible for priests to marry. Nevertheless, 60 percent of the fifteenth-century parish priests in Brabant (a southern province in the Netherlands) had a domestic partner, often with children. There was also a fine—a church sex tax—but this did not deter people too much.[40] Again, this shows that compliance with rules often left much to be desired.

Gender and Homosexuality

In the Middle Ages, sex was still closely linked to gender, as it had been in antiquity. Sex was about roles. The active partner had a masculine role and the passive partner a feminine role. A woman was expected to lie still and a man to go wild, although it was still commanded that sex in its entirety should be controlled *within a marriage*. In the words of Dutch historian Herman Pleij, "Passionate love and erotic urges were part of adultery, with no thought for offspring."[41] Sex was usually seen as what someone did *to* someone else. If two men were to have sex, only one

---

39. Bos, *2000 Jaar Nederlanders en hun sexualiteit*, 975.
40. Bos, *2000 Jaar Nederlanders en hun sexualiteit*, 980.
41. Pleij, *Oefeningen in genot*, 87.

could act as a man (active) and the other as a woman (passive). And the same would apply to women. There were no categories such as gay or straight, and it was mainly about what one *did*, not so much about sexual preferences. As far as homosexuality and forms other than heterosexuality were concerned, it was less about "preferences" or a "different category," but rather about the *action*, and for this the word "sodomy" was used. Gradually, people became less tolerant of homosexuality. According to Pleij, Petrus Damianus was the first to write about homosexuality, specifically in men, in 1049 AD.[42] In the twelfth century, nobody seemed to be very concerned about this, but that would not last long. From that time on, people began to see homosexuality as unnatural, that is, against God's creation. The church took increasingly harsh measures against sex and sexuality between people of the same sex, and eventually even punished it with death.

The Italian Dominican friar and priest Thomas Aquinas (1225–74) is seen as the greatest philosopher and theologian of the Middle Ages. He based much of his work on the work of the philosopher Aristotle.[43] In his work, the concepts of what is "reasonable" and what is "natural" are central. For example, he could speak of fornication that was either against or in harmony with nature. Incest, for example, was natural and sodomy unnatural. According to him, sex was, in principle, only permitted between a man and a woman who were married to each other and wanted to have children, because that was natural. Sexuality was therefore linked to morality. Aquinas also made very negative statements about women. According to Aquinas, men were superior to women, and he based this on the creation story in which the woman was created from the man and the man from earth. For Aquinas, this meant men had more dignity and women were not created in the image of God. The French writer Christine de Pisan (1364–1430) turned Aquinas's argument around: since man was created from earth, and woman from a human being, the woman was superior.[44]

However, Aquinas's influence was, of course, many times greater than that of Christine de Pisan. European women were arguably treated only slightly better in the early Middle Ages than under Greek and Roman rule. Unsurprisingly, Aquinas's thoughts were not isolated. Herman Pleij frequently quotes from *Roman de la Rose* (Novel of the Rose), the first part of which was written between 1225 and 1230 AD by the French

42. Pleij, *Oefeningen in genot*, 118.

43. Karras, *Common Women*. Compare also Karras, *Sexuality in Medieval Europe*.

44. Pisan, *Livre de la Cité des dames*.

poet Guillaume de Lorris and continued forty years later by Jean de Meung. The latter wrote that, without exception, all women are, in fact, whores, however much they try to hide it. Throughout the course of the fourteenth century, the picture of women did gradually became a little more positive.[45] The ancient idea that natural lust was sinful also began to change. If God had created it, it could not be wrong. It was seen as a prerequisite that there should be complete equality and equal enjoyment on both sides. Late medieval literature praised natural sex; it was seen as necessary for good health, and doctors even began to prescribe masturbation for women when they were ill.[46] Once again, unsurprisingly, this revolution proved short-lived.

Reformation (1500–1700)

Accounts of the Reformation traditionally start with Martin Luther (1483–1546), and this reformer certainly brought about different practices, and a renewal of thinking, in the area of sexuality. Although, he also remained a child of his time. In Luther's time, according to church historian Trevor O'Reggio, three models of sexuality were present.[47] The first model saw reproduction or procreation as the primary purpose of sex. This was also the view of the church. The second model had to do with pollution and focused on impurity caused by sex. It placed strong restrictions on marital relationships and what was allowed therein in terms of sexual practice. In this model, procreation was less important. The third model saw marital sex as a source of intimacy and affection and as a symbol and source of conjugal love.

Compared to the adherents of the other two models, those who understood sexuality in terms of the third model saw sexual pleasure more positively. Different elements of these three models were visible in the Middle Ages in different combinations. O'Reggio explores which model Luther adhered to and whether his views changed over time. It seems to him that Luther adhered to all three models during his life.

Luther took a vow of chastity before entering an Augustinian monastery in 1506 but broke it. In 1525, he married Katharina von Bora, an ex-nun with whom he had six children. For Luther, marriage was a gift

45. Pleij, *Oefeningen in genot*, 77.
46. Pleij, *Oefeningen in genot*, 128, 130, 152–54.
47. O'Reggio, "Martin Luther on Marriage and Family," 195–218.

from God and sexuality belonged within marriage. A bad marriage had to be ended and divorce had to be allowed. The latter went against the morality of the Roman Catholic Church. Having children was important, but sexuality also had other functions, such as reducing stress, preventing adultery, and strengthening intimacy. This is why Luther prescribed that couples should have sexual intercourse twice a week. The German bishop Hans Christian Knuth believes that Martin Luther's love letters to his wife Katharina von Bora were more erotic and passionate than any nighttime television program.[48]

The other well-known reformer, John Calvin (1509–64), saw marriage as a sexual and social relationship. Being together was a clear goal of marriage. This is reflected in how he valued women. In a certain sense, Dutch church historian Mirjam van Veen contends, women are better off with Calvin than with some of his contemporaries. "Unlike the Roman Catholic Church, Calvin believed that sexuality did not by definition have to be aimed at procreation. A woman is not just there to have children. And you can enjoy sexuality, if it happens within marriage."[49] Yet, according to Van Veen, Calvin held double standards. He thought, for example, it was worse for a woman to commit adultery than for a man and that the punishment for a woman should be weightier than for a man. A woman was only allowed to divorce if her life was in danger. With the Reformation, veneration of Mary and other female saints lessened and this contributed to the fact that Christianity remained male-dominated.

Marriage

Under the influence of the Reformers, celibacy was increasingly criticized, and marriage began to become the norm. There was also much criticism of the hypocritical attitude of clergy. There were all kinds of strict rules for the laity when it came to sexuality, but clergymen did not seem to keep to them. The Reformers saw marriage as a vocation. That meant that you had to be of service in your marriage. This was also connected to the "righteousness by works" principle the Reformers were opposed to. Celibacy was seen as work. This was due to the Reformers's more holistic approach to man, in which the body received more attention because the incarnation of Christ was increasingly important. The Reformation

48. "Luther was tot Freud."
49. Mirjam van Veen in Hakkenes, "Vrouw in huis is handig."

criticized dualistic thinking in which the body was less important than the spirit. Yet the centuries that followed showed that dualistic thinking was persistent and still had substantial influence.

In the meantime, the ecclesial rules for conducting a marriage became increasingly strict. At the Council of Trent in 1563 AD, the Roman Catholic Church decided that marriages could only be performed in the presence of a priest and other witnesses. Until then, people thought they could simply go to bed with one another. Bos states that statistics were kept from that time onwards and therefore we know that in some Dutch cities at least a quarter of the women were pregnant before they married. Because of the abolition of confession, there was less control over all the prohibited sexual acts performed.[50]

In the seventeenth century, men married around the age of twenty-eight and women around the age of twenty-five. In the Dutch Golden Age (around 1588–1672), a stable family was important, and marriage was a practical necessity. Young people gathered weekly to meet their respective future spouses. The age difference should not be too great, and the social status of both marriage partners should not differ too much. If you met a nice boy or an attractive girl, you could dance with them and then ask their parents' permission to see if you were a match with him or her. If a promise of marriage was made, then, with the permission of the family—men needed permission until the age of twenty-five, women until the age of twenty—the preparations for the wedding could begin. The material provisions were laid out in a contract signed by the man and the woman concerned, and the couple to be married then registered with the verger of the church. In the seventeenth century, the blessing of the marriage by a minister took place in church or at home. After the wedding feast, the couple was escorted to their bedroom by their guests. In some circles, there were even poets who wrote special wedding songs.

Contraceptives

The history of the condom and its use throughout Europe is fascinating. It started in the sixteenth century, when the venereal disease syphilis reached epidemic proportions. In 1564, the Italian doctor Gabriel Falloppio wrote in the book *Morbo Gallico* that a linen sachet, soaked in a salt or herb solution, offered protection against syphilis. In the eighteenth

---

50. Bos, *2000 Jaar Nederlanders en hun sexualiteit*, 982.

century, silk, linen, and fish bladders were used to make condoms, as well as the appendixes of lambs, calves, and goats. To prevent slipping, the condoms had a ribbon on the open side to keep the membrane tight around the penis. These bladder and intestinal skins could be used several times; some paintings and prints from that time show them hanging on a hook or clothesline to dry. At the beginning of the eighteenth century there was a condom shop in Amsterdam, and the first latex condoms were produced as early as 1839. At that time, the church was against condoms, because their use led to a waste of semen.

Modern Age

The modern age began at the end of the eighteenth century with the Industrial Revolution. This changed the situation of many families, along with scientific discoveries having great influence on existing theories about sexuality. Between 1650 and 1850, the "one-sex model" changed into the "two-sex model." The "discovery" of the clitoris was a problem for the one-sex model. Its existence meant that the woman's vagina no longer corresponded to the man's penis (in the sense that the woman had the same genitals as the man, but on the inside), because "now" there was a clitoris as an external feature. Through medical and biological knowledge, people began to think differently about the bodies of men and women.

In the one-sex model, it was the womb that made women into women; in the two-sex model, the natural is more central. Sexuality was therefore approached more biologically. The clitoris was first associated with procreation and, over time, it was increasingly linked with pleasure. However, this was not necessarily a positive for women. Male dominance was less and less subject to the design requirements, for which previously, before biology interfered, there had always been some kind of medical justification. According to Laqueur, it caused a deritualization of sexuality. The outer magic was replaced by an inner cultivatedness.[51] This had to do with the rise of industrialization, because in the city, magical habits were less and less part of daily life.

The first sex education programs in Europe happened around the time of the Enlightenment. The Enlightenment refers to an era of the eighteenth century, in which human reason had great influence on

51. Laqueur, *Making Sex*, viii.

politics, society, art, and science, and thus also on the way people thought about sexuality. One of the most well-known philosophers, who is seen as the founder of the Enlightenment, was the French philosopher and mathematician René Descartes (1590–1650). Descartes emphasized the difference between body and mind. Emotions were seen as something the body did to people and for which you could therefore not be held responsible. People are responsible for what they think. Following Descartes's thinking, a man could reject responsibility for his erection, unless he had a good reason to get one.

In matters of love, Descartes distinguished between pure intellectual or reasonable love and love as passion. The mind was "sexless." Because this "reasonableness" of sexuality was emphasized, there was probably a greater need for its opposite; in the eighteenth century in particular, attention was increasingly paid to pornography. In spite of all reason, little was known about venereal diseases. It was thought that moisture and cold had an influence and people were advised to wear pants. Regular exercise was also though to prevent venereal diseases. In the Netherlands, there was a popular book by Swedish professor Seved Ribbingh. It was published in 1892 and the twelfth edition came out in 1928. The (translated) title was: *Sexual Hygiene and Some of Its Ethical Consequences*. It said that healthy spouses could have sex three or four times a week. If that was not the case, once a week was enough. Other books gave tips on *when* to have sex. In the morning was not recommended because otherwise one would be too tired during the day. Also, after breakfast or lunch would not be smart because it would interfere with digestion, and it was also not good then because it was light outside. So, in the evening was best. Incidentally, Ribbingh gives a lot of interesting and wide-ranging advice in his book, which gives us a pretty good idea of how people thought about sexuality at that time.

From Nature to Desire

Around the time of the Enlightenment, the view of sexuality began to change, and it was increasingly seen as natural and desirable, as it had been—albeit all too briefly—in the late Middle Ages (see above). Sex was, in many cases, considered the highest attainable form of pleasure. The number of premarital pregnancies rose in the Netherlands. One in five women was already pregnant at their wedding.[52] Nevertheless, societal mores were still clearly evident. Although the Netherlands never had such a pronounced Victorian era as England, there were still strong norms and values. The Victorian era began in 1837 and lasted until 1901. In those days, there was little talk of sex, and conservative thinking reigned. Although, as we shall see, people's practices were often different. Nevertheless, there was an image of men as a kind of prince and women as delicate and vulnerable. They would never talk to a doctor about "female problems." Women were expected to have an interest in music, but they were not allowed to play the flute because the shape one's mouth would make playing it was not feminine enough. Playing the cello was not allowed either, because it was an instrument that had to be held between the legs. The violin was thought to provide an uncomfortable position for a woman's neck. In the end, only keyboard instruments remained. The family was an important concept and occupied a central position in Victorian thinking. However, there was a double standard: there were plenty of prostitutes with no shortage of work.[53]

Developments in the Twentieth Century

At the beginning of the twentieth century, talking about sexuality was still quite taboo. Bos recounts the phenomenon of "window-sex" (also called "night-sex") in Staphorst, a small town in the northeast of the Netherlands.[54] An unmarried man would enter the bedroom of a potential bride to chat for an hour. Later, they could have sex, but it had to be with their clothes on and it had to be limited to kissing, fondling, and mutual masturbation. This was a common practice until the 1940s. Sex and marriage were generally reserved for those who had sufficient means of existence. People who did not have sufficient resources either married at an advanced age or remained unmarried. Then, in the 1950s, the average age for getting married shifted from 28.4 (men) and 25.9 (women) to 26.2 (men) and 23.9 (women).[55] Even though the nineteenth century saw a full and varied erotic life, the theory goes that the social system of the time

52. Trumbach, *Sex and the Gender Revolution*, 10.
53. De Knijff, *Venus aan de leiband*, 237.
54. Bos, *2000 Jaar Nederlanders en hun sexualiteit*, 983.
55. Bos, *2000 Jaar Nederlanders en hun sexualiteit*, 986.

meant that marriage proper was limited to the bourgeoisie.[56] This runs parallel to the economic changes taking place, which were more focused on the individual. In 1911, moral legislation (moral law) was introduced in the Netherlands. This prohibited the distribution of pornography, the sale of contraceptives, and prostitution. Masturbation was seen as medically reprehensible in the early twentieth century. Dutch writer Johanna Breevoort wrote a book about it in 1916 called *Stomme zonden* (Stupid Sins). She wrote that masturbation was punishable in God's eyes, and it would also weaken your body, you would sleep badly, get circles under your eyes, sweat a lot, have headaches, and become moody. She also wrote that chronic masturbators, "onanists" (named for the biblical Onan who spilled his seed on the ground), die at a young age. First, they would stop praying, then they would start hating God, and finally they would end their lives. The book was widely read; in 1936 a fourth edition was published. However, the idea that masturbation was bad did not just come from Christianity. Since the eighteenth century, doctors and educators were convinced that onanism led to spinal disorders, brain inflammation, insanity, and suicide.[57] Conversely, total abstinence could also have serious consequences. Prostitution was, therefore, the least of society's medicalized sexual problems, even though it was forbidden by law.

Homosexuality

By the twentieth century, much had changed in how we thought about gay sexuality. To understand this, we need to go back more than a century. Until 1791, homosexual acts were punishable by death. From 1730 onwards, there was a two-year-long *sodomite panic* in the Netherlands: hundreds of men were accused of homosexual behavior and executed. Many men fled for their lives. France ordered homosexuals to be burned long after the burning of witches had been abolished. Partly as a result of the French Revolution, the horrific punishment was banned. Many European countries, including the Netherlands, adopted this law within the next twenty years. In other countries, such as England, the death penalty was replaced by a prison sentence. Though the Netherlands abolished the death penalty, discrimination against homosexuals persisted. The fight against a particular kind of discrimination started at the end of

56. De Knijff, *Venus aan de leiband*, 236.
57. Bos, *2000 Jaar Nederlanders en hun sexualiteit*, 986.

the nineteenth century and ended with the abolition of article 248bis of the Dutch Penal Code in 1971. This article had been introduced in 1911 and stated: "An adult (21 years of age) who commits fornication with a minor of the same sex whose minority he knows or should reasonably suspect, shall be punished with imprisonment for a term not exceeding four years."[58] For heterosexual contact with a minor, the age of consent was sixteen years. The aim of this law was to combat homosexuality, but gradually there were objections to this. The first mass public gay demonstration in the Netherlands—and probably in all of Europe—was against this article, and took place on January 21, 1969. It is estimated that a total of at least five thousand homosexuals were persecuted based on this article. In 1971, the article was removed from the Code. Having said this, acceptance of homosexuality was still a long way off. The advent of sexually transmitted diseases such as AIDS (1981), and the AIDS epidemic, impacted society's acceptance of homosexuality.

Sexual Revolution and the Second Feminist Wave

Since the 1960s, major changes have taken place in how we think about sexuality, which is why this period is also known as the sexual revolution. In the 1960s, the vision of sexuality changed radically. As early as 1946, a Society for Sexual Reform (NVSH) was founded in the Netherlands, which provided sexual health information and ensured that contraceptives were distributed. In 1966, the association had 200,000 members. In 1963 the contraceptive pill came on the market, which meant that sexuality became increasingly separated from procreation and thus from marriage. Many considered this a liberation, but there was also criticism. The pill did not come about without a struggle. In the medical world, people generally did not want to talk about contraception; doctors had to attend refresher courses well into the 1970s.

In 1911, abortion was banned in the Netherlands, except those performed to save the life of a pregnant woman, but the call for safe, legal abortion became louder and louder. By the end of the 1960s, proper discussions about legalizing abortion had begun. Illegal abortion clinics were set up, but it would take until the end of 1984 for the Abortion Act to come into force. This stipulated that a woman had a five-day reflection period and that an abortion could only be carried out by a specially

---

58. "Artikel 248bis," para. 2.

licensed doctor. In 2022, this reflection period was abolished. In general, the sexual revolution broke through more and more sexual taboos. Apart from the advent of the pill, there were, of course, other reasons for the sexual revolution. Before then, a lot of emphasis was put on the *differences* between men and women, with these differences usually resulting in inequality for women. However, women would continue to fight for equal rights.

The first feminist wave, which occurred during the nineteenth and early twentieth centuries in the western world, had mainly focused on women's suffrage, but the second feminist wave (at the end of the twentieth century) was aimed at economic independence, participation in government, politics, and higher education, an equal position in society, and banning violence against women. In the Netherlands, Joke Smit wrote the article "Women's Unease" in 1967. She was widely supported and, together with others, founded the platform "Man-Woman Society" in 1968. This platform demanded equal opportunities in education. The first action group that developed from the platform in 1970 was that of the so-called "Dolle Minas" ("Mad Minas"). They organized actions or meetings on an almost weekly basis throughout the Netherlands. Other groups were also born, each with its own focus.

Also, the custom of asking permission from parents to get married changed in the 1970s. At least until then, you were not allowed to marry before the age of twenty-one. This sometimes led to interesting situations. In Scotland, this rule did not apply; there, you could marry from the age of sixteen without permission. The result: couples fled to Scotland to get married. In Scotland, you could be married by any Scot in the presence of two witnesses.

The Church and Sexuality

According to Grenz, the sexual revolution cannot be seen separately from the process of secularization.[59] He argues that sexuality was privatized partly as a result of secularization. A person's sexuality became a personal matter. As an example, the last time a kind of "folk court" was held in the Netherlands was the nights of November 11 and 12, 1962. A man and woman suspected of adultery were driven around on a farm cart and

---

59. Grenz, *Sexual Ethics*, 9.

mocked by the villagers.[60] After that time, sexuality became something for the individual. The sexual revolution, of course, had an immense impact on Christianity. Christian counter-reaction to the sexual revolution led Christians to clearly define a "Christian" morality.

Until the nineteenth century, the church had largely determined which norms and values applied. Gradually, doctors took over that role in society. The medical world was not always sure how to deal with sexual diversity, but it did gain more and more authority. However, in the Netherlands, it was the church that played a major role in opening up discussions about sexuality. In 1952, the Dutch Reformed Church stated that sex is a gift from God and that masturbation should not be made a major issue.[61] It also stated that contraceptives were permissible. But, as mentioned above, many Christians became even more conservative in response to the sexual revolution.

Many believe that the sexual revolution brought about more freedom, but that remains to be seen. Foucault (1926–84), who studied the history of thought systems, argued that we are actually less free than ever. Culture puts pressure on what we do and think with regard to sexuality. Even if it concerns a "free" sexual morality. Beatrijs Smulders, a well-known Dutch midwife, demonstrates this in the book *Bloed* (Blood), which she published in 2021.[62] Sexual abuse and all kinds of other undesirable things, both in the church and in society, just as easily happen in our time of free sexual morality as they have in other times, and we still see far too much of it today (see chapter 1).

Mid-Term Review: The Profit of History?

What does this overview of history mean for our thinking about sexuality? We must be careful not to compare the different centuries too easily, or to compare them with the perspectives of our present times. However limited the overview may be, one thing has become clear, and that is: throughout history, people have thought differently about gender, sexuality, marriage, and everything connected with these issues. In any case, the history of Christian thinking about sexuality cannot be seen in isolation from Greek and Roman culture. You could also ask questions about the

---

60. Bos, *2000 Jaar Nederlanders en hun sexualiteit*, 994.

61. Bos, *2000 Jaar Nederlanders en hun sexualiteit*, 993.

62. Smulders, *Bloed*.

meaning of history the other way round, that is, focusing on the possible positive or negative influences of Christianity. De Knijff poses this question in his book *Venus aan de Leiband*. According to him, marriage is the highest order, a gift from Christianity for a full experience of sexuality. From an ethical standpoint, De Knijff argues for the positive influence of Christianity on sexuality. For him, the evidence is in the institution of marriage, with its roots in antiquity and lasting throughout European history. He also argues for the connection between marriage and fertility. The act of love symbolizes (or even is) the total surrender and readiness for fertility.[63]

A look into history, however, also shows very clearly that the church used its power to put sexuality in a negative light and to control people, especially women. What is also clear is there was a double standard, with women being seen as the cause of temptation and then punished the most. This overview shows that gender plays a major role in our thinking about sexuality. Throughout history, men have dominated public life and women's voices have been silenced. We mainly know what men thought and how they lived. That Christianity has wrestled with sexuality throughout history is clear. Spirituality, reproduction, and marriage also appear to have been themes that strongly determined people's choices.

In the past century, the church has had less and less influence on sexual morality. Much has happened in the areas of women's rights, gay rights, reproduction and reproductive rights, medical developments, and marriage. These changes are not isolated and cannot only be called positive, even though scientific developments have made a huge positive contribution to understanding the way sexuality "works." We will discuss some of these scientific developments in the next chapter.

Questions for Discussion

- What things struck you while reading this chapter on history? What struck you in particular and why?
- In the early church, we encounter people who did everything they could to avoid sexuality in their lives. What do you think about that?

---

63. De Knijff, *Venus aan de leiband*, 262.

- How do you value the role of the church throughout the ages when it comes to gender and sexuality? How do you see its role now around these sensitive topics?

- Herman Pleij points out that, in the Middle Ages, sex was often seen as "something someone did *to* someone else" and, in the centuries before that, a distinction was made between an active and passive role. Nowadays, there is more attention on the fact that sex is a vulnerable interaction in which equality and reciprocity play a major role. What could this mean for many of our discussions today?

- Where does history take us when we read about the distinction between men and women, especially when it comes to the image of female sexuality, which was not seen in a very positive light?

3

Gender, Sexuality, and Modern Science

Introduction and Selection of Key Topics

How DOES MODERN SCIENCE view human sexuality? What theoretical perspectives does science use? In the last century, many new insights have been gained from which much can be learned. The number of articles that have appeared in the media in recent years, and also the nature of those articles, shows how many misconceptions are still around today about sexuality and gender. There is also a lack of scientifically informed opinion pieces and stories about people's experiences, about homosexual relationships and gender, and about the sociocultural and biological factors that influence people's experience of sexuality.

In an article in the Dutch newspaper *NRC*, with the headline "Men always want sex and other sex myths on the chopping block," sexologist Ellen Laan discusses several persistent myths.[1] Expertly and based on years of research—Laan was a professor at the Amsterdam University Medical Centre—she discusses the results of decades of research into sexual behavior on the basis of a number of assumptions. According to Laan, men and women differ very little from each other as sexual beings; libido (the man as a vessel full of lust that has to be discharged to prevent

1. Laan, "Man heeft altijd zin."

overpressure) is not an issue, testosterone is not a "macho hormone" at all, "blue balls" (the myth that if a man has an erection, he has to have an orgasm because otherwise he gets blue balls) do not exist, and *last but not least*: only true equality between men and women helps. There is a whole story behind each of these assumptions but, even more so, a world of long and patient research. It would be interesting to introduce Laan's propositions into an average church discussion group. How would that conversation go? Laan points out essential elements in the formation of public opinion about sexual behavior and that, as we will show in this chapter, there is a lack of clear information in many areas to do with sexuality. That omission fosters misunderstanding and misinterpretation.

In this chapter, science comes into play as a specific lens through which we look at the complex relationships between gender and sexuality and the influence they have on behavior and perception. This lens should help us to better understand the complexity of the phenomena of gender and sexuality and, above all, we look for scientific theories and models to map it all out. What views are available that might help us better deal with the many practical problems and questions associated with gender and sexuality? We continue our interpretative task (see preface) with the key question: why is this happening? At the end of our journey in this chapter, we summarize the importance of these findings.

We start with a more focused presentation of gender and its related concepts, and then look specifically at different medical and social science perspectives. We have made a deliberate choice as to the order of this discussion. We begin, in the next section, with a more general framework relating to two main currents that often determine discussions on gender and sexuality: *gender essentialism* and *gender constructivism*. We will then continue with an overview from a more medical and biological perspective. At that point, we will also consider the background to biological sex. We discuss biological sex variations that are related to this, and we also pay attention to insights concerning gender identity and gender expression and show how we can understand sexual orientation. In the concluding paragraphs, we discuss insights from psychology and neurology as well as anthropological, sociological, and philosophical notions. In doing so, we make a choice for a more orderly whole.

Between Your Ears or Legs

Gender is between your ears and not between your legs.

—Chaz Bono

Justin Lehmiller quotes this statement by Chaz Bono, a transgender man, in an attempt to describe what the term "gender" means.[2] The statement characterizes the idea that gender identity is a matter of how one thinks about oneself: it is primarily one's own interpretation (based on a variety of things, e.g., hormone levels) of gender. Lehmiller introduces this quote because he wants to explain the difference between biological sex and gender identity. During lectures, he regularly asked students to name one characteristic that made them call someone a man or a woman. Invariably, most of the students present come up with the answer: a man has a penis and a woman a vagina. The other, smaller number of students maintain that it must be the presence of testicles or ovaries, or that it is mainly biological differences, such as the production of testosterone or estrogen, that are decisive. Lehmiller argues that this does not yet answer the question "what makes someone a man or a woman?" There seems to be a tension between what is "present at birth" about gender, genes, sexual orientation, etc., and what can develop based on the socialization of a person in a specific context with specific values and norms. Is gender and everything associated with it—complexity and variation—now a kind of "construct," something that is "created" or develops? Or should we stick to the approach in which everything is fixed from the outset (at conception or during pregnancy) and must therefore remain the same; a kind of "essence" that is immutable? It will become clear that these are, perhaps, contradictory currents, and that we can learn a lot from them—certainly in the church—for our discussion.

In chapter 1, we wrote about gender, and the related discussion around it, by way of introduction. Gender and sexuality are both part of a much broader context and play a role in different sciences and in different cultural contexts.[3] The concept of "sexuality," and related concepts, such as gender, but also terms such as homo-, hetero- and bisexuality, are directly related to European modernity. The term "homosexual," for

2. Lehmiller, *Psychology of Human Sexuality*, 116.

3. Thatcher, *Redeeming Gender*; and Thatcher, *Oxford Handbook*. We refer to these publications regularly in the course of this book.

example, first appeared in 1869. Similarly, the term "gender," used as a grammatical term since the fourteenth century, only gained a different and broader meaning, as we know it today, in the middle of the twentieth century. "Gender" became a subject of academic study, but mainly in the context of philosophical and social-scientific theorization.

It is important that we gain a better understanding of how sexuality, sex, and gender are connected. The gender spectrum, as we have present-ed it (see the *genderbread person* in chapter 1), illustrates this in a helpful way even though much of it can still be discussed and critiqued. It may also help if we place the discussion about the relationships between sexu-ality, sex, and gender against the background of a broader discussion, and with a view to the kinds of perspectives and lenses we are looking for in this chapter. Two theoretical perspectives play an important role in the current discourse. With Adrian Thatcher, we distinguish between *gender essentialism* and *gender constructivism*. These are two different ways of looking at gender, sex, and sexuality.[4] We will briefly elaborate on these concepts because they are foundational to further discussion of scientific perspectives and how they interrelate.

Gender Essentialism

This school of thought assumes that men and women are born with specifically different characteristics. Gender and sex are mostly seen as a matter of biological determination rather than of cultural determination. Gender and sex are, in fact, identical in this view.

From this perspective, it would be argued that there are only two fixed sexes, namely male and female, with fixed patterns of relations be-tween these two, because (and this is the line of thought) that is how God created them. In a chapter about scientific perspectives, a religious or Christian interpretation may seem out of place, but it does connect with the characteristics of an essentialist approach. According to this perspec-tive, it is God's intention that members of one sex long for or desire mem-bers of the other, the *opposite* sex. It is their *essence*. Gender essentialism then, in theological discussions of gender, refers to the view that God cre-ated humankind in two distinct sexes. Our created nature is either male or female and this cannot change (and, in this view, this is in conjunction with an emphasis on biological fundamentalism and determinism). Sex

4. Thatcher, *God, Sex, and Gender,* 3–49.

and gender are fixed from creation and birth, not only in a medical and biological way, but also in a *theological* sense: God wanted it that way. The desire of a woman for a woman or of a man for a man does not match with the created order as God intended it. We were created to be heterosexual so that the opposing definitions of man and woman can be maintained. In practice, adherents of this perspective point out the primary complementarity of man and woman. That is, men and women complement each other, based on an understanding of gender and sex as established in the order of creation.

Gender Constructivism

This is the view that nothing is fixed when it comes to sex and gender: in short, everything is constructed. Constructivism (or a constructivist view) then stands for a set of views that do not see gender as revealed or created by God, but rather as social and historical constructs in society. Societies produce relationships, and men and women relate to each other based on constructed patterns of norms and values. Thatcher relays how both theology and religious people have drawn from both sources (social and historical).[5] Theologically speaking, therefore, there is a great deal of attention paid to the "brokenness" of people, along with all sorts of stereotypes that do not do justice to the uniqueness of people.

In this context, the views of the American philosopher Judith Butler are important, and her publication *Gender Trouble* managed to stir up some people's emotions.[6] According to Butler, gender is not something *essential* (belonging to an essentialist conception), but something that is "performed." Gender has a certain degree of performativity: the language we use to describe something also functions as a form of social action. Thatcher uses the following example to explain Butler's point: When the bride says to her groom, "With this ring I wed thee," that is an example of an act of language by which the bride performs something. According to Butler, we become the men and women we are by an endless and everyday repetition of gendered acts. Butler speaks of *doing gender*, rather than *being gender*. There are, of course, many influences that affect us and shape us. Butler wondered how it was possible that gender identities in

---

5. Thatcher, *God, Sex, and Gender*; and Thatcher, *Redeeming Gender*, 3–49.

6. Butler, *Gender Trouble*. See also and in general: Alcoff, *Visible Identities*; Chodorow, *Femininities, Masculinities, Sexualities*.

different cultures were often shaped along similar (normative) lines.[7] Her answer to this question should not be surprising. The insistence on what was masculine and feminine was shaped by the culturally enforced repetition of opposing gender identities.[8] According to Butler, how gender was experienced had to do with the impact and power of culture. In the light of Butler's work, the term "sexual orientation" came under pressure.

Butler is part of a broader movement called post-structuralism, which also included philosophers such as Foucault. They both rightly point out the influence of language and power in relation to gender and sexuality. Neither language nor power is neutral but reveals assumptions about the way we see and value life and certainly about how we think about relationships. For example, anyone who names a child has a certain power over the newborn child, for the child cannot refuse the name (at least until they are older). Naming, giving language to certain phenomena, always goes hand in hand with a certain power and authority. In essence, this is no different regarding gender and sexuality.

Language

Thatcher explains that in medical science, for example, a whole language field has been developed around the concepts of "heterosexual" and "homosexual."[9] Kathleen M. Sands, professor of American studies and religious studies, makes the helpful distinction between *homosexuality* (referring to identity) and *homoeroticism* (referring to practice and "lifestyle") because of different manifestations and meanings in different cultures.[10] She not only describes the conceptual history, but also the excesses surrounding and the oppression of groups of homosexuals in the context of Christianity. As we have mentioned, the term "homosexual" dates back to 1869, and the term "heterosexual" dates back to 1892. "Heterosexual" was, at first, the term for people who had sex without the desire to procreate. However, it soon became a norm, a measuring rod along which other sexual behavior was measured as deviant.[11] In

7. See van Heesch, *Ze wisten niet of ik een jongen of een meisje was*. Van Heesch gives a very insightful view of the history and development in medical and psychological science of sex variations.

8. Van Heesch, *Ze wisten niet of ik een jongen of een meisje was*, 9–41.

9. See Siker, *Homosexuality and Religion*, 3–31.

10. Sands, "Homosexuality, Religion, and the Law"; and Sands, *God Forbid*, 3–31.

11. Thatcher, *God, Sex, and Gender*, 24–25.

popular or vernacular speech, language related to sexuality plays a major role in how we think about it. Words such as "fuck," "screw," etc. reveal a kind of tyranny of phallocentric (focus on the penis as an image of male dominance) language whereby women are forced to see the world from a dominant male perspective. As a consequence, we end up with a discourse that is characterized by objectification, violence, and condescending behavior.

Thatcher discusses the three levels at which power plays a role alongside language: 1) at the level of relationships between men and women; 2) at the level of interaction between social institutions and individuals; and 3) at the level of changing relationships with more emphasis on reciprocity. At the first level, we speak of "power over" (women), in the sense that it implies a certain domination and therefore subordination. In relation to gender, this "power over" often takes the form of patriarchal patterns. In many societies, women are then the most vulnerable party, with a minimum of being denied some of their rights and a maximum of being subjected to violence such as domestic abuse and rape. At the third level of power, it is mainly about "power with" (someone or something). This is where there is shared power, in which cooperation, mutuality, consultation, and consensus play a much greater role.

Influential in this conversation is the work of the French philosopher Foucault who, in his three-volume work *Histoire de la Sexualité,* calls attention to the second level at which power plays a role: between social institutions and individuals.[12] According to Foucault, knowledge comes to life through processes of exclusion, in which one acquires knowledge by excluding others in relation to that knowledge. The government exercises power over its citizens through the institutions it allows. Foucault sees power playing a role everywhere, often through institutions and networks. For example, think of advertisements on television, the branding of products that we do or do not need but nevertheless buy, and also the type of clothes that we wear. Global corporations exert a high degree of social power over people, and they therefore determine part of our identity. This type of power is tangible and demonstrable in the field of human sexuality. Foucault's analysis is poignant, but also open to justified criticism. For example, the question is whether his vision of power does not, in fact, make resistance to power (also in the field of gender and sexuality) impossible. To what extent can people resist the deterministic character of

12. Foucault, *Histoire de la Sexualité,* vol. I, *La Volonté de Savoir; Histoire de la Sexualité,* vol. II, *L'usage des Plaisirs; Histoire de la Sexualité,* vol. III, *Le Souci de Soi.*

power, by means of institutions, in our society? Abuse of power, of course, does not only happen at the level of institutions, but also in families and relationships.[13] After this somewhat broad-sweeping introduction, we will now move to the contributions of the various sciences.

Extremes or Grey Areas

Heleen Zorgdrager, professor of gender studies at the Protestant Theological University in the Netherlands (PThU), pays attention to the tension between essentialist and constructivist approaches. In an online publication entitled "Back to Nature? A Feminist Theologian on the Verge of Conversion," she expresses her own doubts about gender identity as a social construct and moves more strongly toward the vision that assumes a biological basis for gender identity.[14] Decisive for Zorgdrager are studies that increasingly point to a biological basis for gender dysphoria (the experience of a mismatch between one's physical/biological sex and the gender identity that differs from it), and also, for example, studies that show that homosexual behavior is hereditary to a factor of 30 to 40 percent.[15] The worldwide leaning to a renewed attention to traditional family values, that emphasize the binary nature of man and woman (see, for example, the recent Roman Catholic document "Male and Female He Created Them"), also motivates Zorgdrager's need for a theological response.[16] According to her, we cannot ignore the newer biological insights from an evolutionary perspective. We take Zorgdrager's contribution as a call for caution when it comes to jumping to conclusions about the relationship between nature (essentialist) and nurture (constructivist). New insights could lead to both approaches needing to adjust their primary positions.

Thatcher, too, notes that although the two movements are described as two extremes, it is worth remembering that there are many intermediate

13. Thatcher, in *God, Sex, and Gender*, 28, refers to the ways in which the New Testament depicts Jesus, more as someone powerless than as the powerful ruler (cf. 1 Cor 1:18). Of course, Jesus had a certain power over and agency in people who followed him and looked out for help, etc. At the same time, he lived intentionally in uncomfortable relationship with the rulers and institutions of his time.

14. Cf. Zorgdrager, "Terug naar de natuur?"

15. Zorgdrager, *Tussen Hooglied en #MeToo.*

16. Congregation for Catholic Education, "Male and Female He Created Them."

positions.[17] On the one hand, not every theologian who considers themselves an essentialist will claim that desire and procreation are eternal constants, but that they are matters of great importance throughout human history. The strength of this thinking is that it can protect us from going along with the ebb and flow of culture uncritically, for there are many values in various (Christian) traditions that still promote the good life. Perhaps these value-based traditions also put human sexuality in perspective and contribute to a healthy restraint of human desire. On the other hand, there are good arguments for various tenets of constructivism. We could make the claim, for example, that God has given people a responsibility to develop good relationships, leaving it up to us how best to do this. Of course, this then emphasizes human freedom (with healthy accountability) in a different way.

Important in this debate is the consideration that when things tend to get difficult it is almost always related to the opposition between these two approaches to gender and sexuality. At the heart of this is the fact that many religions and religious movements may be inclined to express themselves in a way that fits in with an essentialist approach, while the more secular debate on gender is increasingly based on a constructivist view. This tension, and all the problems that go along with it, becomes even clearer in recent responses to the work of the Canadian neuroscientist and sexologist Debra Soh. In her 2020 book *The End of Gender*, Soh tries to debunk myths about gender, sex, and identity in our society.[18] Her view is that gender has only a biological basis and is certainly not a social construct. According to Soh, we have been infected by feminist scholars such as Simone de Beauvoir and Judith Butler. It is very clear that Soh misrepresents feminist thinking and generalizes too easily.[19] But what is more problematic is that her thinking is used and applied uncritically by numerous representatives of the more essentialist views (compare chapter 1). According to Soh, gender politics are harmful as they shape a strong push to conformity and run the risk of impacting the mental health of trans and other nonbinary individuals. She argues that gender politics reject scientific evidence with regard to the differences between men and women, and that gender theories lack empirical evidence and are mostly based on political and cultural ideologies. While we sympathize with Soh's critical assessment of specific and early treatment of

17. Thatcher, *God, Sex, and Gender*, 17–32.
18. Soh, *End of Gender*.
19. See Lorenzen, "Radical Feminist Review."

young children and teenagers, we believe that she ignores the complexity of both nature and nurture in their delicate interplay. It would be too soon to conclude that biological sex is the sole determinant of gender. The role of socialization, cultural norms, and power dynamics needs to be taken into account. In general, Soh's argumentation is, in many ways, nurtured by a strong negative response to her own negative experiences as an academic. The boldness with which Soh presents her views may give some the confidence to think that science is backing up the more essentialist views and that gender identity is only a postmodern figment of mind. Unfortunately for them, this is not the case and tensions between the two paradigmatic views remain. In reality, the various approaches to gender seem to blend and blur, and the contrast between the more essentialist approaches and the more constructivist approaches is less clear. This fact does not necessarily make conversations around gender and sexuality easier either. However, it can dissuade us from jumping to conclusions and making judgments about people in different situations.

Biology, Genetics, Sex, and Gender

What light do the life sciences shed on the complex phenomena of gender and sexuality? As we have already pointed out in the previous paragraph: it is not an unambiguous story. In an interesting and convincing essay, biogeneticist and theologian Neil Messer shows that there is a great variety of views on sex variation, the origin of human sexuality, and variations in sexual behavior based on heredity (behavioral genetics). Behavioral genetic studies of homosexuality are not left out of the equation either.[20] We see his conclusions as essential to the discussions we aim to address with this book: there is a lack of constructive dialogue between biologists and medics, for example, on the one hand, and social scientists and theologians, for example, on the other. Critical objections from the social scientists are quickly dismissed as anti-scientific trickery by neuroscientists, while social constructivists accuse biogeneticists of holding to a discourse of power. Of course, this is a case of the pot calling the kettle black, but at the same time this is a major problem. Unless the various branches of science work together, we will not get much further than pitting the different viewpoints against each other. The development

20. Messer, "Contributions from Biology," 69–87.

of new models with which to view these complex issues is, of course, decisive for the development of a constructive dialogue.

It is of the utmost importance that scientific knowledge is used and mapped well to address complex issues, even if it questions our assumptions. Lehmiller points out that biological sex is "the function of three distinct components: chromosomes, gonads and hormonal levels."[21] It is these three components that are largely responsible for the "biology" of men and women. In an overview, this differentiation looks as follows:

Level of differentiation	Male	Female
Chromosomal sex	XY	XX
Gonads	Testicles	Ovaries
Hormonal sex	Androgen	Estrogen
Sexual anatomy	Fully developed penis and scrotum as well as their corresponding internal reproductive structures	Fully developed vulva, as well as corresponding internal reproductive structures

Table 3—Sequence of biological sex differentiation[22]

Chromosomal sex refers to a specific combination of chromosomes in our genes, which are, in part, responsible for biological sex. Usually, chromosomal sex is determined at conception, when a male sperm cell fertilizes a female egg cell. Egg cells normally carry a single X chromosome, while sperm cells usually carry a single X or a single Y chromosome. When the combination is XX, the development of the fetus will usually result in a female form.[23] When the combination is XY, the development will usually lead to a male form. Hormonal sex refers to the hormones released by the gonads: androgens and estrogens. Both are released by men and women, but in a different balance. Usually, the female body produces more estrogen, and the male body produces more androgen. Lehmiller shows that hormones are not only responsible for the development of internal and external genitalia, but they also have a major influence on the way the brain of a fetus develops in the womb.[24]

21. Lehmiller, *Psychology of Human Sexuality*, 117.

22. On the basis of Lehmiller's model.

23. Compare Chess Denman's work, especially *Sexuality*; Lehmiller, *Psychology of Human Sexuality*.

24. Lehmiller, *Psychology of Human Sexuality*, 118.

Hormones have a serious impact on the development of a more male or female brain before birth. A specific part of the brain, the hypothalamus, is strongly affected by prenatal hormones. It plays an important role in the regulation of sexual behavior. A part of the hypothalamus, which contains reliable sex differences, is called the *preoptic area* (POA). Research has shown that this area is larger in full-grown men than in adult women. Another part of the hypothalamus is now believed to be responsible for gender identity. The eventual development of "typically" male or "typically" female bodies requires a kind of "cooperation" between chromosomes, gonads, and hormones. Practice shows, however, that the interaction of chromosomes, gonads, and hormones does not always develop a "typically" male or female body (or person, for that matter). In these cases, we speak of intersexuality.[25] Thus, biological sex is, in reality, an extremely complex and varied phenomenon. Some people, for example, are born with external and/or internal genitals that are not "typically" male or female. Following the work of Margriet van Heesch, it is therefore better to speak in terms of sex variation. Lehmiller gives a helpful overview of these variations.[26] We summarize salient characteristics of the different variations in a table below.[27]

---

25. Lehmiller, *Psychology of Human Sexuality*, 119.
26. Lehmiller, *Psychology of Human Sexuality*, 121.
27. Lehmiller, *Psychology of Human Sexuality*, 121.

Biological sex variations			
Type	Description	Gender identity	Sexual Orientation
Klinefelter's Syndrome	Most common is an XXY chromosome combination; male anatomy with some female characteristics	Usually male	Same gender attraction is no more common than it is among biological males
Turner Syndrome	Singular X-chromosome, feminine body and genital appearance, no functioning internal reproductive structures; sexual activity relates to start of puberty	Female	Not linked to same-gender attraction
Complete Androgen Insensitivity Syndrome	XY-male but insensitive to (male) androgens; female genital appearance, usually not detected until puberty	Female	Attraction to men
Partial Androgen Insensitivity Syndrome	XY-male who responds partially to (male) androgens; genitals appear to be a mix of male and female structures	Male or female	Variable
5-Alpha Reductase Deficiency	XY-male, unable to convert testosterone into dihydrotestosterone; has testes but has female genital characteristics until puberty	Usually female during childhood, male starting at puberty	Most attraction to women
Congenital Adrenal Hyperplasia (CAH)	XX-female with deviant hormone production; masculine genital appearance	Usually female with "masculine" interests	Most attraction to men

Table 4: Biological sex variations

The Story of David

Some decades ago, the New Zealand psychologist John Money presented his theory of gender-neutrality. Based on his research, he was convinced that every human being was initially a kind of blank page regarding his or her gender. Money contended that it seemed that every child is born with a kind of possibility to be either male or female. Which way the child will ultimately develop, he was convinced, will be determined by its environment. Money tested his theory when he met a very concerned mother who did not know what to do when her son's penis had been severely damaged by an incorrectly performed circumcision. He advised the parents to raise their young son Bruce as a girl. Bruce was castrated on Money's advice and was given the name Brenda. For a longer period in his adolescence, he was also given female hormones. Money then recommended an operation to change his sex and create a vagina. Money then monitored the situation for several years and met with Brenda annually to evaluate her progress. In his reports, in articles in leading journals, Money reported that Brenda's change was a resounding success, proving the theory of gender-neutrality. However, the facts did not support the claimed success. Brenda did not really see herself as a woman. She did not want to dress like a woman and preferred to hang out with boys. She felt depressed, had great difficulty adapting, and became suicidal. As a teenager she resisted hormone treatments and refused surgery to complete her transformation. During this period, her parents decided to speak the truth about the accident and what had happened since and, shortly afterwards, Brenda chose to adopt a male gender identity. From then on, he called himself David and eventually underwent operations to become the man he always felt he was. Things did not end well for David. On 4 May 2004, he committed suicide.[28]

The story of David Reimer is an impressing and sobering one on several levels and sits right at the heart of the different stages of development of scientific knowledge and experiments regarding sex variation. It shows the complexities of the nature and nurture discussions and the impact these have on real people. David's parents and doctors did not just try to teach him a specific gender. They also changed his genitals and gave him treatments. All of this proved insufficient to overrule his feeling that he was a male after all. Van Heesch also states: "The most important lesson

28. See "David Reimer." Compare also van Heesch, *Ze wisten niet of ik een jongen of een meisje was*, 9–44.

Reimer taught us was that his fate could never justify the irreversible medical interventions on children with a gender variation."[29] We will attend to the impact of these practices below.

Gender and Sex Variations

So far, we have mapped out how we can look at gender in different ways (and with different conceptual theories). However, there is more to explore about *practice*, in which we find a great deal of variation and complexity. Van Heesch and Lehmiller pay attention to the confusion that often exists around the question on what basis we know whether someone is a man or a woman. Both cite the example of the South African athlete Caster Semenya, who won the world eight-hundred-meter race in Berlin in 2009. Her fellow athletes demanded a gender test because of her angular look and voice. The Dutch newspaper *Volkskrant*, on August 19 of that same year, was headlined, "The World Doubts: Is Semenya a Woman?" A huge riot arose, with the athlete coming under increasing pressure, especially when it was revealed that a test (under the pretext of a doping test) had already been carried out without her knowledge at an earlier stage. Sadly, Semenya became an object of medical science. Diversity then soon became a rare disease. In this case, we are witnessing a power struggle over the body of an athlete, and it raises the legitimate question of how knowledge about sex variations is generated, especially when it leads to the exclusion of people.

A second important theme (besides the importance of understanding the two broad currents of *gender essentialism* and *gender constructivism*) is, as described above, the historical development of ideas around sex variation. Although, on the one hand, this is to some extent already part of a more medical-anthropological lens, on the other hand we feel that the history of dealing with sex variation is a good framework for our discussions in this book because it also shows (in addition to the possibilities and insights) the limitations and downsides of medical science. For this reason, we will give a brief historical overview of these developments below.

Margriet van Heesch takes us on this historical journey of discovery, with various sources and related developments in knowledge. She

---

29. Van Heesch, *Ze wisten niet of ik een jongen of een meisje was*, 31; translated by the authors.

shows that knowledge about sex development has increased considerably in the past decades, and she also elaborates on lessons learned in medical and psychological science. Below, we follow van Heesch in her historical analysis.[30]

Van Heesch reviews the various paradigms that have been influential in the field of sex variation in recent decades. To this end, she divides the past decades into five periods: from 1900–1950, 1950–70, 1970–90, 1990–2000, and finally 2000–2014. It is a thorough account of the multifaceted quest for a decisive answer to hold on to and its corresponding knowledge about gender.

Historical Analysis

In the first period (1900–1950), two models of thinking alternated. On the one hand, it was generally thought that a person's sex was biologically determined (biological determinism) in the gonads and could therefore be predicted, while on the other hand, it was assumed that an individual would eventually develop into a man or a woman of his or her own accord. In the first model, it was thought that ovaries and testes made the woman or man, irrespective of the behavior and the appearance of the body. In the second model, doctors, such as Fritz Kahn, were very influential in the idea that parents and doctors had a supportive role to play, but that the right sex would undoubtedly "show up" at some point in time.

In the subsequent phase (1950–70), these two models remained of great influence. The development of gender identity either took place through education (the so-called optimal-gender-for-education protocol, based on later falsified research by the New Zealand psychologist John Money), withholding of information, and surgery, or through a process of its own, in which an approach similar to that of Kahn was chosen: just wait, sooner or later the right gender will develop. Although knowledge about the effects of prenatal hormones increased, according to van Heesch, the idea that children were born psychosexually neutral remained unchanged. It was precisely in this period that the emergence of what can be called a sociocultural determinism was observed.

Gradually, in the following period (1970–90), the biological deterministic views are subjected to more criticism. Sociocultural determinism made its appearance. Feminists expressed the opinion that such

---

30. Van Heesch, *Ze wisten niet of ik een jongen of een meisje was*, 88–109.

views (especially the aforementioned binary thinking about man and woman and gender) blocked the social position of women. This gave the discussions another turn, whereby a biological fundamentalism dominated conversation, according to van Heesch: biology no longer had the final say, but it did provide the basis on which gender is shaped differently per context and culture. Constructivist thinking about gender definitely received a boost from this. The attention paid to people sharing their own stories and raising their own voices was increasing.

In the phase that followed (1990–2000), the influence of postmodern thinking can increasingly be seen, according to van Heesch. Biology was increasingly seen in perspective alongside other insights and, partly due to the influence of Foucault, it was placed in the framework of power structures. The constructivist framework soon gained priority, and research was carried out about a possible third gender. Fausto-Sterling proposed that there should even be five gender identities and others as many as eight. Van Heesch labels this paradigm the "categorical paradigm." It is striking how earlier claimed scientific insights, especially regarding the parenting model considered proven by Money, largely ended up in the bin. Van Heesch demonstrates that it became clear that the paradigm in which sex and gender were seen as highly creatable, mainly produced stigma, trauma, and new taboos.[31] A new paradigm is emerging, biological constructivism, which emphasizes the combination of neurobiological and social aspects in the development of gender.

Van Heesch also characterizes a last phase, up until the end of her research (2000–2014). She notes that in recent years, contradicting views are still tumbling over each other. In 2003, Money's parenting protocol still proves to be influential in the Netherlands, and van Heesch gives examples of shocking practices, and confusion about concepts and descriptions of different sex variations. The question is: how can we prevent burdening people against their will with a label that only stigmatizes, such as the (however well-intentioned) attempt to speak of disorders of sex development (DSD). Who has the right to speak of a "disorder?" A general practitioner or specialist? Or the patient? A more positive development is that more and more different research sources can be linked with each other, with the aim of being able to name or determine a gender identity.

Van Heesch continues her analysis with a large collection of life stories of people with gender variations. She shows that the lack of

31. Van Heesch, *Ze wisten niet of ik een jongen of een meisje was*, 104.

knowledge, or the prevailing norms for masculinity and femininity in many cases, led to shame, identity problems, and (self-)rejection. Many of the personal stories are characterized by denial of personal identity, as there was a "constant attempt not to want to know that there might be something special about my body."[32] Reading the stories, one recognizes the patterns as described by van Heesch: in many cases, limited medical knowledge had more authority than experience for the people struggling with their gender identity. This *knowledge-asymmetry*, identified by van Heesch, often led to a lack of alternative definitions of the self. With a view to better counselling, van Heesch expresses the hope that more attention will be paid to long-term sociocultural and medical research and to an early sharing of crucial information with children who are affected. She hopes for recognition of the marginalization of people living with gender differences. She poses an important challenge to factors in society that influence stigmas surrounding gender variations: binary gender thinking, reproductive imperatives, heteronormativity, homophobia, the so-called coital imperative, and the "curable" nature of intersexuality (all terms used by van Heesch). We share van Heesch's opinion that these discourses should indeed be questioned and analyzed, especially in church circles, because of the great impact these frameworks have on people. This does not mean that we embrace unhelpful gender ideological notions, as we are aware of, for example, teenagers in high schools being immersed in unguided gender conversations that can have a huge impact on their well-being. It is clear that this is not what van Heesch had in mind at all. Careful examination of assumptions seems even more crucial now.

The Story of a Mother

In the spring of 2014, a Dutch mother posted a remarkable message on a private international Facebook group for people with gender variations. "Dear friends, I just need to vent my heart." She had gone to see an endocrinologist for her three-year-old child with a provisional diagnosis of "gonadal dysgenesis and ambiguous genitalia." The endocrinologist was concerned about the mother's attitude and wanted her to see a psychologist. First, the mother had to stop thinking that her child showed a sex variation, as he was "just a boy." "And . . . oh, and one more thing, I shouldn't talk to my friends and family about my son's condition [. . .] not to mention the fact that I have to see a psychiatrist because [as] parents we don't want surgery and the

---

32. Van Heesch, *Ze wisten niet of ik een jongen of een meisje was*, 60–63.

doctors do." The mother can't get over it: "So the advice in the Netherlands is *deny* and *lie*! I am stunned!"[33]

Variations in Gender Identity, Expression, and Orientation

In chapter 1, we described the different concepts we use as working definitions in this book. Gender identity is defined there as "a person's own and individual perception of whether he or she is male or female." We defined gender expression as "the way in which gender is displayed through behavior, interaction, and appearance." In the meantime, it has become clear that we can speak of a much broader gender diversity. In practice, we see variations in the way gender is expressed. We do not want to simply pass over a term like "cisgender," which refers to people whose gender identity matches their birth sex. The term is usually used to refer to the opposite of "transgender."

We have chosen here to focus mainly on transgender, as this term refers to a very broad group of individuals, which transcends culturally defined gender categories. The term "transgender" usually refers to people whose assigned sex at birth does not correspond with their experienced gender identity. This has included people who call themselves transsexual or transgender, people who "cross-dress," drag queens, drag kings, and others who do not identify as male or female. A distinction is made here between transvestism and cross-dressing. A man who is masculine in terms of his physical sex and gender identity, but exhibits feminine behavior in terms of his gender role, had been referred to as a "transvestite." A "cross-dresser" is usually a heterosexual man who imitates the appearance of a woman by dressing in a traditionally feminine way. When a man expresses himself in a feminine way, they have sometimes been referred to as a drag queen. When a woman expresses herself in a masculine way, they have sometimes been referred to as a drag king. In the past, being transgender was assessed as a *gender identity disorder*.[34] Gradually, the term "gender dysphoria" has been used, with the following criteria being essential:

---

33. Van Heesch, *Ze wisten niet of ik een jongen of een meisje was*, 53.

34. Van Heesch, *Ze wisten niet of ik een jongen of een meisje was*; Lehmiller, *Psychology of Human Sexuality*, 130.

- A perceived mismatch between gender expression and physical characteristics;

- A deep desire to be of the opposite sex and to be treated as such;

- A desire to be able to move away from his or her primary and secondary sexual characteristics and to have the primary and secondary sexual characteristics of the opposite sex;

- The belief that feelings and behavior are typical of and belong to the opposite sex;

- Clinically observable stress and functional limitation, and feelings of incongruence. Gender dysphoria is not considered a clinical problem unless the patient is under severe stress about it.

Lehmiller points to the distinction between *male-to-female* trans people (MTF) and *female-to-male* trans people (FTM). An MTF transsexual is assigned male at birth (AMAB) but sees themself as a woman; an FTM transsexual is assigned female at birth (AFAB) but sees themself as a man. The views on the origin of transsexuality are complicated. There may be a neurological basis, related to the influence of prenatal hormones. The patterns of attraction to men and women in these groups are diverse. Treatment of adult transsexuals is often complex and lengthy, ranging from surgical intervention (vaginoplasty, removal of uterus and ovaries, reconstruction of the clitoris into a penis, phalloplasty, etc.) to intensive psychological counselling. Surgical intervention does not simply take place, but is preceded by long-term psychological assessments and discussions, focusing on motivation and possible conflicts. Complex hormone treatments and major surgery to the genitals are only carried out after careful consideration.

In addition, we cannot leave out another group of people, namely those who see themselves primarily as *genderqueer*. This group places itself largely outside a binary classification of male/female. Sometimes members of this group will characterize themselves as *bigender*, with a high degree of change in role behavior in different contexts, moving strongly between male and female roles. Others may characterize themselves as *asexual, aromantic,* or *nonbinary,* for example. What is clear is that for many people who consider themselves genderqueer, there is an idea that gender identity is not so much a fixed identity state, but rather flexible and changeable. For many, *being queer* is an expression of a continuous search process in which they find themselves, especially if it is unclear where they might be on a spectrum of being transgender.

Sexual Orientations

In chapter 1, we outlined how we intend to use the different concepts relating to sexuality and gender. It is important to consider not only variations in gender identity, but also different sexual orientations. In the first chapter, we defined sexual orientation as "the unique pattern of sexual and romantic desire, behavior, and identity expressed by a person." We will use this definition in this section when describing the content of several sexual orientations. We are aware that it is important to look at different orientations through a broad lens, because identity, behavior, and attraction differ per individual.[35]

For many people, there are only three categories of orientation: heterosexual, homosexual, and bisexual. However, research shows that sexual orientation is best seen on a continuum. But, bearing this in mind, generally, people do not fit into the famous scale developed by Kinsey (see Figure 3) with two extremes: exclusively heterosexual and exclusively homosexual. And the research has moved on from here.

(0)	(1)	(2)	(3)	(4)	(5)	(6)
Exclusively heterosexual	Heterosexual, incidental homosexual tendencies	Heterosexual, more than incidental homosexual tendencies	Bisexual, equally heterosexual and homosexual	Homosexual, more than incidental heterosexual tendencies	Homosexual, incidental heterosexual tendencies	Exclusively homosexual

Figure 3: Kinsey scale

In this section, we will not discuss the various theoretical explanations for the emergence or development of sexual orientation. We note that there is a multiplicity of explanations, ranging from psychological theory (in line with Freud, for example), biological and hormonal theory (regarding brain function or genetic explanations), to evolutionary theory and biopsychosocial theory (with much attention to sexual fluidity when it comes to orientation). Instead, we will give a brief overview of different orientations or preferences.

---

35. Lehmiller, *Psychology of Human Sexuality*, 145–46.

Kinsey and his colleagues assumed that every person experiences at least some degree of sexual attraction. This turns out not to be true. There are individuals and groups of people who describe themselves as "asexual." Richards and Barker point out that although this is a relatively new group identification, the experiences underlying this characterization have existed for much longer. It seems difficult to determine the number of people who identify as asexual. Estimated percentages are between 0.5 and 1.5 percent of the population.[36] Within the asexual community, there is also great diversity. Carrigan points to a wide variety of attitudes toward sexual behavior, ranging from aversion and dissent to positive and romantic attraction, including, for example, hetero-romantic, bi-romantic, and pan-romantic.[37] Research points to the importance of describing similarities and differences between the groups of people who identify themselves as asexual. Definitional issues are extremely important, even if it means carefully identifying what an asexual orientation is not. Richards and Barker point out that there is some confusion surrounding the term. Asexuality is often equated with (an attraction to) celibacy or a deliberate choice to live a life of celibacy. The result can be that an *absence* of sexual attraction is confused with the *choice* to *intentionally* abstain from sexual activity. It is important that the experiences of people who characterize themselves as asexual are taken seriously and in their respective choices, be they directed at being less sexually active or living a life in celibacy, potentially even with a level of felt pressure regarding the relationship between being homosexual but not choosing to enact their sexual orientation.

BDSM (BONDAGE, DISCIPLINE [DOMINANCE, SUBMISSION], SADISM, AND MASOCHISM)

BDSM has undoubtedly become better known through the erotic novel *Fifty Shades of Grey* and the subsequent film adaptation of the book.[38] However, there is still a public perception that those who engage in BDSM must have a history of abuse in some form. A well-known example of BDSM is *spanking*: being tied up in a certain way and suffering verbal

36. Richards and Barker, *Palgrave Handbook*, 7.
37. Carrigan, "How Do You Know," 3–19.
38. James, *Fifty Shades of Grey*.

humiliation in the process. Lehmiller points out the general distinction that is made between *masochism* and *sadism*: masochism refers to sexual gratification through receiving physical or psychological pain; sadism refers to deriving sexual satisfaction from inflicting physical or psychological pain on others. It seems that there are many misunderstandings about people who express their sexual experience in this way. Research shows that in most cases, people practice BDSM in mild forms, which do not involve extremes. Recent research also shows that at least 10 percent of the population is generally interested in BDSM practices.[39] In the scientific debate on BDSM, the question of classification often arises. Should the "need" for or enjoyment of BDSM be seen as a deviation, a psychiatric illness, a perversion, or simply as adult entertainment? Many of the practices seen in connection with BDSM are still classified as a paraphilic disorder within DSM-5, the classification system for mental disorders and illnesses. The term "paraphilia" refers to a deviant sexual interest in which a person is aroused by deviant activities, objects, or persons who are incapable of consenting to them.[40]

A "disorder" is assumed when personal functioning is impaired or when harm is done to others. As far as "paraphilic" activities are concerned, these are mainly exhibitionism, voyeurism, sadism and masochism, fetishism (such as excitement by lifeless objects), transvestism, and pedophilia. Websites emphasize that paraphilia is punishable as soon as damage is done to another person. Opinions vary widely. Since 2013, changes have been made to the DSM-5 classification regarding paraphilia. The aim of these changes was to better distinguish between a nonnormative sexual interest and a disrupted sexual interest. The DSM-5 publication points out that most people with an atypical sexual interest do not have a mental disorder. To be diagnosed with a paraphilic disorder, people must feel personally stressed about their interest, engage in sexual behavior that causes psychological stress, injury, or worse to another person, or not be consensual.

The responsible DSM-5 working group changed the term *sexual masochism* to *sexual masochism disorder*, with the aim of being able to distinguish between atypical and disturbed sexual behavior.[41] In a certain sense, therefore, we can speak of a shift toward a practice in which BDSM is not immediately judged to be pathological (that is, BDSM by default

39. Lehmiller, *Psychology of Human Sexuality*, 336.
40. Turley and Butt, "BDSM," 24–41.
41. Compare "Paraphilic Disorders."

as an illness or disorder). This trend is also referred to by Richards and Barker. It is striking that BDSM has more recently been seen as a form of recreation by adults, with specific conditions and rules. Other researchers hold the opinion that the comparison between BDSM and practicing extreme sports (boxing, rugby, etc.) should be drawn, because in the latter category no pathologizing appears to be present.

BISEXUALITY

The term "bisexual" is generally used in western cultures to refer to individuals who are attracted to more than one gender. The term is not without its problems for researchers because it is not always clear what exactly is meant. Sexologists, for example, tended to focus their attention on the gender identity of the person with different and specific desires. They suspected that nonheterosexual desires were anchored in gender identity. For example, a woman with masculine traits would be attracted to other women; a man with female traits would be attracted to other men. If a person experienced attraction to both men and women, this would indicate that this person also possessed male and female characteristics. However, the term used was not bisexuality, or even intersexuality, but the obsolete term "hermaphroditism."[42]

A well-known sexologist of the nineteenth century, Karl Heinrich Ulrichs, held a specific theory of a third sex. According to him, the fetus develops during pregnancy in such a way that a differentiation in sex takes place so that either a heterosexual man, a heterosexual woman, or a homosexual "third sex" develops. This third gender could then neither be characterized as male or female. The result: female souls in male bodies and male souls in female bodies.

It is interesting to note that the various waves of research and scientific insights succeed each other. For example, a later sexologist, Von Krafft-Ebing, believed that bisexuality arose under the influence of evolutionary processes and that, in connection with this, it should be seen as an immature stage of development from which all kinds of other sexual orientations emerge.[43] In this view, everyone would have some degree of bisexual "potential." Gradually this perspective changed, partly because

---

42. For more general background see Storr, *Bisexuality*; Oosterhuis, *Stepchildren of Nature*; Richards and Barker, *Palgrave Handbook*.

43. Richards and Barker, *Palgrave Handbook*, 42–58.

one-sided binary thinking, with male and female as two opposites on one continuum, was questioned. From the mid-1980s onward, research increasingly focused on a critical appraisal of that long-standing dichotomy from earlier research. In older research, it was noted, bisexuality and bisexual behavior were explained away as features of a transitional phase (see above), evidence of a psychological or mental problem, or even evidence of the denial of one's homosexuality on the basis of internalized homophobia. Slowly but surely, bisexuality was seen as an orientation that should be distinguished from homosexuality and thus as an identity of its own.

The fluidity of human sexuality, gradually and over time, was beginning to be seen as a given. Stereotyping is still present in abundance, however. Lehmiller points to the fact that the idea that bisexuals are actually homosexuals who do not dare to come out is still circulating. Lehmiller also points to recent studies with different test groups that show convincingly that bisexuality exists. Bisexuality indicates a complex identity that is undoubtedly experienced differently by different people.[44] The study that Diamond carried out a few years ago is also interesting: of the group of women who identified themselves as bisexual, almost 90 percent were found to be in a long-term monogamous relationship.[45] The myth that bisexual people could not have long-term relationships was thus challenged.

HETEROSEXUALITY

Earlier in this book we pointed out the normative character of heterosexuality and the fact that heterosexuality has a strong normative function in society. In fact, it refers to the view that there are normative assumptions in society regarding gender: there are two sexes, male and female, and only attraction between the opposite sexes is acceptable. We call this heteronormativity.[46] Heteronormativity structures social and religious beliefs and organizations in society, influences policy, and is literally the norm, because it determines who is inside, but also who is outside. In short, heterosexuality is the norm. Interestingly, in much of the psychological literature, heteronormativity is not an object of discussion or

44. Lehmiller, *Psychology of Human Sexuality*, 145–49.
45. Diamond, "Female Bisexuality," 5–14.
46. Warner, "Introduction," 3–17.

research, it is a given.[47] What received most attention in research and study was what deviated from that norm. The question that can justifiably be asked is whether a broader and more in-depth analysis of heterosexual behavior could not, in fact, yield many new insights. The term was first used in the last half of the nineteenth century. Katz shows that at a certain point the term was even used to describe the variety of feelings an individual had for both sexes. In today's terms, we would now characterize this as bisexuality.[48] Von Krafft-Ebing, discussed above, used the term to describe a sexual instinct directed toward procreation (reproduction). "Normal" sex was therefore sex with a person of the opposite sex.

Both Von Krafft-Ebing and Freud saw homosexuality as a version of heterosexuality: the latter was normal and good, the former abnormal and bad. A first historical departure from this thinking only occurred around the middle of the 1960s when, under the influence of the second feminist wave, heterosexuality was increasingly seen as a mechanism responsible for the unequal treatment of men and women and even disadvantaged women. Biological sex was increasingly distinguished from culturally transmitted gender (identity). The influence of constructivism is immediately visible here. The ideology of heterosexuality (as the result of a social construct) was seen as the way in which heterosexual domination came about. The work of Adrienne Rich is well known: she emphasized that women were not born heterosexual but were forced into a heterosexual mode by the social system that expected obligatory heterosexuality from them.[49] Biological approaches, interestingly enough, were of course excluded and rejected.

Homosexuality

It is important to mention at the beginning of this paragraph that although we are discussing homosexual orientation, we are making a distinction between gay men and lesbian women, because they are not the same. In a publication written by Richards and Barker, but also in many other studies, a distinction is carefully made.[50] In this section, we will briefly discuss a number of important themes related to homosexuality.

---

47. Farvid, "Heterosexuality," 92–108.
48. Katz, as cited in Farvid, "Heterosexuality," 92–108.
49. Farvid, "Heterosexuality," 92–108.
50. Richards and Barker, *Palgrave Handbook,* 77–79; Carroll, *Sexuality Now,* 45–46.

It is notable that although older sexological and psychological research made a concerted effort to arrive at a more inclusive understanding of what characterizes gay men, much of this research contributed to the stereotyping of gay men as strongly feminine. Many of the discussions and prejudices relate to what the terms "masculinity" and "femininity" mean. This is not only true for gay men. Connell points to the fact that this group of men can suffer from both oppression and privilege. According to Connell, this results in a constant conflict about what exactly "manliness" is.[51]

Homosexual men are forced (in the West) into a value system of masculinity to which they have not contributed, and which is not part of their lived experience either. Riggs rightly puts his finger on the problem when he states that, in general, talking about "gay men" as if they were a single category is problematic. Opinions vary widely as to the types of intimacy and even whether these intimacies should be pathologized or not. Or is it merely a variation within the various forms of human intimacy in general? Presumably, there is a much greater variation, as is the case with other sexual orientations and their corresponding expression.

Freud, in his own way, was clear about this. He saw homosexuality as a specific reaction to the separation of the young child from its mother, with the subsequent imposition of an external "law" by the father. This view was later, of course, frequently distorted and deformed into the familiar trope that "gays have had a strong mother and a weak father in their formative years." In our time, we have seen that this vision also strongly figures in the debates over conversion therapy. There has been a lot of discussion about this in the public domain again recently, partly as a result of an investigation by the Dutch government. Those debates are not isolated and happen as well in the US and Australia, for example and in many ways, these discussions have become highly politicized. A Dutch study revealed that there are at least fifteen organizations in the Netherlands that claim to be able to "cure" homosexuality. This study speaks of a variety of practices aimed at "suppression, discouragement and change, by speaking of Sexual Orientation and Gender Identity and Expression Conversion Efforts, in short SOGIECE."[52]

Others believed that homosexuality should not be approached any differently than to, say, a biological anomaly such as color blindness.

51. Riggs, "Gay Men," 77–91.

52. Bureau Beke/Ateno, "Voor de verandering." This is the Dutch study, but other studies are available. Cf. "Report on LGBT Conversion Therapy Harms."

Homosexual men have a similar range of "masculine" behaviors as their heterosexual counterparts. The idea that homosexual men who are more focused on receptive anal sex are more passive or feminine has been disproved by recent research.[53]

Lesbians

What applies to developments in research on and knowledge of homosexuality often also applies to homosexuality as expressed by lesbians. Here, too, we see a transition from initial pathologizing to acceptance, and a better understanding of the variations in sexual expression. As Sonja Ellis writes, it becomes clear, for those who have studied them, that lesbians come in all shapes and sizes.[54] It is also interesting to note that not all women who feel attracted to women both emotionally and sexually define themselves as lesbians. Some would rather say that they are bisexual, or even pansexual or heterosexual. Time and again, the diversity of human sexuality, as well as its fluidity, is demonstrated.

Increasingly, research on lesbians has focused on issues of identity, relationships, parenting, and health. Until the late 1970s, there was hardly any adequate theorization of lesbianism.[55] Where it did occur, the assessment of lesbian orientation was often seen as the result of derailed and distorted socialization and upbringing, and requiring compulsory psychiatric treatment for a so-called cure. In connection with the removal of homosexuality from the DSM classification in 1973, the emphasis shifted to a more positive approach and acceptance of lesbian relationships and expression. The contribution of researchers such as Kitzinger, who denounced the oppression of lesbians but also managed to demonstrate the extent to which social and political systems influence the way people express their sexuality, was important.

Psychology and Neuroscience

A very different lens through which we can view human sexuality is psychology. Again, we are aware that we cannot possibly describe all the developments from psychology in this summary. Yet it is important to

53. Riggs, "Gay Men," 77–91.
54. Ellis, "Lesbian Psychology," 109–28.
55. Ellis, "Lesbian Psychology," 109–28.

emphasize the multidisciplinary nature of this book. Whether we start from a theological, anthropological, philosophical, biological, or any other scientific discipline, the fact is that sexuality and gender must be studied from several angles if we want to do justice to its diversity. We therefore see these psychological notions, and the lessons from many decades of research, as an attempt to highlight a specific way of looking at human sexuality, and the same applies to neurology and brain science. Our key question here is: how do psychology and neuroscience look at human sexuality and gender? We follow different schools of thought in order to provide what, we hope, is a good overview. Where necessary, we take an excursion through a specific movement or author.

The first name that comes up when talking about the psychology of sexuality is of course Sigmund Freud (1856–1939). The Austrian father of psychoanalysis systematized new insights into the unconscious like no one before.[56] He was convinced that the sexual drive (libido) is one of the most important forces in human existence. According to Freud, the human personality consists of *id*, *ego*, and *superego*. In short, human development is a vulnerable interplay of these three, where *id* stands for pleasure and need, with little regard for what others need. The human *ego* develops later, in interaction with the environment and, together with the also-developing conscience (*superego*, with social and parental values), keeps the *id* in balance. Carroll gives a good example of the relationship between the different parts of the personality according to Freud.[57] Imagine this, she writes: A woman (or a man) from a very conservative religious background wants to wait to have sex until she is married. One evening she is out with her boyfriend, and they become intimate (an action of the id according to Freud). It feels good, but soon she realizes (the ego comes into play) that she and her boyfriend are about to have sex in the car. She reconsiders and, having been brought up with the idea that sex before marriage is not desirable, she feels guilty (superego). The ego, or core of the personality, must therefore be able to maintain the balance, because otherwise (according to Freud) the superego takes over all behavior and someone becomes permanently paralyzed by feelings of guilt.

Most controversial was Freud's theory concerning psychosexual development, and not only for people with Christian beliefs. Freud developed his theory in parallel with his research into the structure of the

---

56. Callaghan, "Contributions from Psychology," 88–104.
57. Carroll, *Sexuality Now*, 24–25.

human mind.[58] His well-known theory of seduction was that hysteria was a result of traumatic experiences surrounding early seduction. This theory was not at all new, but it added an extra element by pointing to the consequences of early exposure of children to sexuality.[59] Ultimately, Freud himself rejected this theory, although other scholars picked it up again. Freud identified different phases (oral, anal, phallic, latent, genital) along which sexual development proceeds. Each phase is characterized by several specific developments and problems arise when this phase does not progress properly.

The first six years of development are crucial, according to Freud, and many problems that arise can be traced back to the phases associated with them (oral, anal, phallic, etc.). Freud argued that during the phallic phase (between the third and sixth year of life), children go through either an Oedipus complex (a boy's sexual attraction for his mother and hatred of the father) or an Electra complex (a girl's sexual attraction for her father based on psychological traumatization due to the lack of a penis). At the end of this phallic phase, Freud noticed, boys and girls identified with the same-sex parent and then displayed either male or female behavior.

The controversial element in Freud's theory lies in his views on the experience of sexuality in children.[60] The presence of sexuality in childhood, and not only in adolescence, was for many in Freud's time too difficult, and a bridge too far. It is important to note that Freud's theory emerged at a time when there was great cultural pressure regarding sexuality.[61] Open conversations about sexuality were taboo. In the meantime, Freud's theory has also been widely criticized by various other scholars. The theory seems partly unscientific and is difficult to repeat through new research. Moreover, major questions have arisen concerning the clients Freud consulted for his research.[62] Furthermore, and not unimportantly, Freud's theory is full of sexism. His views on penis envy

---

58. Denman, *Sexuality*, 66–76.

59. Denman, *Sexuality*, 66–76.

60. Carroll, *Sexuality Now*, 25. Callaghan, "Contributions from Psychology," 88–104.

61. Carroll, *Sexuality Now*, 25.

62. Carroll, *Sexuality Now*, 25. Lehmiller, *Psychology of Human Sexuality*, 8–26; and Callaghan, "Contributions from Psychology," 88–104.

(also related to the Electra complex) suggest that women are incomplete due to the lack of a penis.[63]

Gradually, the emphasis shifted from the study of the unknown unconscious of human sexuality to the empirical investigation of visible behavior. With this, the more behavioral theories came to the fore. The central idea here is that behavior (and thus also sexual behavior) arises from specific experiences and that people can learn to replace bad behavior with new (and better) behavior, for example, by means of specific forms of conditioning. Lehmiller provides a helpful example.[64] First of all, a stimulus must be identified that causes specific behavior. For example, if someone's genitals are caressed, sexual arousal will occur. The next step is then to associate a new stimulus with the stroking that does not cause the arousal. This form of classical conditioning with the aim of stimulating different and new behavior is limited because it cannot explain all sexual behavior of people. Other forms of influencing and conditioning were therefore developed with the help of rewarding or punishing desired/ undesired behavior. This so-called *operant conditioning* was also applied by a limited group of therapists with the aim of changing homosexual behavior into heterosexual behavior. The therapy form, a kind of "conversion therapy," uses physical punishment, among other things, when homoerotic stimuli are present. The therapist shows a client erotic photos of the same sex and at the same time administers electric shocks to the genitals, with the aim of creating aversion. Lehmiller and others point to the fact that there is no valid scientific evidence to date that this form of therapy is actually effective; rather, the opposite seems to be the case.[65]

From a more social psychological angle, attention is drawn to observational learning. The central idea here is that whenever we see others displaying certain behavior that is rewarded, we are likely to imitate it. The emphasis here is, of course, on modelling behavior. The influence

63. Carroll, *Sexuality Now*, 25. Lehmiller *Psychology of Human Sexuality*, 10.

64. Lehmiller *Psychology of Human Sexuality*, 11–12.

65. Lehmiller, *Psychology of Human Sexuality*. Compare Haldeman, "Gay Rights, Patient Rights." For the sake of further clarity, we refer to the aforementioned Dutch study "Voor de verandering," that addresses the harmful impact of conversion therapy. The report shows a variety of normative views people with a nonheterosexual orientation had to respond to. The report summarizes their findings: "A non-heterosexual orientation is: (1) a sin (also when there is no sexual practice); (2) an evil power people need to be set free from; (3) a disease that needs to be cured and healed; (4) something people need to learn to live with, without the related sexual practice ("it is a cross people have to bear"). The last view especially is often combined with the strong suggestion that it is strongly advisable to lead a life of celibacy.

of the media (internet, music, film, TV series, etc.) is interesting in this context. In a subsequent chapter (chapter 6) we will discuss these related influences in more detail, but it seems clear that the way in which sex and sexuality play a role in the media has a modelling effect and can therefore also teach or stimulate certain behavior. Positive and negative role models are both present, but research shows that sex is often presented in a risky and unrealistic way.[66]

Another well-known theory of sexual behavior is the so-called *exchange theory*. The core of this is that sex is a source of exchange in heterosexual relationships, in which women are usually seen as the "sellers" and men as the "buyers." The theory also assumes that female sexuality has a greater value than male sexuality and this would give women more sources of exchange than men. According to this theory, there is more demand (from men) for female sexuality. There would therefore be a kind of cost-benefit analysis that underlies a relationship.[67] Like Lehmiller, we question the one-sidedness of this theory because there is plenty of other research that indicates a reciprocal willingness to put self-interest second in a sexual relationship.

Although sociopsychological theorization offered many new insights, attention gradually turned to theories in which the human personality is central. These psychological theories, which focus on the development of the human personality, deliberately give more attention to the intrapsychic factors that are considered responsible for sexual behavior. In this context, the *Big Five* personality model has become well-known, with an emphasis on five distinct factors, each of which can in turn be related to sexual behavior. These factors are (briefly summarized): emotional stability, extraversion, openness to (new) experience, mildness, and thoughtfulness.[68] The idea behind this theory is that it is possible to get a fairly reliable picture of someone's personality by looking closely at these five different factors or traits. These personality characteristics were then linked to their possible relationship to sexual behavior. It is striking that the characteristics extraversion and mildness/altruism were most consistently associated with sexual behavior.[69] For example, a high degree of extraversion often appears to be linked to having more than one sex partner and taking risks in that direction. A low degree of

66. Gunasekera, Chapman, and Campbell, "Sex and Drugs," 464–70.

67. Lehmiller, *Psychology of Human Sexuality*, 15–16.

68. Lehmiller, *Psychology of Human Sexuality*, 17.

69. Lehmiller, *Psychology of Human Sexuality*, 16.

altruism was often linked to having sex with someone other than their regular partner, and in combination with the use of drugs and alcohol.

Both high and low levels of interpersonal warmth appear to enable people having multiple sex partners. Low emotional stability seems to be associated with engaging in unprotected and risky sex. Other studies building on this personality model point to additional factors such as erotophobia and erotophilia.[70] These two extremes on a continuum would show how individuals have either strongly positive or strongly negative emotions toward sex. The perspective offered by these and other more personality-oriented theories is attractive, but the question is, of course, what is being measured: personality or attitude? And how do personality and the biological or genetic components relate to each other?

Lehmiller points to a more recent development that focuses on the evolutionary aspects of sexual development and behavior. He shows that only in the last three decades scientific studies have begun to elaborate on the much older evolutionary thinking (e.g., Darwin) concerning human sexuality.[71]

Evolutionary psychologists promote one core notion in particular: people have a strong internal motivation to produce as many offspring as possible. According to these psychologists, in order to achieve this goal, people have gradually developed specific preferences regarding physical and psychological characteristics that our (future) partners should have. Thus, there would be a developed selection pressure that ensures the match with the right (sex) partner. For example, heterosexual men would mainly be attracted to women with an hourglass-shaped body and long silky hair. The (many) previous generations have developed these preferences, according to this theory.

Another important element in this approach is the assumption (based on long-term research) that men and women have separate mating behavior. This seems to be related to the differences in investment that men and women must make to conceive a child together. For example, the investment of men is usually minimal compared to that of a woman. Theorists say that this would also explain why it is in men's

---

70. Erotophobia can be described as a specific phobia for sexuality or sexual relationships; erotophilia is a personality trait that influences how a person responds positively or negatively on signals of a sexual nature. In general, persons with an erotophilic posture will respond more positively to and think more positively about sexuality compared to those who do not have that posture. See Macapagal and Janssen, "Valence of Sex," 699–703.

71. Lehmiller, *Psychology of Human Sexuality*, 19–20.

interest to have sex with many fertile women; this way, they increase their chances of successful reproduction. This would explain the behavior of many modern men: they want many sex partners and pay excessive attention to their appearance.

Women, on the other hand, must make a much bigger investment: a pregnancy normally lasts nine months and then there is a lot more to be done. This would explain why modern women look for a reliable man, who remains faithful, has a high social status, and a good job, etc. Interestingly, there is quite a bit of evidence to support this theory. Problems are also plentiful: If reproduction is so important, why should anyone be anything other than heterosexual? The question is also to what extent these preferences can be traced back to social and cultural factors, in which certain behavior is seen as desirable for men or for women.

In his concluding remarks on the contribution of psychology, Callaghan writes that there is much to be learned from psychology and especially from psychological research.[72] He holds the opinion that, in general, theologians have hardly considered the variety of data that has surfaced. From Freud it can unmistakably be learned that sexuality has a much more comprehensive influence on human existence than is generally assumed. At the same time, human sexuality cannot be reduced to the release of biological tensions or even to one phase of life. The insights of the various theoretical models are many, as are their limitations. There is also a clear emphasis on the strongly relational nature of human sexuality. In our view, psychology, too, points to the need for reflection on the image of humans: which image of humans and, within this, of human sexuality, is in the foreground? More about this in the next section.

A brief glance into neuroscience provides a very nuanced picture. On March 30, 2019, the Dutch newspaper *Trouw* headlined an article about the differences between men and women with respect to the brain: "Men and women are not that different, argues renowned British brain scientist Gina Rippon: 'Gender is something we teach ourselves.'"[73] The author of the article, Nicole Lucas, shares Rippon's basic views. In a more recent publication, Rippon states that the differences between the brains of men and women are small and that no far-reaching conclusions can be drawn from this. Rippon argues this in *The Gendered Brain*.[74] She does

72. Callaghan, "Contributions from Psychology," 88–104.
73. Lucas, "Zo verschillend zijn mannen en vrouwen niet."
74. Rippon, *Gendered Brain*.

not dismiss the classic theory of *nature* (what is naturally and biologically/genetically predisposed) and *nurture* (what is learned, developed as a result of learning processes, culture, and environment), but nuances it by pointing to the *plasticity* of the brain.

The brain, says Rippon, is constantly changing under the influence of experience. In the *The Gendered Brain* Rippon refers to a study among taxi drivers in London. In order to qualify for a license, the drivers have to prove that they know the map of London. The study showed that the brains of those who are still in training differ considerably from those who have been doing the job for years. Rippon points to a major breakthrough in recent years: the discovery that the brain is much more proactive and anticipatory about gathering information than previously thought. It is not the case that the brain only reacts when new information comes in, but it generates predictions about what is coming next, based on previous patterns from previous situations. We could say, says Rippon, that the brain is constantly making images that help it to "navigate"; it is a kind of high-end satellite navigation.[75] Rippon points out that even babies absorb social information at a fast rate, making connections, and registering what is important. They are tiny social sponges that absorb the necessary cultural information very quickly. To illustrate this, Rippon gives the example of a remote village in Ethiopia, where researchers had several sealed boxes with new laptops delivered. The laptops contained a limited number of games, apps, and music, but without any instructions. The researchers observed what happened. It took four minutes before a child opened a box and found the on-off button. In the next five days, every child in the village was able to use forty or more apps![76]

Rippon in no way disputes that there are biological differences between men and women (and therefore also in relation to sexuality or in the experience of it) but emphasizes the interaction between disposition and environment. A world in which gender and the ideas about it are central will develop a human brain that functions based on the prevailing ideas. In short: the prevailing ideas about what is normative for typically male or typically female behavior will leave their traces in the brain.

Rippon aptly summarizes: "With input from exciting breakthroughs in neuroscience, the neat binary distinctiveness of these labels is being challenged—we are coming to realize that nature is inextricably entangled

75. Rippon, *Gendered Brain*, 112.
76. Rippon, *Gendered Brain*, 14.

with nurture. What used to be thought fixed and inevitable, is being shown to be plastic and flexible; the powerful biology-changing effects of our physical and our social worlds are being revealed. Even something that is 'written in our genes' may come to express itself differently in different contexts."[77] For Rippon, one thing is clear: there is no such thing as a typical male or female brain. With this, she puts the debate about gender and sexuality into perspective and offers room for nuanced views, whereby the dominant binary thinking is not only questioned, but also put into a broader context.

Anthropology and Sociology

In the previous section, the need for reflection on the image of humankind was already discussed. Both anthropology and sociology are important in this context. For anthropology, thorough reflection on cultural systems of meaning is central. Anthropology is concerned with (religious) culture. Social and political networks and, of course, the people involved in them, are increasingly playing a role in this. Gender and sexuality are preeminently issues concerning the way people assign meaning, especially in a variety of religious cultures.[78] Our perception of ourselves is inextricably linked to it.

Denman explores how changes in family structures are studied within anthropology.[79] He notes a clear shift from a "patrilineal" society to a society characterized more by self-chosen kinship. In a patrilineal society, a family structure changes when a man marries a woman. In fact, the woman's ties to her "native group" are then cut and she joins her husband's group. In traditional contexts, marriage is accompanied by a transaction (a dowry). In most cases, divorces are rare and any children are seen as belonging to the father's group. Sexuality is mainly aimed at reproduction, at controlling female fertility, and at securing the bloodline. In the social form in which one can choose kinship, it is not certain that one is a member of a group: women can inherit, still have rights in the group in which they were born, and can also divorce much more easily and frequently. Sexuality in this way is seen much more as a resource for women themselves. This shift throws a special light on the

77. Rippon, *Gendered Brain*, 15.
78. Stewart and Coleman, "Contributions from Anthropology," 105–19.
79. Denman, *Sexuality*, 38–43.

recent Nashville Declaration (2019), which also caused a great deal of controversy in the Netherlands and in other countries. Although there is, and may be, a difference of opinion regarding gender and sexuality, the debate seems to be linked to this observed shift toward other forms of living together and social structures, and the difficulty that religious communities have with this. The erosion of traditional forms of relationship is certainly partly a consequence of the shifts identified by Denman and, as it were, calls for the recalibration of traditional forms. In the Nashville Declaration, these are explicitly found as a reaction.

Anthropology studies how gender and sexuality influence the cultural and social order, often linked to myths and rituals that are discussed in that worldview. For example, what is generally seen as male and female is expressed in connection with creation stories. For example, the Old Testament story about the garden of Eden, in which the fate of Eve and all her descendants was irreparably determined by her curiosity, has long been read—also in an anthropological sense—as an explanation for male-female relationships and even for the religious status or position of women. Similar interpretations are also present in other cultures. It is interesting that where anthropologists, based on research, found a kind of "third gender" (neither male nor female, but something else), this was often accompanied by an attribution of spiritual power to the group.[80] The *hijra* in India (also in Pakistan and Bangladesh) are a well-known example. Born as men, they live as women, and often in communities. The question is whether they can be seen as transgender persons. In any case, they often act as ritual workers with a special spiritual power to bless or curse others. They are also exposed to discrimination and violence because there is no legal protection for them.[81]

Other religious practices are better known. For example, the Jewish Bar Mitzvah is an example of collective gender construction (*coming of age rite*). A Jewish boy who turns thirteen reads from the Torah and from that moment is responsible to God and promises to keep the law. He has become a "son of the law." Incidentally, the ritual does not only play a role in ultraorthodox circles, as is sometimes suggested. In liberal circles, a similar ritual is performed with girls of the same age; they become B'nai Mitzvah, "daughters of the law."

---

80. Stewart and Coleman. "Contributions from Anthropology," 105–19.

81. We refer to chapter 2 in which we mentioned the fact that women often lost their gender.

Considering these anthropological examples, what is true for gender is certainly also true for sexuality: in connection with views on gender, sexual practices also differ from culture to culture. Stewart and Coleman point to those religious contexts where sexual abstinence is seen as a spiritual force. For example, large groups of Hindus on pilgrimage appear to be abstinent. During their pilgrimage, they honor the celibate god Ayyappan, who they see as the result of this celibate lifestyle. On the way back from their pilgrimage, they visit large numbers of beach resorts. Stewart and Coleman's research shows that there is a relationship and a kind of interaction between sexual practices and social identity. Unfortunately, celibacy often does not have a positive ring to it, as it has become too intertwined with sanctioned religious authority in an ecclesial context. And sexual abuse often takes place in hierarchical power relationships, with extremely destructive consequences.

Therefore, sensitivity to what anthropological data has to tell us seems to be extremely relevant. At the same time, it also insists that we take the influence of our own cultural baggage on our view of gender and sexuality seriously. A better understanding of cultures that are foreign to us often provides an advantage in understanding one's own practice and normativity.

Denman rightly points out that there is no such thing as a "sociology of sexuality."[82] With a view to what we might call a history of the sociological approach, he refers to Hawkes, who contends that it was mainly the Enlightenment that questioned the immediate connection between sexuality and sin.[83] It was around the time of the Enlightenment that the idea that sexuality is an animal activity came up for discussion. Nature and everything connected with it was seen in a more positive light, and so were sexual behavior, prostitution, adultery, etc. It is also clear from her overview that sexual expression in the lower social strata of the population was not as common as it had been in the past. Women, and forms of sexuality other than heterosexual coitus, were suppressed.

In the nineteenth century, not a lot changes. Even then, female sexuality seems to be dominated by male sexual activity. This may have been related to the fact that women were no longer economically dependent on marriage and men's fear of losing control. Denman also draws attention to the British sociologist Anthony Giddens. Giddens reflects,

---

82. Denman, *Sexuality*, 49–55.

83. Hawkes, as cited in Denman, *Sexuality*, 50.

in a specific way, on the social roots and implications of the modern discourse on gender and sexuality. He explores the connection between the highly individualized interpretation of life with an emphasis on individuation and self-development and the way in which this influences personal choices, especially where sexuality is concerned. This contrasts sharply with a premodern context in which traditional norms and values were decisive. For Giddens, it is certain that the rise of romantic love relates to the modernization of society and to the social and individual construction of self. The norm is: the story of two lovers and two lives and their relationship, almost independent of what surrounds them.[84]

Giddens also notes the emergence of a "plastic sexuality," a sexuality separated (some would argue liberated) from an intrinsic relationship with procreation and mainly focused on the development of personal identity. According to Giddens, "plastic sexuality" is linked to social trends from the eighteenth century, when the size of the family was gradually reduced. This development continued around the 1960s when contraception was widely introduced. Giddens has a much more positive view of this than Freud. For Freud, sexuality is an unregulated force, for Giddens it is (certainly when it comes to its plasticity) an opportunity for the development of civilized citizens. It is striking that Giddens's vision shows many traits of a constructivist approach. For example, it needs to be noted that he sees sexuality primarily as a lifestyle: it is more about social conditioning and personal choice and less about biology. In the light of what we discussed earlier in this chapter, this is questionable. Once again, it is as if the phenomenon is being looked at in a one-sided way, without the various perspectives being related to each other.[85]

Midterm Review—What Significance Do These Perspectives Have?

In this chapter, we looked at the phenomenon of human sexuality through different scientific lenses. What struck us immediately was the great diversity of visions and opinions. We have tried to map out the landscape a little better by clarifying concepts (e.g., gender and sex variations), but we have also shown here and there how each scientific branch has slowly but

84. Denman, *Sexuality,* 49–55.

85. See Lindsey, *Gender Roles,* for a more extensive treatment of sociological concepts and views with regard to gender.

surely formed its own vision. What is important to us—and here we agree with Messer—is the need for a structured dialogue between biologists, medics, social scientists, and theologians.[86]

To give an example: if, on the basis of scientific research, it is almost certain that there is a biological-genetic basis for gender fluidity, in which the boundaries between what we usually call typically male and typically female appear to be much more fluid, then it is inevitable that religious people and churches will have to discuss these various forms of relationships with each other. This is for a later chapter, but this should even come up in theological discussions about what transcends gender, if we still want to take a transcending unity in (the body of) Christ as a starting point. That conversation, then, also transcends the fairly flat and one-dimensional conversation about chromosomal sex (or gender), visible gender variations, and possible sexual orientations. At the same time, our anthropological reflections show how much has changed in relation to what is normative in the context of family structures. Of course, this raises many questions regarding the social cohesion or cohesiveness of society and one can rightly be concerned about that. Anthropologists make us sensitive to the social forms in which gender and sexuality take their place. The difficulty that exists in many religious communities around shifting patterns of norms and values (from a patrilinear society to "looser" connections) cannot be seen separately from their difficulty with recent views on gender and sexuality, in which gender fluidity plays a role because not everything can be placed in binary schemes. These newer notions no longer fit into patrilineal contexts.

Questions for Discussion

- In this chapter, we made a distinction between gender essentialism and gender constructivism. To what extent is this a helpful distinction in the many discussions about gender and sexuality?

- At what points does this chapter challenge you to think more deeply about your own assumptions and beliefs about gender and sexuality?

- Do you know people who struggle with sex variation? Thinking also of the stories we wrote down from Margriet van Heesch's study, how important is it to know people who struggle with this?

86. Messer, "Contributions from Biology," 69–87.

- In the context of sexual orientation, we also briefly touched on the discussion of conversion therapy. To what extent is this an issue in your own context?

- The different scientific visions discussed in this chapter require much more dialogue. How do you think this necessary dialogue could be further stimulated? What is needed for it to happen?

4

Gender and Sexuality
in the Bible

Introduction

IT GOES WITHOUT SAYING that the role of the Bible is significant in discussions about sexuality and gender in Christian circles. At the same time, many of these discussions are complex because it proves to be really difficult to be aware of the different assumptions we hold while reading the Bible. The practice is that verses are frequently quoted and related to each other, without sufficiently looking at the nature and scope of these verses, passages, and texts in their own context. The question "what does the Bible say about sex?" seems too shortsighted if, at the same time, another question is not given sufficient space: what is the nature and scope of the book that we call the Bible?

This chapter is about the connection between these two questions. First of all, we ask ourselves which material, which texts, that we find in the Bible help us to better understand the reality of human sexuality and gender. And second, how do we read these texts with an idea of their nature and purpose, how they might have been intended to be heard, and in what context they were transmitted? It will soon become clear that when we delve into various themes, they cannot be understood separately from individuals and groups of people who believe in God. In many ways, our relationship with God, and the ways in which people frame this relationship, plays a role in the way sex and sexuality are thought about. That in itself is an interesting fact. What is surprising is that a rather diverse picture emerges from the different biblical texts. In this chapter, we try to portray a "unity in diversity" in an honest way, while at the same time not avoiding tough questions.

In conversations about the Bible and sexuality, we clearly move along with the waves of culture. For theologians, this is a very important fact. Theologians need to be aware of the impact that language and social change have on notions of "sexuality" and "gender" and on their related practices. When we look for the role of theology in relation to gender and sexuality, this means carefully looking at the ebb and flow of modern views, convictions, and their development.

This means that we cannot simply read late-modern views, especially those of the last few decades, back into biblical texts as if they (for example, the views on two sexes) have always been present in the Bible. This also means that theology can play a role by not simply adopting modern concepts of sexuality and gender. A critical counter-voice is also necessary. Those who want to better understand sexuality and gender in relation to the Bible must be prepared to take seriously the impact of social change on relationships and their development. It may be experienced as shocking or as liberating, but the fact is that in the space of one generation we have seen big shifts regarding how we understand homosexual intimacy. It is no longer seen as a crime and, so far (by 2023), thirty-four countries have legalized same-sex marriage. But much has changed for heterosexual relationships as well. Simply think of the liberalization of divorce and abortion, the decrease in the number of marriages, the increase in registered partnerships, equality between men and women as marriage partners, the disappearance of the obvious relationship between marriage and having children, and, finally, caring for children has become a greater challenge. We can value these changes differently, but the fact remains that this is the context in which we read the Bible today.

First, we focus on the question of how we read the biblical texts. What approach do we then choose and what does this mean for the ways in which we deal with the various themes? On the basis of a number of themes, we will then show how our chosen approach can be applied. We then continue our search with a discussion of a number of concrete texts and themes. The final part of this chapter is devoted to the question of whether and how theology helps in our discussions about sexuality. What does it provide, and what kind of reflection generally supports better conversations? This chapter focuses on the *normative* task (see preface). The key question here is: what should (ideally) be going on? We look for building blocks in the Bible and biblical theology that can contribute to a normative framework for gender and sexuality. We will soon discover that this is not a simple goal to achieve and that much depends on the lenses through which we read the Bible. We will make a choice for those reading lenses and use them as we move toward chapter 5.

How Do We Read the Bible?

We read the Bible through a certain lens, influenced by the times we live in. But that does not mean that in the twenty-first century there is only one way in which people read the Bible. There is much discussion about *hermeneutics*, and rightly so. Increasingly, it is important to talk about the rules with which, or perhaps better about the lenses through which, we read and the ways by which we do justice to the texts. Most scholars agree that we cannot go about claiming just about anything when it comes to interpretations. So, what kind of (general) approaches can we distinguish, bearing our sexuality and gender in mind?

American theologian David Jensen broadly distinguishes three approaches.[1] The first approach positions the Bible as a guide to sexuality, in which certain texts are selected to determine what is and is not allowed in the area of sexuality. In a way, this turns the Bible into a kind of rule book, leaving little room for various contexts and discussions. A second approach assumes that the Bible is inadequate to guide us and that it is out of date for many subjects, including sexuality. We live in different times, so we should not use the Bible as a guide for the twenty-first century. Doing that would be selling both our contemporary age and the Bible short. The third approach takes a different track, seeing the whole Bible as a *narrative of desire*, a story that expresses God's desire for creation and all humanity. In that narrative, sexuality is a facet within other relational expressions.

We will briefly discuss these three approaches and then make our own choice. In the first approach, the emphasis is on using the Bible as a handbook. The general rules are considered clear and unambiguous and

1. Jensen, *God, Desire, and a Theology of Human Desire*, 1–16.

much depends on the assumption that sex is good in one context and bad in others. Genesis 1 and 2 are often used and, in this view, in these chapters, marriage is held up as the norm. Everything (sexual) outside of marriage must be seen as wrong. The relationship between Adam and Eve is the model and norm for good sexual relations.[2] It is this order of creation that norms sexual behavior: sex is permitted only within the marriage relationship between two partners of the *opposite* sex. Within this approach, this pattern continues to play a role in the interpretation of many biblical texts.

Sex outside of marriage should be regarded as suspicious and as not in accordance with the created order as intended by God. According to this view, it not only damages existing marital relationships, but also the community itself (in Paul's language the "body of Christ").[3] Within this approach to the Bible as an ethical handbook, homosexuality is rejected. Texts in the Hebrew Bible, especially Leviticus 18 and 20, are directly applied to today's society, and the specific context in which these texts were passed on hardly matters. The well-known text (among several others) from Paul's letter to the church in Rome (Rom 1:26) also plays an important role in the condemnation of homosexuality. In this approach, the conclusions are often sharp: the rules are abstinence *before* marriage and fidelity *in* marriage, with any other form of sexuality being idolatry. The problems with this approach mainly revolves around an almost acontextual interpretation of the aforementioned and other texts. We will discuss this in more detail later in this chapter.

The second approach starts from a conclusion: biblical texts on sexuality are problematic because they have little or no relevance for the world today. One of the major problems is the essentially patriarchal setting in which the texts originated. The patriarchal world of the past, with hierarchical laws, where women were seen as property, cannot possibly determine what we should think today, because we live in a very different time and context. This approach causes the Bible to fade into the background. The language of the Ten Commandments, for example—think especially of the commandment not to desire your neighbor's wife—is full of notions of self and property. We will explain this further, but this approach assumes that this language mainly evokes an unequal discourse of power and therefore cannot dictate how we should live today.

2. Cf. Gen 2:24–25.

3. 1 Cor 6:15; 10:16; 12:12; 12:27; Eph 4:12.

It is noteworthy, according to the adherents of this approach, that the rules are directed more to women than to men. In the pastoral letters, for example, young widows are presented as more susceptible to "sins of the flesh" than others: "As for younger widows, do not put them on such a list. For when their sensual desires overcome their dedication to Christ, they want to marry. Thus they bring judgment on themselves, because they have broken their first pledge" (1 Tim 5:1–12).

The impression we get from this text is that the writer is strongly advising his audience not to allow young widows to make promises of abstinence. They would do better to remarry. The suggestion that could be made is that women are possibly more inclined to sexual vices than men (as it has been interpreted throughout much of history; cf. chapter 2). The question is whether the text makes a comparison between women and men. Adherents of this second approach will stress that texts like this (and many others) have strongly influenced Christian conversations and practices around gender and sexuality. It is all about male privilege versus a secondary status for women (cf. chapter 1). From this perspective, women are guilty because of their responsibility for the presence of sin (Gen 3:12; 1 Tim 2:12–15), and therefore must be silent in church (1 Cor 14:34), and are also often presented as the epitome of unfaithfulness and fornication (Hos 2–4; Rev 17). According to this approach, the texts have a strong patriarchal bias and thus have their own history of interpretation (Eph 5:22–23; Col 3:18–19). For many contemporary theologians, the patriarchal context of these texts is a bridge too far: the underlying values cannot be accepted as guidelines for marriage and sexuality without question in the here and now. At the very least, these underlying values need to be clarified and reconnected to today's questions and values. In this context, Jensen rightly points to the fact that the tension between *agape* (often associated with divine love) and *eros* (more often associated with sexuality and eroticism) does not help, certainly not when these are played off against each other.

The third and final approach has a completely different starting point. The Bible is central as a *narrative of desire*. From beginning to end, the Bible emphasizes the importance of relationships: relationships with God, relationships among people, relationships with creation, and so on. The Bible brings these stories about the various different relationships to our attention, and the core of these is always shaped by desire. God desires to share his life, love, and grace with us. The Bible is full of desire. We can read the Bible in such a way that it is one extensive narrative of desire. This means that biblical texts that at first glance seem to have nothing to say about sexuality do say something about it. The creation stories demonstrate this. Everything is good, even very good, it sounds like the refrain at the beginning of Genesis. Everything is made, created, for relationship with God and creation.

God does not create out of shortage, but out of abundance—abundance of goodness and desire. Out of goodness and abundance, the first human couple longs for each other. The disruption of the story of desire is hard, especially when this same human couple chooses to possess apart from God. The shadow of this choice may lie mostly in the thought that God (precisely in his abundance) is in fact holding something back from them, not giving them everything. And so, they choose the wrong side of things. Those of us who know the story know that it did not end there, but God kept alive this longing for deep and ongoing relationship. In this context, Jensen speaks of "the covenant as an anchor in this world," in which God continues to search and long for deep connection with his people.

The New Testament breathes this continuous quest, Jesus is the total embodiment of God's longing for fullness and relationship. This is expressed in the many stories of the New Testament. The story of the woman who suffered from menorrhagia (Matt 9:20–21) is well known. She approaches Jesus and thinks: if I can only touch his outer garment, I will be healed. Jensen states that the language used here is very precise. The touching of the edge of the garment can be read as a euphemism for sexual touching. Her bleeding isolates her, and makes her unclean. She has a deep longing for touch and healing.[4] In this same line of thought, there are more examples of a strong focus on desire; think of the resurrection stories in which "touching" plays a major role (Mary, Thomas; John 20). Further on in this chapter, we will see how this narrative of desire is also reflected in other parts of the New Testament, up to the last book of the Bible, Revelation.

Jensen gives a clear overview of these three approaches. They should be seen as a kind of typology, an idealized description of the ways the Bible is dealt with. Reality, of course, is always more complex and unruly. Jensen rightly seeks to escape from a view of the Bible as a regulator of behavior and also from an approach which pushes the Bible into irrelevance for our present time. This second view benefits no one and, moreover, it does not do justice to the character of the Bible. It is clear where his

4. Jensen, *God, Desire, and a Theology of Human Desire*, 1–16.

preference lies: an approach to the Bible as a *narrative of desire*—God's desire to be in relationship with his creation. Sexuality is embedded in that narrative of connectedness, intimacy, and relationship. From that perspective, sexuality and sex cannot be consumer goods; rather, they are intertwined with deeper connections to and knowledge of those whom we love.

We want to connect with and draw out Jensen's third approach: the Bible as a narrative of desire. Our search through different parts of the Bible shows that there is enormous diversity within this approach. Jensen's approach functions as a reading aid that enables us to do justice to the different historical and scientific lenses we have explored so far. This does not imply that diversity is now a particular norm, which then necessarily leads to the conclusion that biblical texts do not have much to say about norms and values, or that would prevent the development of a sexual ethic. Jensen's approach shows us that there is indeed a normative framework and that the central focus on desire offers something to hold together and anchor the different lenses we have observed and provides an authoritative orientation.

The thinking of British theologian Adrian Thatcher is also important for us throughout this chapter (and the next). We choose to integrate Thatcher's work here because of his starting point and its direct application. He chooses to approach the Bible as a witness to the revelation of God in Jesus Christ.[5] The Bible bears witness to God revealed in Jesus. Others tend to argue that the Bible and Jesus together embody God's truth. Thatcher's starting point is consistent with the way Jensen endeavors to read the Bible in relation to gender and sexuality. In a general sense, Jensen helps us by giving us the overarching reading lens or framework—a narrative of desire. We take a look at the Hebrew Bible and New Testament through this lens and within this framework. As will become apparent, this provides a very diverse and more expansive picture.

Diversity and the Big Picture in the Hebrew Bible

Jensen has already pointed out that in discussions about the Hebrew Bible and sexuality, the creation stories from Genesis 1 and 2 are often used as a starting point, and where marriage is presented to us as the ultimate norm. It is this creation order that sets the standard for sexual

5. Thatcher, *Redeeming Gender*.

behavior: sex is only permitted within the marital relationship of two partners of the opposite sex. This is the dominant discourse within the church. As a representative example, this view is strongly held by American theologian Richard Davidson.[6] According to him, Genesis 1–3 form the normative framework for what can be said about human sexuality in the rest of the Hebrew Bible. Davidson refers to this "pattern of Eden," which he characterizes as the divine design.[7] He thus develops his considerations according to what happened *in* the garden of Eden, what took place *outside* the garden of Eden, and what happens next in a kind of *eschatological return* to the garden of Eden. In a final sense, the Song of Songs functions in this scheme as the canonical "holy of holies," one of the most authoritative texts on human sexuality, with (according to Davidson) enormous implications for today's issues.

It is no surprise there is no place for homosexuality or bisexuality in his thinking, since sexual differentiation is set by God in the order of creation. The argument is that this given differentiation stems from the polemic against the deification of sexuality, which was so prevalent among Israel's neighbors, where the sexual activities of the (fertility) gods were a dominant motif.[8]

Ken Stone points out that the texts in the Hebrew Bible show a more complex picture than Davidson and others claim.[9] It is too easy to read the texts of Genesis (and other texts for that matter) as prescribing the traditional Judeo-Christian model of marriage and sexual relations (a marriage of one man and one woman) without exception. The first chapters of Genesis point out the importance of a reproduction-oriented heterosexuality in the context of ancient Israelite society. However, scholars are increasingly coming to the conviction that the Hebrew Bible reveals a wider variety of perspectives on sexuality and gender. In the reflections from the Hebrew Bible that we offer in this chapter, we try to do justice to that variety.

6. Davidson, *Flame of YAHWEH.*

7. Davidson, *Flame of YAHWEH,* 6–7.

8. Davidson, *Flame of YAHWEH,* 18.

9. Stone, "Marriage and Sexual Relations," 173–88.

Sexuality and Marriage in the Hebrew Bible

Stone states that the Hebrew Bible is often seen as one of the sources confirming the traditional view of marriage and sexual relationships. In that view, there is a strong emphasis on heterosexuality and procreation-oriented monogamous relationships.[10] As already indicated, texts such as Genesis 1:26–28 and 2:22–25 play a major role in this, and reception history indicates these texts tended to be interpreted in ways that confirmed this hermeneutic. Stone shows that we are dealing with a much more complex picture. We could, once more, argue that the opening chapters of Genesis point to the importance of procreative heterosexuality for the ancient society of Israel. However, an overview of the entire Hebrew Bible shows that there is much less continuity to this argument and, in a general sense, there is a broad spectrum of perspectives on sexuality, gender, and family relationships. It is important to note that the many texts that show this broader perspective originated at different points in time and are often hundreds of years apart.

The language used to describe marriage and relationships in Genesis 1–3 is striking. In Genesis 3:6 the terms "husband" and "woman" are used as a translation from the Hebrew terms *ish* and *ishah*.[11] The question is, of course, which language the Hebrew Bible uses to refer to something like a *marriage*. In most cases, we encounter expressions like those used, for example, in Genesis 4:19: "Then Lamech took for himself two wives: the name of one *was* Adah, and the name of the second *was* Zillah" (NKJV). Words such as "take" (Gen 11:29; 28:9; 36:2), "give" (Exod 2:21; Judg 3:6), or "bring" (Gen 29:23) are used as well.

Although it cannot be simply said that marriage is the only type of relationship in which property and ownership can be expressed, it is clear that women often came under the authority of men and that men were usually the primary actors in the creation of marriages.[12] Marriages were arranged, in most cases, with the male heads of the family in the lead (e.g., Isaac and Rebekah, Gen 24; Dina, Jacob's daughter, Gen 34; Jacob, Moses, and also David negotiated directly with the fathers of their future brides, Gen 29:15–30; Exod 2:21; 1 Sam 18:17–27). Biblical scholars like Michael Coogan, for example, point to this and similar social structures

10. Stone, "Marriage and Sexual Relations," 173–88.

11. Compare the English text in the NIV.

12. Stone, "Marriage and Sexual Relations," 175.

and conventions, evidencing that women were subordinate in family structures and in many ways they were considered inferior.[13]

Within this patriarchal society and its structures, women, daughters, mothers, sisters, and so on were subordinate. Coogan notes that even when some women are significant in the stories, they are still not mentioned by name. We never hear the names of Noah's wife, Lot's wife, etc.[14] Husbands and fathers actually had a lot of power over their wives and daughters. In Gen 18:12, Sarah calls her husband Abraham "lord" (*adon* in Hebrew) and a few chapters later, in Gen 20:3, she calls him "master" (*baal*). The same terms are used many times in relation to possessions and property. The influence of these specific texts can be traced as far back as New Testament times, in this case in 1 Pet 3:1 and 6.[15] Coogan also refers to Exod 21:7–11, where we can read that a father could get rid of his daughter by selling her as a slave. The new "owner" is bound by specific regulations in the care of her and if he does not comply, the woman is "free" to leave the new owner. It is clear that women are at the mercy of men, who determine for them what is right and wrong; after all, they had the legal right to do so.[16]

In this context, we can speak, along with Stone, of a clear gender hierarchy.[17] Women simply do not "take" or "give" husbands in the Hebrew Bible. Marriage is usually a transaction between men, although mothers are often involved in arranging a marriage (e.g., Gen 21:21). This is reflected not only in the terms "taking" and "giving," but also in Hebrew words such as "baal" and "adon." The word "baal" is used to designate God's rival, the god Baal, and this simple fact already proves strict hierarchical thinking: a male spouse is compared to a god. Husbands are "lord and master" over their wives. Another example of this is Deut 24:4, where we read: "her first husband, who divorced her, is not allowed." The Hebrew term translated here with "husband" is once more "baal."

Stone rightly contends that translations can be misleading, because the original meaning of the Hebrew word sometimes disappears

---

13. Coogan, *God and Sex*, 28.

14. Coogan, *God and Sex*, 27.

15. "Wives, likewise, be submissive to your own husbands, that even if some do not obey the word, they, without a word, may be won by the conduct of their wives, . . . as Sarah obeyed Abraham, calling him lord, whose daughters you are if you do good and are not afraid with any terror."

16. Coogan, *God and Sex*, 29.

17. Stone, "Marriage and Sexual Relations," 175.

completely. That is the case here. In the Hebrew text of Exod 20:17—"You shall not covet your neighbor's house. You shall not covet your neighbor's wife, or his male or female servant, his ox or donkey, or anything that belongs to your neighbor"—masculine linguistic forms are used to warn a male audience. This commandment applies to a male Israelite who covets things that belong to another male Israelite, including slaves and animals. Marriage was thus seen as part of an exchange between groups of people, in which men played a dominant role. Crucial and often necessary alliances were thus formed (e.g., Gen 34:13–24). Stone points out that even where there is real love between the two marriage partners (e.g., Isaac and Rebekah, Jacob and Rachel, David and Michal), economic and hierarchical assumptions or conditions are simultaneously at play.[18]

Marriage was essentially a contract, and Coogan points out that in most cases the Hebrew term *berît* (used for covenants between God and Israel) is used for the commitment.[19] The contract had two phases. The first phase concerned the betrothal, *kiddushin*, in which the future bride was legally transferred by her father to her future husband. The woman in question was then formally already the "property" of her "fiancé." Usually, after a short period of time, the second phase began: the actual marriage.

It should not surprise us, since the transactional character of marriage plays such a prominent role that we find numerous examples of men who have several wives. Lamech and Jacob each have two wives, and Esau seems to have several. But the list does not end there: Ashur, Abraham, Gideon, Elkanah, Saul, David, and last but definitely not least, Solomon. It is not so much a question of *polygamy* (multiple marriages), but of *polygyny* (several wives). In Deut 21:15–17a we even read: "If a man has two wives, and he loves one but not the other, and both bear him sons but the firstborn is the son of the wife he does not love, when he wills his property to his sons, he must not give the rights of the firstborn to the son of the wife he loves in preference to his actual firstborn, the son of the wife he does not love. He must acknowledge the son of his unloved wife as the firstborn by giving him a double share of all he has." Exodus 21:10 also leaves no room for ambiguity: if there is a second wife, the man must not neglect his first wife. Coogan also points to the presence of polygyny. Abraham, for example, besides Sarah and Hagar, had another wife, Keturah, with whom he had six sons (Gen 25:1–2). Gideon, too,

18. Stone, "Marriage and Sexual Relations," 177.
19. Coogan, *God and Sex*, 64.

produced many offspring, according to Judges 8:30: "He had seventy sons of his own, for he had many wives." Coogan explains the importance of offspring in society at that time: it was a matter of the survival of a family. In any case, the legislation in Deuteronomy took this into account (Deut 21:15–17).[20]

Although having several wives was apparently permitted, this did not mean that these women all enjoyed the same status. Stone refers to the Hebrew term *pilegesh*, which is often translated as "concubine," which indicates a sexual relationship rather than marital rights. It seems there is a close relationship between *pilegesh* and the Greek term *pallake*, a woman (not a marriage partner) with whom a permanent sexual relationship was maintained.[21]

Susan Ackerman, in her study of the term *pilegesh*, shows there may be two categories to be distinguished: one group that refers primarily to a woman of secondary rank (e.g., Judg 19:3, 26–27) and one group that refers to women who are part of the husband's harem, but are not actually spouses.[22] We encounter this last category with Saul, David, Solomon, and Gideon. It is reported that they had both wives and concubines. They were not married to the concubines (Judg 8:30–31; 2 Sam 5:13; 15:16; 16:21; 19:5; 21:11; 1 Kgs 11:3).

Even though, according to Stone, we do not know much about the values and norms that determined the lives of the *pilegeshim*, we can assume that the term reflects a system of marriage and sexuality in which men had several permanent sex partners. In practice, especially rich and affluent men could afford to have several concubines. Thus, having several wives and concubines often indicated great wealth, status, and power (e.g., 2 Sam 3:1–5). The fact that in the Hebrew Bible there is such a clear recognition of polygyny, and descriptions of its often negative influence (the abuse of power with regard to women), is used by some to suppose that monogamy was therefore preferred. A difficulty with this interpretation, however, is the story in which the prophet Nathan condemns David's adultery with Bathsheba. From this narrative it can be clearly deduced that God gave David several wives (2 Sam 12:7–8). In the same text, it is also clear that God will give David's wives to another (2 Sam 12:11). It is therefore difficult to purge this recognition from Old Testament theology which argues for the preference of monogamy (or monogyny).

20. Coogan, *God and Sex*, 72.
21. Stone, "Marriage and Sexual Relations," 178; and Coogan, *God and Sex*, 7.
22. Ackerman, *Warrior, Dancer, Seductress, Queen*.

Another aspect of marriage and sexuality in the Hebrew Bible is incestuous relationships and other problematic unions. In a number of texts, it is clear that not all marital unions are permitted or that there should be a sexual relationship. Leviticus 18 gives clear stipulations: no sexual relationship with your mother, or another wife of your father, your sister or half-sister, your aunt, your daughter-in-law, your sister-in-law, etc. However, inconsistency is noticeable here, because the marriage between Abraham and Sarah in Genesis is labelled as positive, while according to Gen 20:12 both have the same father. This marriage would not have been permitted on the basis of Lev 18:9 and 20:17. Leviticus 18:18 prohibits sexual contact between a man and two women who are sisters. However, such a relationship creates the twelve tribes of Israel: Jacob has children with both Leah and Rachel. Mixed marriage of Israelites with non-Israelite women is given significant attention in a number of texts but, again, we do not get a consistent picture. Moses has both a Midianite wife (Exod 2:16–22), Zipporah, and a Nubian wife (Num 12:1). When Miriam speaks out against this, she is punished by God and must stay outside the camp for seven days.

Another example is that Samson's parents oppose his desire to marry a Philistine girl. In the same text, it is immediately clear that God instigates this, though, admittedly, in order to find a reason to enter into battle with the Philistines (Judg 14:1–4). And not the least example is the story of Ruth. She is a Moabite who marries an Israelite and becomes the great-grandmother of David (Ruth 4:18–22). There is no uniformity: sometimes these marriages are condemned, sometimes they are not.[23] So, we can conclude from this that we witness several forms of relationships in which sex for men did not only take place in a monogamous relationship. For women, other rules applied.

Adultery and Prostitution

In the Hebrew Bible, adultery was regarded as a serious matter. Both the man and the woman involved in adultery ran the risk of being killed (Lev 20:10; Deut 22:22). Again, the assumption is that the married woman is under the authority of her husband. In this context, the husband has exclusive rights to the sexual relationship with his wife. The offence of a man committing adultery with a married woman is directed against the

---

23. Coogan, *God and Sex*, 77–78.

man who has the authority over the woman with whom the other man committed adultery. Adultery was, in fact, a form of dispossession.[24] In addition, inheritance was endangered by adultery because it interfered with the patriarchal structure. Adultery was thus the first step in an unlawful appropriation of property; it called the rights of the husband to have exclusive sexual access to his wife into question. The theme of dispossession also plays a role in David's relationship with Bathsheba (2 Sam 11). What is striking in this story is God's judgment, through the prophet Nathan, on what David has done.

Interestingly enough, a married man does not commit adultery when he has a sexual relationship with a prostitute. His female partner (the prostitute) is not married and is not under the authority of another man.[25] Incidentally, it is assumed today that apart from this toleration of prostitution, there was no sacral prostitution in Israel. Stone contends that prostitution led to the stigmatization of women. Moreover, in Deut 23:17–18 we read: "No Israelite man or woman is to become a shrine prostitute. You must not bring the earnings of a female prostitute or a male prostitute into the house of the LORD your God to pay any vow, because the LORD your God detests them both." Simply put, this meant that money earned from prostitution could not be used to pay for a vow in the temple.[26] At the same time, prostitution was condoned.

Others rightly point out that, in the context of a patriarchal society, women who did not have a father, husband, or male relative to offer them protection often did not have many other choices for survival. This, of course, in no way justifies prostitution. Coogan shows that the Hebrew word cannot always be unambiguously translated as "prostitute," but must also be associated with women who were sexually active outside a formal marriage.[27] As an example, he refers to Gomer, the wife of the prophet Hosea. She was sexually active, but probably not a prostitute, although the older translations of Hos 1:2 suggest this. Nuances are important here. Coogan addresses Lev 19:29: "Do not degrade your daughter by making her a prostitute, or the land will turn to prostitution and be filled with wickedness." Ultimately, according to Coogan, the purity of the holy or sanctified land is at stake here. Either way, there is a religious stigma.[28]

24. Coogan uses the term "expropriation," *God and Sex*, 53 (e-book version).
25. Stone, "Marriage and Sexual Relations," 180–81.
26. Stone, "Marriage and Sexual Relations," 182.
27. Coogan, *God and Sex*, 163.
28. Coogan, *God and Sex*, 165.

Also interesting are texts like Prov 29:3 and 6:26. In the first text, the author states that visiting prostitutes leads to the squandering of their father's fortune. In the second, a comparison is made between the cost of a visit to a prostitute on the one hand, and a possible attempt by a woman who belongs to her husband at a relationship with another man, on the other hand. Prostitution is thus at least less costly and also less problematic than potential adultery, if we understand the text correctly. In the Hebrew Bible, we come across countless examples of problematic and incestuous relationships, abuse, and rape. Here are just two well-known examples; the two Tamars: Tamar and her relationship with Judah (Gen 38) and Rahab (Josh 2), and in 2 Sam 13 Amnon's rape of his sister Tamar. In both stories, questions of sex (or more accurately, rape) between family members are addressed. Finally, Coogan also points out the role that women and possibly prostitutes played in the stories of Samson (Judg 14–16).

Divorce

Deut 24:1–4, often referred to in discussions of divorce, is, in fact, not directly dealing with divorce.[29] The focus is on the remarriage of a woman from whom a man has previously divorced. The exact reason for this is not clear. Coogan suspects that here, as in other texts, issues of inheritance may play a role.[30] In fact, it appears to be an existing divorce practice in ancient Israel. The translation of Deut 24:1–4 is somewhat ambiguous in more recent Bible translations. We read, "If a man marries a woman (the Hebrew text uses "baal," lord, master), who becomes displeasing to him because he finds *something indecent* about her, and he writes her a certificate of divorce, gives it to her and sends her away from his house" (NIV). The NKJV translates this as: "When a man takes a wife and marries her . . . because he has found *some uncleanness* in her." The term "something indecent/some uncleanness" appears only once elsewhere in the Bible, in Deut 23:13, where it refers to inappropriate nudity

29. "If a man marries a woman who becomes displeasing to him because he finds something indecent about her, and he writes her a certificate of divorce, gives it to her and sends her from his house, and if after she leaves his house she becomes the wife of another man, and her second husband dislikes her and writes her a certificate of divorce, gives it to her and sends her from his house, or if he dies, then her first husband, who divorced her, is not allowed to marry her again after she has been defiled. That would be detestable in the eyes of the Lord. Do not bring sin upon the land the Lord your God is giving you as an inheritance."

30. Coogan, *God and Sex*, 71.

during defecation. Coogan believes that in Deut 24:1–4, it is a kind of abbreviated expression for (a form of) adultery.[31] At the very least, it can also be read figuratively as shame, disgrace, and uncleanness.

Exod 21:8 suggests, as a reason for divorce, "if she does not please the master who has selected her," and Deut 22:13 speaks of if the man "dislikes her." In the remainder of that chapter, it becomes clear that the virginity of a newlywed woman was considered extremely crucial for the marriage. From the context, it appears that the man in question wrongfully accused his new wife and put her reputation as a virgin at risk. He has sown doubt about her virginity and that is an offense. It is probably less about the woman's reputation and more about her father's, because he did not protect his daughter's honor. Divorce is not allowed in this setting. A similar prohibition of divorce applies to a man who rapes a virgin (Deut 22:28–29). In addition, priests were not allowed to marry a divorced or defiled woman. Such a marriage did not fit in with the required ritual purity (Lev 21:7).

Coogan also discusses the well-known (in Christian circles) and complex text from Mal 2:13–16. Given the importance of this text, we will consider it at some length. We read:

> [13] Another thing you do: You flood the LORD's altar with tears. You weep and wail because he no longer looks with favor on your offerings or accepts them with pleasure from your hands. [14] You ask, "Why?" It is because the LORD is the witness between you and the wife of your youth. You have been unfaithful to her, though she is your partner, the wife of your marriage covenant. [15] Has not the one God made you? You belong to him in body and spirit. And what does the one God seek? Godly offspring. So be on your guard, and do not be unfaithful to the wife of your youth. [16] "The man who hates and divorces his wife," says the LORD, the God of Israel, "does violence to the one he should protect," says the LORD Almighty. So be on your guard, and do not be unfaithful.

The question is how then the crucial verse 16, which is often translated with "I/He hate(s) divorce" and which sounds absolute, must be understood. Clearly it is not translated thus in the NIV used here. Coogan also wonders how this text, and its often-claimed absoluteness, is to be understood, particularly with other texts, such as Jer 3:7b–8a: ". . . and her unfaithful sister Judah saw it. I gave faithless Israel her certificate of

---

31. Coogan, *God and Sex*, 71.

divorce and sent her away because of all her adulteries." How does this metaphorical and symbolic language relate to the text from Malachi? Coogan applies the context of the fifth century BC in his interpretation of this important text. According to him, we must read the text against the background of *exogamy*: marriages outside the group. The passage would then mainly refer to Jewish men who divorced their Jewish wives with the intention of getting married to non-Jewish women.[32] These gentile women may have been very young and may have been "trophies." Spiritual leaders such as Ezra and Nehemiah would have opposed such intermarriages (Ezra 10:2–3).

Later, in Ezra 10, people confess their guilt collectively. In the text, we find a long list of those who had married *foreign* women. In contrast with exogamy, Coogan elaborates on the importance of *endogamy*.[33] The choice of a bride was largely based on belonging to the same ethnic and therefore religious group.[34] An interesting example of the way in which a marriage outside the group could lead to problems is seen with Jezebel, the daughter of the king of Tyre. Jezebel was married to Ahab, the king of Israel (1 Kgs 16:31–33). The (religious) identity of the group and its convictions can then come under discussion (Deut 7:1–11). It thus seems very likely that the text from Malachi refers to the phenomenon of exogamy rather than to a general provision regarding divorce. Stone shows that there is some inconsistency on the issue of mixed marriages.[35] As mentioned above, Moses had both a Midianite wife (Exod 2:16–22) and a Nubian (possibly Ethiopian) wife (Num 12:1). Moses's sister Miriam is punished when she and Aaron speak negatively to Moses about his Nubian wife. Samson's parents speak negatively about his desire for a Philistine wife, but the narrator leaves no room for doubt: God is responsible for the relationship (Judg 14:4).

Sexual Pleasure

Sexual desire is not labelled as negative in the Hebrew Bible. A newlywed man does not have to join the army and he can stay at home for a year

32. Coogan, *God and Sex*, 75.

33. Endogamy is the practice of marrying within a specific group. The norm of the group determines who belongs and who does not. Endogamy is the opposite of exogamy.

34. Coogan, *God and Sex*, 51.

35. Stone, "Marriage and Sexual Relations," 184.

to make his wife happy (Deut 24:5). What is Ruth's intention when she sleeps in Boaz's "bed" in the middle of the night (Ruth 3)? Naomi advises her to get ready, go to the threshing floor, and lie down at the feet of Boaz. We read: "When he lies down, note the place where he is lying. Then go and uncover his feet and lie down. He will tell you what to do" (Ruth 3:4). It is clear that it was not customary for a woman to lie down at night with a strange man.[36] Does the expression "uncover his feet and lie down" have a sexual connotation? Whatever the case, Ruth stays with him all night, until dawn. And in Gen 18:12 we also find positive connotations around sexuality, although Sarah points out that she and Abraham are already at an advanced age.[37]

About Nudity

In Gen 2, we read about the creation of (the) woman; that she is taken from the man. Verse 24 says that they will again become "one flesh" and this refers to having sexual intercourse. Remarkably, in Genesis 2:24 there is not a single word about possible offspring that could result from the unification of their bodies, though this is discussed in Gen 1:28. Gen 2:24 seems to refer to a purely sexual union, not related to procreation. In Gen 2:25, the last verse of chapter 2, it is mentioned that Adam and his wife were both naked, but were not ashamed of each other. Nakedness was thus part of the good creation. It stands for open-mindedness, perfection, unity, and openness. The serpent who appears on the scene in the following verses is cunning (in Hebrew the same root as the word for "nakedness"). In the conversation with Adam and Eve, he tells them that their eyes will open as soon as they eat of the fruit (3:5). That indeed happens (in verse 7), and then they notice that they are naked. Apparently, they were not even aware of it before. Beyond that observation,

36. Others would want to contend that because Ruth and Boaz are called "righteous" the chance they would have had sexual intercourse is very small. We leave this here as a question. Cf. Coogan, *God and Sex*. Coogan states that the referral to "laying at his feet" is an explicit referral to the genitals. In this context, he refers to the circumcision of Moses by his wife Zipporah (Exod 4). God attempts to kill Moses (because he had not been circumcised?) and Zipporah then cut's the foreskin of her son's penis and touches Moses's feet with it. According to Coogan, "feet" symbolize "penis." Of course, we do not contend that whenever there is mention of "feet" in the Hebrew Bible they refer to a penis.

37. "So Sarah laughed to herself as she thought, 'After I am worn out and my lord is old, will I now have this pleasure?'"

their awareness of nakedness is now a sign of shame and guilt: the other has become a threat, and now this nakedness testifies to alienation from each other, to distance. Where nakedness was good before, it must now be covered. We also read this in other texts in the Bible. Think of the story of Noah who gets drunk and is naked (Gen 9:20–27). Cham, the father of Canaan, shares this with his two brothers who then cover their father without seeing him. Noah then curses Cham. Nakedness has become a disgrace since the fall and, in a symbolic sense, often refers to low status. But that is definitely not part of God's good creation. Dutch theologian Frank Bosman links what he calls "the innocent nakedness of the gardens of Eden and Song of Songs" with the nakedness of Jesus on the cross.[38] Although, in this section, we mainly focus on the Hebrew Bible, we briefly discuss the meaning of Jesus's nakedness here. The nakedness of each crucified person emphasized his or her vulnerability. We should not be too eager to provide Jesus on the cross with some kind of loincloth, says Bosman, because in all likelihood there was none. But neither should we see the nakedness of Jesus as the nakedness of a child in the manger. According to Bosman: "Jesus's life is a penetrating reflection of the desperate credo of Job: *I was born naked, and naked shall I die.*"[39]

Bosman also demonstrates that in art history (especially in the Renaissance) we can find clear examples of the many artists who indulged in depicting the most vulnerable part of our existence, and of Jesus's existence: our nakedness. Bosman writes:

> Naked he dies on the cross. Naked, He is taken down from the cross by a few people, including the faithful Mary Magdalene, and laid down in a rocky grave. When, according to the stories, Jesus rises from the dead on the third day, the first witnesses, men as well as women, find the death cloths rolled up in a corner of the tomb. Then they witnessed several appearances of the resurrected Jesus. This Jesus is just as naked as when he hung on the cross. He had left the death cloths behind. And how else could sweet unfortunate Thomas be invited to put his finger into Jesus's pierced side? (John 20:24–31).[40]

38. Bosman, *God houdt van seks*, 42; translated by the authors.

39. Bosman, *God houdt van seks*, 42; translated by the authors.

40. Bosman, *God houdt van seks*, 43; translated by the authors.

The Positive Image in Song of Songs

The most affirming and positive image when it comes to sexual desire is, of course, found in Song of Songs. There is no doubt that the Song of Songs is the most sensual, erotically charged poetry in the Hebrew Bible. Sexual desire and pleasure are attributed to a female speaker without any form of stigmatization. Even, and perhaps especially, with the use of metaphors and symbols, space is given to physical and female experience as nowhere else in the Bible. In the Song of Songs, there are also voices to the contrary, such as when it becomes clear that certain figures (like her brothers) regard female sexual freedom as suspect (8:8–9). Is this a sort of protective urge or the guarding of sexual purity (cf. Gen 34:14)? And when the woman is looking for her lover at night, she is beaten by the guards of the city (5:7). Scholars such as LaCocque have claimed that the woman of Song of Songs wrote this text precisely in order to change the negative image of (her own) female sexual experience in society.[41] Coogan states:

> The Song of Solomon is one of the most lyrical and most fasci-
> nating of those voices. In the foreign country that is the biblical
> world, the Song is a garden of earthly delights—full of blos-
> soming lilies, fig trees, grape vines, and henna shrubs, turtle-
> doves, foxes, and gazelles, apples, raisins, and pomegranates,
> cypresses, cedars, and palm trees—a veritable Eden. And the
> delights are not just those of nature: it is a place where sex—
> unmarried sex, sex for its own sake and not just for reproduc-
> tion—is celebrated.[42]

An interesting analysis is also given by theologian David Carr, who places the Song of Songs in the context of the Near East and its love poetry.[43] In general, Carr's explanation of Song of Songs does not differ much from Coogan's approach. What is interesting is the successful attempt to break through the traditional paradox between a spiritual and a sexual reading of Song of Songs. Carr rightly points out the important connection that exists between these two dimensions: whoever talks about sex must also be willing to talk about the soul.

---

41. LaCocque, *Romance, She Wrote.*
42. Coogan, *God and Sex*, 26 (e-book version).
43. Carr, *Erotic Word.*

Cleanliness and Promiscuity

In her impressive study *Body, Gender and Purity in Leviticus 12 and 15*, the German Hebrew Bible scholar Dorothea Erbele-Kuster deals extensively with the relationship between language, the body, and gender in the Hebrew Bible and with a view, especially, to the two chapters from Leviticus mentioned in the title.[44] She aims to explore how a specific reading of these texts shows the impact on our understanding of sexuality, gender, and the body. For her, it is crucial that relatively little attention has been paid to a feminist-anthropological reading of these texts. She writes about the *gender unawareness gap*, a gap that needs to be filled because it paints a more nuanced picture of the scope of these texts.

Fortunately, several studies have been published in recent years by female scholars, in which this theme is given the attention it deserves. Lev 12 and 15 are part of a larger body of texts that begin in chapter 11. The themes range from what animals may or may not be eaten to skin diseases, and from provisions relating to birth to unclean liquids leaving the body. Lev 11–15 are, in turn, part of the larger whole of chapters 11–26, which deal with purity and holiness. The (sexual) body must be culturally pure for God if man is to be close to God. God's holiness must, as it were, be reflected in that body (Lev 11:44; 19:2). For Erbele-Kuster, attention to the physical, in its relationship to God, is not a neutral matter. Rather, the body and gender are produced and transmitted through language and culture.[45] The body and gender identity emerge from social and religious contexts, in which they are also standardized in a ritual sense. She also notes that a number of different interpretations of the purity rules have been proposed in recent decades, and some are more congruent than others.

Historical-theological approaches attempted to reconcile the prescriptions in Leviticus as part of an identity process in which Israel had to distinguish itself from the surrounding pagan religious cultures. In this point of view, the driving force behind the regulations would be the rejection of the fertility cult and its embedded religious aspects. A completely different approach is based on the idea that we must presuppose a magical worldview, in which the regulations show a stage of development from a form of pantheism to monotheism. In this sense, uncleanness should be associated with demons and legislation in the wider ancient Near Eastern

---

44. Erbele-Kuster, *Body, Gender and Purity*.

45. Erbele-Kuster, *Body, Gender and Purity*, 2–3.

society. A third view emphasizes an ethical model, in which inculcating awe for the lives of animals is the purpose of the regulations.

Others point out the medical and hygienic importance of the rules. A sociological approach focuses mainly on the impact of these rules on strengthening priestly power structures. This view incorporates the idea that the rhetorical structure of Leviticus is mainly aimed at confirming the Aaronic priesthood.[46] The most influential view in more recent times is undoubtedly Mary Douglas's.[47] From a cultural-anthropological perspective, she showed that the purity regulations represent a social-religious system that aims to align the inner and outer worlds. The rules bring order to people's experiences, clarify religious practices, and reduce discomfort. The rules form a symbolic system, limit what can and cannot be done with a body, reflect the social order and, on this basis, bring stability. Later, Douglas nuanced her view and linked it more strongly to a literary approach. She then states that the provisions regarding purity in Lev 11–16 are a further elaboration of the first nine chapters of the book of Genesis.[48]

Eve Levavi-Feinstein agrees to a large extent with Erbele-Kuster, though from a broader analysis of Hebrew texts and with a specific focus on "purity and pollution" in relation to sexuality.[49] She also notes that not a great deal of attention has been paid to this theme, even though a considerable number of texts do specifically make a connection between sexuality and purity. For Levavi-Feinstein there is a clear relationship between the terminology referring to purity and impurity on the one hand and concepts such as virginity, adultery, and rape on the other.[50] Moreover, she sees a relationship between offensive and illicit forms of sex, and considers the question of temporary uncleanness as a result of intercourse or ejaculation. In any case, it goes without saying that "purity" and "pollution" were important concepts in ancient Israel.

The Hebrew verb *tm'* appears frequently in the Hebrew Bible, as does the noun *tame* (uncleanness) associated with it. Levavi-Feinstein explores the idea that the various terms associated with uncleanness should be connected primarily with a sense of disgust.[51] "Pollution must then

---

46. Erbele-Kuster, *Body, Gender and Purity*, 2–3.
47. Douglas, *Purity and Danger*.
48. Douglas, *Leviticus as Literature*.
49. Levavi-Feinstein, *Sexual Pollution*.
50. Levavi-Feinstein, *Sexual Pollution*, 2.
51. Levavi-Feinstein, *Sexual Pollution*, 7.

be understood as having its roots in disgust. Levavi-Feinstein therefore interprets uncleanness and pollution (*pollution* also in her terminology) from that perspective. The verb *ṭm'* describes a negative and contagious quality that is the product of disgust. The use of the verb and its associated terms is present in the Hebrew Bible in many varied forms.

However, the terms used in relation to pollution are not negative per se, as they may refer to the *risk* of pollution without immediately stating that the activity associated with it is prohibited. Beliefs about pollution do not necessarily prohibit the behavior that could lead to it. Sexual intercourse leads to ritual uncleanness, but of course it is not forbidden; one simply had to cleanse oneself afterwards (Lev 15). Levavi-Feinstein points out that the language used in the Hebrew Bible in connection with cleansing focuses mainly on women: men defile, women are defiled. The same background plays a role here, as we discussed earlier in this chapter: in the context of the Hebrew Bible, women are also sexually the property of men; sex outside marriage defiles the woman and ruins the man.[52]

How does virginity play a role in the Hebrew Bible? Virginity before marriage was very important, but apparently only for women.[53] There are numerous examples of women in the Hebrew Bible who did not have a relationship with a man, but rarely do we find references to a man who did not have a sexual relationship with a woman. When Abraham is looking for a wife for his son Isaac, his servant comes into contact with Rebecca. The narrator of Genesis then reports: "The woman was very beautiful, a virgin; no man had ever slept with her" (Gen 24:16). Coogan highlights another example of a prominent virgin, Jephthah's daughter.[54] Jephthah, according to Judges 11, was himself conceived with a prostitute (11:1). As a result, he had to flee from his brothers, who had no intention of sharing their father's inheritance with a man who was the son "of another woman." His brothers had literally (and legally) disowned him by sending him away.[55] In this situation the elders of Gilead come to him because a war has broken out with the Ammonites (11:5). They want him to lead the battle against the Ammonites. On the condition that he will be their leader, he agrees. On the way to the battle, he makes a promise to God that if the Ammonites are defeated, he will give the first thing that comes to him after the battle to God as a burnt offering (11:30–31).

52. Levavi-Feinstein, *Sexual Pollution*, 158.

53. Coogan, *God and Sex*, 30.

54. Coogan, *God and Sex*, 26.

55. Coogan, *God and Sex,* 26.

When the battle is over and the Ammonites have been defeated, Jephthah returns victorious. He is welcomed with dancing and drumming, his daughter leading the way (11:34). The shocking conclusion is that he keeps his promise and he will have to sacrifice his daughter, his only child. She is given permission to go to the mountains for two months to grieve over her virginity (11:38). When the two months are over, Jephthah carries out his promise. There is no divine intervention here, as in the story of Isaac; the girl's name is not even mentioned, nor is her death condemned. Coogan argues that part of the tragedy is that the daughter dies a virgin and thus never had children. Because of the fact that a woman's primary role was locked up in marriage and motherhood, there is hardly a positive view of lifelong virginity.[56]

Although adultery is an offence against the man to whom the woman belongs, the woman is not spared. Her uncleanness as a result of the adultery is considered very negative. Numbers 5 outlines the procedure for this situation. The language that runs through the section like a refrain, for the woman who may or may not have committed adultery, is the language of *contamination* (vv. 13, 14, 19, 20, 27, 28, 29). It is unclear if, and how often, this procedure was actually carried out. In a text like Deut 22:13–21, attention is also drawn to what should happen to a woman who is (accused of being) no longer a virgin at the time of her marriage. Apparently, after the wedding night, a man can suddenly take a dislike to his wife and accuse her falsely (22:14). There seems to be no rules for men who are sexually active before marriage.

Diversity and the Big Picture in the New Testament

Benjamin Dunning, in *The Oxford Handbook of New Testament, Gender and Sexuality*, examines the place of gender and sexuality in the New Testament and early Christian literature.[57] Similarly, Colleen Conway looks to these starting points for a helpful discussion.[58] A central question is how concepts we use today (sex, sexuality, gender, sexual acts, etc.) relate to the world of the New Testament. It is clear that historians, anthropologists, philosophers, and many other theorists have tried, in recent

---

56. Coogan, *God and Sex*, 29. Regarding virginity, the assurance one wanted to have about who the father of the child was, played an enormous role.

57. Dunning, *Oxford Handbook*.

58. Conway, "Masculinity Studies," 77–93.

decades, to clarify the various cultural backgrounds, political systems, and religious embedding of these concepts. Biblical scholars have made their own contributions on the basis of their interpretations of the transmitted texts in the Hebrew Bible and New Testament.[59] New and in-depth insights from feminist scholars (we will discuss this later) have contributed to an increase in the complexity of how we understand texts that already had a long history of interpretation. Specifically, our question focuses in on how concepts such as sex, gender, sexual differentiation, sexual acts, and sexuality were actually understood and enacted.

Considering the well-known verse Gal 3:28 ("There are no longer Jews or Greeks, slaves or free, male or female; you are all one in Christ Jesus"), we must ask ourselves what kind of claims can be made concerning gender and sexuality.[60] It seems that (in terms of interpretation) an apparently logical division of humanity into two groups—male and female, masculine and feminine—has been abolished since the coming of Christ. At the same time, we have to deal with the influences of both the Hebrew Bible and Greco-Roman thought. But, a critical reader will note, what about a text like 1 Cor 11, where the same Paul seems to aim at keeping the differences pretty much intact? Moreover, can we easily apply our modern concepts of gender and sexuality to these texts? In general, thinking about gender as it has developed in recent decades has left its mark on the interpretation of texts.

In chapter 3, we explored how much the tension between nature and nurture plays a role in dealing with gender and sexuality. This means that, with our modern reading glasses on, we cannot simply accuse Paul and other authors of arbitrary interpretations or contend that they would not have been able to go against the existing views on what was "masculine" and "feminine." In this chapter it will be necessary to be sensitive to the complexity of the texts and to the now-prevalent consensus that gender in antiquity was primarily a spectrum with gradations in what was seen as masculine and feminine.[61] In what follows, we will discuss various themes that emerge from the New Testament. First, we will discuss Jesus and gender.

---

59. In this context, we mention the work of Loader, *Sexuality in the New Testament.* Loader starts with an introduction about the impact of context for understanding key New Testament texts and then explains a series of core texts.

60. Compare Neutel, *Cosmopolitan Ideal.*

61. Dunning, *Oxford Handbook.*

Sexuality and "Marriage" in the New Testament

Sex According to Jesus—Jesus and Gender

What can we find, for our search, around the person of Jesus or in the stories that have been written about him and his actions? To what extent is there a pattern in those stories that can help us better understand what we are dealing with in terms of gender and sexuality in our time?

Thatcher starts his chapter on "Jesus and Gender" by describing his goal: to make a theological contribution to the field of gender discussions so that human relationships can be seen in the light of Christ's redemption.[62] Thatcher, we are convinced, rightly places this particular discussion in this particular framework because it functions as a kind of ultimate test. If we believe that Christ has redeemed us, then this must have an undeniable impact on us and all our relationships, and that includes gender and sexuality. Redemption is the work of God in Christ (Eph 1:9); there is a direct connection between the incarnation of God in Christ and the "incarnation" of concrete love and righteousness. Theology often falls short when it comes to this concrete connection between thinking about the incarnation of Christ and its implications for human sexuality. The core beliefs of the Christian faith, which in many respects are too one-sidedly expressed in masculine language, can be formulated in such a way that oppression disappears and hope is offered.[63] It would be unhelpful to repeat parts of chapter 1 here, but it is about how tensions can be resolved between an (ancient) androcentric (with masculine aspects as the focus) anthropology with one nature (i.e., the "one-sex" theory) and, for example, a (modern) complementary anthropology (man and woman are two different sexes, but they are complementary). A solution must be sought for a more *transformative* understanding of what it means to be human. But then viewed from a unity, and in such a way, that men and women use their specific characteristics and qualities. The typically transformative character of God's actions in creation and recreation (God transforming us into the image of Christ) must be linked to this.

The question is, of course, where we see this connection in the gospel or even directly in the person of Jesus. Thatcher rightly states that the transformation brought about by God in Christ is far more encompassing

---

62. Thatcher, *Redeeming Gender*.

63. Erwich, "Practical Theology."

than just the field of gender; we are not arguing about that. However, those who seek with care will find, even if a number of problems have to be overcome. How can we get a clear picture when we consider that most of the stories about Jesus, including his interactions with women, were written by men? Jesus did not write the gospels personally. Moreover, it is not very difficult to violate Jewish religious traditions of Jesus's time: we have already established the place of and attitudes toward women.[64]

That is precisely why it is interesting to see how women are portrayed in the various gospels. It is certain that Jesus, as we meet him in the gospels, was aware of the sexual politics of his time, especially because he takes an impressive stand against the way in which patriarchal power abuses and exploits women (e.g., Matt 5:27–30). Jesus is touched by the woman who suffered from menorrhagia (Mark 5:24–34 and parallel examples in the Synoptic gospels). He is on his way to heal the twelve-year-old daughter of a synagogue leader and then comes into contact with the woman who has lived in physical and, especially, social isolation for twelve years (the number twelve is of great importance in Jewish tradition because of its associations with wholeness and completion).

In a deeply symbolic sense, we witness here what it meant to be a woman and to be Jewish, from the young woman who has just had her first period to the older woman whose periods do not stop.[65] In Jewish tradition, the older woman is permanently unclean and everything and everyone she touches is unclean too (Lev 15:25–27). Jesus is thus also unclean by her touch and puts his own reputation at risk for her. Jesus acknowledges her existence by addressing her in public and also calls her "daughter," saying: "Your faith has healed you" (5:34). No one had stood up for this "outcast" and certainly no one had accepted her into God's household. This is comparable to another woman, again without a name, in Mark 7. This woman has the wrong gender, the wrong nationality, and the wrong religious background. She is a single parent with a daughter who is believed to be possessed by demons. Another example we can mention is Jesus's sharpening the interpretation of the Torah when he addressed the committing of adultery in Matt 5:27–30 (part of the Sermon on the Mount). His transformational interpretation is: "But I tell you that

---

64. Thatcher, *Redeeming Gender*, 121–22.

65. We cannot exclude other valid interpretations. It is well possible that there were no issues regarding the elderly woman's cycle, but that something of a different nature was happening.

anyone who looks at a woman lustfully has already committed adultery with her in his heart" (5:28).

According to Thatcher, it is conceivable that Jesus is resisting the view of men, that women are themselves to blame for sexual harassment. No restrictions are placed on women's location, dress, visibility, or behavior. Instead, Thatcher argues, Jesus seems to call on men to take responsibility for their own thoughts and behavior and thus control themselves and their behavior.[66] Thatcher shows that although women were not part of the circle of the twelve Jewish disciples, they travelled with Jesus and served him.

In every Gospel we find the story of Jesus's anointing by a woman (Mark 14:3–9 and parallel). And those who reread the story of Mary and Martha may discover that Mary was in all probability a disciple, not a passive listener at the feet of Jesus, but precisely because of this attitude and posture, this made her a disciple. Women also play a major role in the resurrection narrative and their loyalty is often contrasted with the unbelief of male followers. Thatcher concludes his search with a closer analysis of a number of well-known encounters in the Gospel of John: the Samaritan woman, the woman accused of adultery, Mary the sister of Lazarus, and Mary of Magdala.

Amy-Jill Levine similarly asks us to pay attention to reading the gospels through a different lens, one in which seemingly fixed gender roles are broken, or at least put them into perspective. She points to Jesus's attitude to marriage and his relativization of the role of fathers and husbands. He calls into question typically male privileges by instructing his followers to serve one another. Not the image of the warrior, but that of the child comes to the fore (Mark 10:15; Matt 19:14; Luke 18:17). Levine argues that, in this way, Jesus's male followers are robbed of their male *identity markers*.[67] Thus, we might read the nature of Jesus's struggle with his imminent death just before his arrest (Matt 26:36–45; Mark 14:32–42; Luke 22:39–46) as a compromise with normative male stoicism. Similarly, his cry of desolation on the cross (Matt 27:46) could suggest a loss of male status. Female roles also take on a different perspective. Although Jewish and Roman societies were fundamentally androcentric and patriarchal, in the gospels, women are given much more space and their position is not limited to working at home and caring for children. Women followed

66. Thatcher, *Redeeming Gender*, 123–24.
67. Levine, "Gospels and Acts," 295–314.

Jesus, played a role in his protection (Luke 8:1–3), and travelled, even as missionaries. Women had financial resources, were entrepreneurs (Lydia, Acts 16:14), were the first witnesses to the resurrection, etc. Inscriptions show that they had leading functions in synagogues and acted as teachers and prophets. More can be said about this, but it is clear that there is a very diverse picture.[68]

Although Levine's view is sympathetic, it raises the question: does the image that emerges from this diversity of texts in the New Testament indicate ambiguity for *all* genders (not only from a binary perspective)? In general, there seems to be room for a wide range of various gender roles. In an extensive essay, Conway discusses different interpretations.[69] To begin with, she points to the influence theorists, such as Laqueur, have had on our understanding of the way in which sexual diversity was perceived in antiquity.[70] As discussed in earlier chapters, people often reasoned from a singular gender model (from male to less masculine): free men at the top, the less perfect versions of men below (women, slaves, etc.). The benefit of Laqueur's thinking was that we may be less inclined to import contemporary thinking about sexual diversity back into classical texts.

This certainly applies to the New Testament, too. Masculinity was defined above all by the criterion of being in control of one's own desires, passions, and lusts.[71] It therefore had to be proven in competition with other men; thus, masculinity was always a "work in progress." Biblical scholars have published an enormous number of studies in recent decades that have focused on the theme of "masculinity" in the Bible. Peter-Ben Smit outlines, in an introductory study, how different models

---

68. Brooten, *Women Leaders*.

69. Conway, "Masculinity Studies," 77–93.

70. Laqueur, *Making Sex*. Laqueur has received serious criticism. Thatcher refers to Helen King, for example, who contends that Laqueur's position is too reductionistic. King argues that he has downplayed the evidence for the "one-sex model." She also states that the similarities and differences between scrotum and womb need to be seen differently than Laqueur sees them. King also argues that Laqueur too easily embraces a constructivist view (cf. chapter 3), which was the dominant view in the late seventies and eighties of the last century. Thatcher is not insensitive to this criticism, but takes the fact that for a long time gender was a very unstable phenomenon in antiquity as his starting point. In addition, theorization regarding the sexual body remained highly ambiguous. *Cf.* Thatcher, *Redeeming Gender*, 50.

71. Ivarsson, "Vice Lists," 163–84.

of thinking about masculinity have developed and which perspectives have played a role in these developments.[72]

We may pause here, before going into more detail, and ask: what does all this searching bring us? As far as we are concerned, the answer is this: Yes, Jesus called twelve men to be his disciples. And as Jewish men, they represented the twelve tribes of Israel, but Jesus's interactions with and approach to women is unprecedented! This is completely new in a world where women were seen as imperfect and inferior men. Their perceived inferiority was expressed in all sorts of ways, but Jesus brings them into God's family and into the wider circle of disciples, and respects them fully—as the many encounters show. Thatcher argues convincingly that women are true disciples, whose faith, devotion, and perseverance sometimes exceeded (and exposed) that of the apostles.[73]

Can we say that Jesus himself casts a different light on what should be seen as male and female? What, for example, does a story like Jesus washing his disciples' feet mean with regard to gender?[74] All the emphasis is on Jesus's serving, and giving himself away in love. Whoever wants to rule must learn to serve; whoever wants to be the most important must learn to be the least. It is a total reversal of the existing order, and his act makes the prevailing power structures subject to criticism. It seems to contradict the masculine power patterns we encounter in the Greco-Roman world.

Conway has astutely pointed out that the ways in which Jesus is presented are sometimes ambiguous.[75] On the one hand Jesus is presented as the one who surpasses the power and glory of the emperor, and on the other hand we see Jesus's agony on the cross as a story of humiliation and "emasculation." In other examples, Jesus compares himself to a woman (Luke 15:8–9), and to a hen that takes care of her chicks (Matt 23:37).[76] And it is well worth paying attention to the way the Johannine Jesus's gender is constructed. Conway points out that while Jesus is presented as the one who has perfect control over circumstances, others have no authority over him except God, his Father. Furthermore, Peter-Ben Smit

72. Smit, *Masculinity and the Bible*, 4–13.

73. Thatcher, *Redeeming Gender*, 131.

74. See John 13.

75. Conway, *Behold the Man*.

76. One could argue that the other story in Luke 15, the parable of the lost coin, does not receive necessary attention. Like the story of the prodigal son, this story also gives an image of God. See also Leene, *Triniteit, antropologie en ecclesiologie*.

picks up Conway's work and, by "deepening some of Conway's insights into the structure of Jesus's masculinity, argues that Jesus's death on the cross deconstructs this masculinity, which makes any form of "macho Christology" impossible, and "opens up doors toward alternatives."[77]

Through God's interventions in God's world, things are turned upside down. What is great is small and what is weak is strong. Jesus is Lord, *kurios*, but in a completely different way than usual rulers. He does not rule through domination or control. His way is the way of *un-mastery*. This is the foundation (and also the tension) of the dialectic that lies between humiliation and exaltation. Both are present and necessary. We find these in the often-quoted passage Phil 2:6–11:

> Who, being in very nature God, did not consider equality with God something to be used to his own advantage; rather, he made himself nothing by taking the very nature of a servant, being made in human likeness. And being found in appearance as a man, he humbled himself by becoming obedient to death— even death on a cross! Therefore God exalted him to the highest place and gave him the name that is above every name.

It is striking that Jesus is often called "the human" instead of "the man." In the context of Jesus's time, a woman could not be a rabbi, but his masculinity is not necessary for his plan of redemption. The language of Father and Son refers to the relationship between them, namely one of complete equality, and less to gender or sex. And, as we read in many places in the Bible (e.g., John 4:24), God transcends gender, so we must be careful not to fall into the trap of seeing God as male.[78] There are theologians who argue for the use of different language to describe God, but it is questionable if this is a good solution. It remains important to use relational words, but that makes avoiding language that is colored by sex and gender difficult. Furthermore, there is a range of metaphorical language used for God, for example when God compares Godself with a birth-giving woman/mother in Isa 66:13 and 42:14. And God's mercy (God being the merciful, *el rachoem*) is related to the Hebrew word *rechem*, which means "womb."

The role of Mary is also interesting in discussions of Jesus's gender. Jesus had an earthly mother, he spoke of a heavenly father, and Mary has often been characterized by the church as the example of the perfect virgin woman who was at the same time a mother. Arnold Huijgen

77. Smit, "Jesus and the Ladies," 1–15.

78. Leene, *Triniteit, antropologie en ecclesiologie*.

discusses this impossible expectation in his book about Mary. Mary, the perfect virgin mother, is also portrayed as the new Eve.[79]

When raising questions about Jesus and gender, Karen King does not start with a close biblical reading, like Thatcher, but takes a different approach.[80] She does not set out to "reconstruct" Jesus's gender, but concentrates on how Jesus is presented as a man, circumcised Jew, virgin, husband, and eunuch. It is clear from the outset that the most reliable historical sources are silent on whether Jesus was married or had any kind of sexual relationship.[81] According to King, we must understand the Greco-Roman world with its coded gender protocols. Following Craig Williams, she writes that a "real man" was in perfect control of his fears and desires, ruling over others and their bodies; an "effeminate" man was dominated by these things and by the bodies of others.[82] Self-control was also of a masculine nature; sexual desires and fears had to be conquered. This hegemonic masculinity could often only be realized by a certain elite.[83] The vast majority of people were on a spectrum toward the "unmanly" (subordinates, women, slaves, and children). It was not out of the question that this "unmanly" group could exhibit masculine behavior, but having male genitalia was no guarantee of masculinity.[84] Masculinity was never a singular fixed identity, but rather an "unstable condition" that could be made and granted, or removed and taken away. The individual's gender status was permanently exposed to that risk and could not be viewed separately from economic and social status, ethnicity, age, and (local) culture.[85] King explains that circumcision is an example of something that threatens masculinity. In the Jewish tradition, Jesus's circumcision marked his full participation in the covenant as a Jewish man; however, from the perspective of the Greco-Roman culture, it was a barbaric act that rendered him ethnically inferior and feminized him.

Throughout the gospels and early Christian literature, we are given differing depictions of Jesus. Earlier in this chapter we pointed out this tension. The gospel writers often present Jesus as a man of humble origins from the unpopular area of Galilee. He leaves his family and goes out to

79. Huijgen, *Maria*.
80. King, "Jesus," 407–27.
81. King, "Jesus," 407.
82. Williams, *Roman Homosexuality*.
83. Hegemonic as aimed at dominance over.
84. King, "Jesus," 408.
85. King, "Jesus," 408–9.

preach, has no fixed abode, and is poor. He ends up on a cross as a slave. These are not exactly the images that help spread his message in a world dominated by a male elite; it is the greatest possible anti-story. At the same time, Jesus is portrayed as the obedient son and the righteous slave, possibly reversing some of that same anti-story.

King gives two examples that illustrate this complexity: the Gospel of Mark and the Book of Revelation.[86] We have already seen how Jesus's treatment of women differs from what was usual at the time. King shows us that there is an emphasis on Jesus's authority (exorcism of demons, healings), which is not unlike the ideology of the Roman rulers, but in Mark's gospel this is also a subversion of Roman imperial ideology. And, as we have outlined, there are images of masculinity that are in competition with each other. Jesus uses language and rhetoric that fits with the expectations for masculinity, but he is also the crucified slave who is abandoned by everyone.

The book of Revelation, of course, has its own complexities.[87] According to King, in Revelation we see a cosmic Jesus who appears in various forms: that of an angel, a lamb, the Son of Man, and a rider on a white horse. The progression of images is interesting: in chapter 1 Jesus is an angel, in chapter 5 a lamb (certainly not a man), and in chapter 19 a super warrior, almost hyper-masculine. We could even say that at the end Christ is again depicted in male images, while the enemy is given female features.[88] King also points to attempts to read the book through the lens of what has been called "the penetration matrix," that is, those who penetrate are seen as masculine and those who are penetrated are seen as feminine or, more accurately, as unmanly. Through this lens, Christopher Frilingos argues the figure of the lamb destabilizes binary categories of male and female.[89] The pierced lamb (Rev 5:6) stands "as if slain" and is thus represented as feminine/unmasculine. Lynn Huber also moves in this direction:

> The one who can open God's scroll, the one who conquers, is the epitome of weakness and passivity, an animal slaughtered as a sacrifice. Presumably penetrated or pierced (Rev. 1:7) and put on display in the midst of the throne room, the Lamb's body is

86. King, "Jesus," 410–412.

87. Cf. Friesen, *Imperial Cults*; Kovacs and Rowland, *Revelation*; and Huber, "Revelation," 349–69.

88. King, "Jesus," 407–27.

89. Frilingos, *Spectacles of Empire*.

feminized; for, according to the protocols of Roman gender, only feminized bodies, including the bodies of slaves and the defeated, are placed before the penetrating gaze of others. In this way, the Lamb redefines what it means to be a victor, an ideal man.[90]

In chapter 14, however, this passive figure takes on the active role of one who "penetrates," focusing on the enemies and their awaiting judgment. The martyrs are characterized as female because of their suffering and ex-ecutions, but at the same time they represent a male victory through their perseverance. It becomes clear how in such a reading, different dominant images are held very closely to each other, and sometimes even contradict each other. Passive resistance by male virgin martyrs (Rev 14:4: "these are those who did not defile themselves with women, for they remained virgins") is presented as a legitimate masculine position.[91]

It is striking that these stereotypes of masculinity and femininity do not always fully apply and are applied differently in different bibli-cal texts. For example, men are also metaphorically the bride of Christ. According to King, who cites Conway to reinforce her argument,[92] the violence in Revelation comes close to absurdity because it surpasses the civilized manliness of Roman imperial rhetoric. From this perspective, God's way and that of the lamb almost ridicule the power of the emperor. It forms a counter-script, even down to the gory depiction of divine ven-geance. In this way, both hyper-masculinity and resistance are linked; we could even say this is "feminine."

For those interested in the broader discussion on how gender is presented in Revelation, we refer to the work of Huber.[93] She takes the position that Revelation uses the dominant cultural ideas of masculinity and presents them in a way that is *consistent* with the dominant culture. The aim however, according to Huber, is to create a counter-image to the "real" man who can only succeed in life if he marries and has children. Huber's ultimate example is that the 144,000 male virgins challenge the dominant Roman perception of masculinity. They have not engaged with women and follow the lamb, even to a state of gender ambiguity, and in Revelation 19 these virgins become the bride.

---

90. Huber, "Revelation," 349–69.
91. Frilingos, *Spectacles of Empire*, 192.
92. Conway, *Behold the Man*, 174; Conway, *Sex and Slaughter*, 222–38.
93. Huber, "Revelation."

A word of caution is helpful here, we think. Although the perspectives of Huber and others sheds a new light on these texts, we think it is problematic to interpret the entire book of Revelation only through the lens of gender.[94] We are convinced that the focus in Revelation is on the abuse of power by the Roman Empire and within which the emperor claimed ultimate divine power. Of course, in this framework of abuse of power, the ambiguity surrounding gender does play a major role, as discussed above. John used the images and stereotypes of his time precisely for the purpose of questioning the hierarchy and power structure, for the benefit of the whole world. Steven Friesen writes about this in his analysis and from this starting point:

> In Revelation, space and time centered on the absent throne of God, which was accessible only through worship. To those who were not deceived by the claims of empire and who were faithful until death, Revelation promises unending worship in the eternal presence of the Lamb and the One seated on the throne. John was on a collision course with the imperial way of life. John's vision of the world has implications beyond his first century setting, for John was not simply anti-Roman, he was anti-empire. His understanding of his world produced a religious critique of hegemony that transcended his particular historical location.[95]

King continues her analysis with a reference to early Christian literature in which Jesus is described as divine wisdom and as a mother.[96] These metaphors are generally less well known, but no less impressive: Jesus in the role of a mother who protects and nurtures her children (in the Odes of Solomon) and Jesus as a divine teacher. An exclusively male Christ seems insufficient for the scope of what Christ does for us. King speaks of *gender coding*: the role of giving birth, breastfeeding, raising children, and sharing divine revelation as a mother—all of these images are applied to Jesus.

It is interesting to see that references to Jesus as husband, virgin, and eunuch are made as well. In terms of discussions of Jesus's sexual and marital status, this is often in a context of rivalry, around rituals, and within the framework of the vision of the church (ecclesiology). These

---

94. Moore, *Untold Tales*; Selvidge, "Powerful and Powerless," 157–67; Jack, "Out of the Wilderness," 149–62.

95. Friesen, *Imperial Cults*.

96. King, "Jesus," 412.

discussions have been used to support controversies, give direction to the spiritual formation of people, or contribute to the formulation of theological views. In many cases, a connection is made between the chastity of the faithful and their relationship to Christ, whether married or not (cf. 2 Cor 11:1–5 and Rev 14 and 19, in which Christ as a marriage partner is indicated primarily in a metaphorical sense).

An emphasis on the virginity of Jesus is found in both church fathers Clement of Alexandria (125/150–215) and John Chrysostom (347–407), with reference to the superiority of a life of celibacy, based on their conviction that Jesus was not married.[97] For Tertullian (circa 155/160–220 AD), Jesus was both a virgin and a eunuch, who was spiritually pure and thus a model for renouncing earthly things, and with eternity as the reward. Tertullian distinguishes between Christ's human marriage to the church (cf. Eph 5:31–32) on the one hand, and his total unmarried "flesh" on the other.

In Matt 19, in the context of a debate about marital relations, Jesus gives his view, which affirms marriage but at the same time tightens the law. Further down in the same chapter (19:10–12), Jesus points to the so-called *eunuchs*. According to Megan DeFranza, the term "eunuch" was a kind of umbrella term for a number of forms of sexual differentiation, which did not correspond to the ideals of masculinity.[98] DeFranza places "eunuchs" in line with other possible gender variations that we are now more familiar with, such as androgen insensitivity syndrome, Turner's syndrome, etc. (see chapter 3).

In an extensive analysis, she claims that the eunuch was a kind of in-between category in terms of gender. In this context, she refers to Augustine, who stated that a castrated eunuch was not changed into a woman, nor was he allowed to remain a man. For Augustine, says DeFranza, the eunuch stood outside the binary order.

The eunuch is a special category, not only because of the alternative it may provide, but even more so because of its relationship to Jesus in the passage from Matt 19. DeFranza believes that as time went by, Jesus's statement was watered down so that it was only concerned with unmarried men. In reality, it concerns three types of eunuchs, which were also known within the rabbinical traditions: (1) those who were born as eunuchs (called "eunuchs of the sun" because they were eunuchs at birth,

97. King, "Jesus," 412.
98. DeFranza, *Sex Difference in Christian Theology*.

when the sun shone on them for the first time); (2) men who became eunuchs by castration; and (3) men who had made themselves "barren" for the kingdom of heaven. This last category has generated perhaps the most discussion. DeFranza shows how, historically, the figure of the eunuch had various positions, ranging from court official, head of household and elite slave, to the marriage partner of Roman emperor Nero. As for their sexuality, they were often used as reliable caretakers for wealthy households because the eunuch was believed to have no sexual desires. DeFranza reasons that there is sufficient evidence to contradict this because it is known from various sources that women did use the eunuchs for their own sexual pleasure because of the lower risk of pregnancy.[99] Eunuchs *represented* what happened when men lost their manhood, but the *practice* was often different. They were considered to be asexual and said to be irrational, manipulative, and full of deceit—just as women were seen to be.

From the ancient Hebrew context, castrated eunuchs were considered foreigners and outcasts; in fact, castration was forbidden in Judaism. Castrated people were excluded from the assembly of Israel (Deut 23:1: "No one who has been emasculated by crushing or cutting may enter the assembly of the Lord"). At best, they could not fulfill the duty of producing offspring. At worst, they were associated with oppressive regimes, prohibited sexual activities, and involvement in the fertility cult. Isaiah prophesies that a time will come when they will be fully part of God's people (Isa 56:4–5: "I will give them an everlasting name that will endure forever"). It is clear that eunuchs did not comply with Roman, Jewish, and Christian ideals of gender, according to DeFranza (through her references to Jewish writings such as the Tosefta):

> Legally other, morally other, sexually other, socially other, religiously other, and ethnically other, eunuchs were "exiles from the society of the human race, belonging neither to one sex nor the other," as the fourth-century Roman poet Mamertinus eloquently portrayed them.[100]

So, following DeFranza, the question is: what did Jesus's audience (according to Matthew) understand when they heard the word "eunuch"? It seems very likely that Matthew added Jesus's words in 19:12 to emphasize Jesus's identification with the messianic visions of Isaiah. In any case,

---

99. DeFranza, *Sex Difference in Christian Theology*.

100. DeFranza, *Sex Difference in Christian Theology*, 62.

these broad themes in Matt 19 were fertile ground for early Christian ascetics. In the early church, "eunuchs for the kingdom" were seen as those who voluntarily left their families and work behind for the eternal reward promised to them. Matt 22:30 was used in support of this interpretation: "At the resurrection people will neither marry nor be given in marriage; they will be like the angels in heaven."

It is not certain whether Jesus consciously associated eunuchs with angels, according to DeFranza, but that is the association that was usually made. Over a long period of time, both in the western and eastern church, boys were castrated so that they could be used as angelic singers. The "castrati" were elite slaves and singers in the church. DeFranza's analysis of history seems apt: Christian writers in both the western and eastern churches have deliberately tried to take Jesus's statements about eunuchs away from castration practices and gender ambiguity. Both traditions have oriented themselves toward the old prejudices regarding masculinity and perfection. If the eunuch was really to represent Christian perfection (and that seems to have been the movement that many wanted to make), it could only be done by changing the way the eunuch was portrayed: changing the eunuch from a symbol of gender ambiguity and femininity into an alternative form of masculinity.

In the west, this masculinity was defended metaphorically: the virtuous virginal life reflected in the language of a fight waged with the devil and demons. In the east, Byzantine writers dared to attribute virtues and sanctity to literal eunuchs.[101] Ultimately, the question DeFranza wants to answer is whether historical accounts of the eunuch provide enough guidance to equate the category of "eunuch" with intersex conditions. At a minimum, her analysis makes clear that people in antiquity were indeed more familiar with gender variations than is generally assumed, and that the eunuch was, in fact, a complement to the spectrum of the "one" male sex.[102]

It is interesting to see her concluding thoughts on Matthew 19. Jesus was not afraid of eunuchs, nor did he belittle them, or speak of them as proof of brokenness after the fall. In a way, eunuchs are presented as a model worth following. Jesus took their shameful identity, which did not fit the gender ideals of antiquity, and turned it around as an identity for his disciples. DeFranza may be stretching her argument a bit when she

101. DeFranza, *Sex Difference in Christian Theology*, 62.
102. Compare chapter 2.

then presents eunuchs as paragons of radical discipleship. It is probably also farstretching to see Jesus as a eunuch, as Tertullian did. However, that Jesus raises questions for traditional ideals of masculinity is certainly the case. Eunuchs leave behind the power of the "pater familias" and exchange honor and prestige for an ambiguous existence. In this sense, we could argue along with DeFranza that Jesus presents eunuchs as a correction to the elevation of human sexuality as the core of what it means to be human. Perhaps her vision is meaningful and life-giving for people with an intersex condition. The story of the Ethiopian eunuch in Acts 8 is particularly striking: He is reading Isaiah 53:7–8, which is about the suffering servant. Philip tells him that these verses are about Jesus. This humiliated servant understands, asks to be baptized, and becomes a believer. We would do well to remember that the first convert from the nations is a eunuch. Codes of conduct concerning masculinity are broken and in a new covenant relationship, represented by baptism, the eunuch becomes a member of a new family and thus gains a new perspective and identity.[103]

Marriage, Adultery, and Divorce

Despite what we may have been told, the New Testament presents quite a nuanced picture when it comes to marriage. It seems that the New Testament writers have different ideas about the value and meaning of marriage. Several independent perspectives exist side by side, creating a polyphony of voices. The descriptions in the Gospels, however, do show a fairly consistent picture of the way Jesus looked at marriage. In the Synoptics (Matt 22:30; Mark 12:25; Luke 20:34), marriage is almost a kind of distraction: "At the resurrection people will neither marry . . ."), divorce must be prevented (Matt 19:9; Mark 10:11–12), and sexual self-control is highly valued. Jesus also seems to clearly conceive of marriage as intended for a man and a woman, as well as being critical of polygyny. The realization that the end of time was near and God's kingdom was coming undoubtedly contributed to the development of this perspective on marriage.[104] Jesus also speaks of new family relationships. In Mark 3:31–35 we read that Jesus's mother and brothers wanted to speak to him while he was with a group of people. He then asked who his mother and

103. Levine, "Gospels and Acts," 295–314.
104. Knust, "Marriage, Adultery, and Divorce," 521–38.

brothers were, and looked around and said, "Here are my mother and my brothers. Whoever does God's will is my brother and sister and mother."

Of course, none of this detracts from the fact that there are differences and nuances in the way marriage and divorce are spoken of in these verses.[105] According to Mark 10:12, divorce can apparently be initiated by a woman as well as by a man. The parallel verse Matt 19:9 does not mention women can initiate divorce. An important difference is that Mark was written with a view to believers in a pagan (gentile) environment and in that context Roman legislation applied, which allowed women to initiate a divorce. The text from Matthew simultaneously allows for exception, and Jesus, once again, (re)interprets Mosaic law. The original ideal of the indissolubility of marriage, under certain conditions, as a commitment for life, is key here. More recent Bible translations translate the Greek term *porneia* with "(sexual) immorality" (e.g., the NIV and NET of Matt 5:32 and 19:9). Only because of *porneia* would being sent away with a letter of divorce be permitted. The term refers to adultery, sexual contact with a prostitute, marriage outside the ethnic group, incest, and perhaps other sexual offences.[106] In a literal sense, the term *porneia* refers to prostitution, since the term for a prostitute is *porne* (female) or *pornos* (male). In a broader sense, the term was also used for unauthorized sex. In Mark 10:12 there seems to be no doubt: divorce is not permitted, and the exception clause is not present.

Coogan connects this to the internal Jewish debate about divorce. The Pharisees got it right, the texts of Deuteronomy do allow divorce, but Jesus reinterprets these and points to Moses's reason for allowing it: the stubbornness of the people.[107] Levine writes: "Jesus's tightening is not, as many sermons assume, aimed at protecting the woman from the rabbinic 'no fault model' (e.g., allowing burnt food as a reason for divorce). The woman was already protected against such practices on the basis of her marriage contract (*ketubah*). Jesus offers a counterpoint to Deut 24:1–4."[108]

It would seem for the apostle Paul, in the same tradition as the gospel writers, divorce is not acceptable (1 Cor 7:10–11) and this on the authority of the Lord himself. Yet that is not the last word for Paul. In 1 Cor 7:15 it

---

105. Coogan, *God and Sex*, 41–44. At the center is the protection of the weak and poor; so different to divorce practices in 2023.

106. Knust, "Marriage, Adultery, and Divorce."

107. Coogan, *God and Sex*, 70; Levine, "Gospels and Acts," 295–314.

108. Levine, "Gospels and Acts."

appears that he considers divorce permissible if, in a marriage between a believer and a nonbeliever, the nonbeliever wishes to divorce.

Homosexuality and Homoerotic Relationships

In Christian circles, hardly any other subject (as far as sexuality is concerned) is currently as controversial as homosexuality. Confusion reigns everywhere, even though the term as we use it today only made its appearance in the nineteenth century, before which it was mainly used for a form of sexual activity (see chapter 3). As soon as the term "homosexuality" is mentioned, difficult discussions begin that often get bogged down in extreme positions and opinions. For some, it is already a bridge too far to even talk about it; that alone, some would argue, could lead to the church going "downhill." Being a Christian and being gay or lesbian are, according to many, incompatible. Let alone their having a relationship. For some, there is an understanding that someone can be gay, but that should not lead to someone "practising a homosexual lifestyle." Anyone who has developed some understanding of the complexity of the issue will immediately sense that, in the language we use and the way we express ourselves about it, all sorts of things are at play.

Do we have to talk about it again? Yes, we should. But not because of pressure from all kinds of lobby groups or from the church itself. We know that people's opinions are not likely to change because of a different interpretation of some difficult biblical texts, although it is important to wrestle sincerely with the different interpretations, such as those we have discussed here. Meeting someone who is, for example, gay or transgender and living in a loving relationship is likely to be more fruitful than having a theoretical discussion.

First, it is important to summarize some concepts before we address three key texts. This is necessary to rise above the noise made whenever Christians have fraught discussions on gender and sexuality. The following points can help provide a framework within which a discussion can take place. Some of these principles have already been discussed in this book.

1. Addressing homosexuality from a New Testament perspective inevitably leads to the identification of a number of hermeneutical problems: the use of terms (such as homosexuality[109]), the historical

109. Zeichmann, "Rethinking the Gay Centurion," 35–54.

distance to the texts we are studying, and the cultural embedding of the text in the context and experience of the time. There need not be a false dichotomy between either rigidly applying these texts to today or concluding they have no meaning for today.[110]

2. Discussions must also be connected with the narrative of "desire" as proposed at the beginning of this chapter (and chapter 5). In doing so, we allow the broader story of God's dealings with humans to resonate throughout discussions of gender and sexuality. Within a narrative of desire as a starting point, there is no room for a homophobic hermeneutic.

3. Any suggestion of an automatic connection between homosexuality and pedophilia must be rejected, as well as the idea that to value a homosexual relationship is to question Christian morality.[111] Sexual abuse and immoral behavior can happen in any human relationship, whether homosexual or heterosexual in nature.

4. In recognizing gender as a spectrum (see chapter 3), in which there is equality and some measure of fluidity, and in which gender identity is visible in a diversity of sexual expressions, we gain a different perspective. This conviction is strengthened by our understanding of, among other things, Gen 1:26–27, in which we do not see God's creation of "man and woman" as a binary fact, but as a continuum within which there is room for diversity. This does not diminish the significance and enormous value of marriage and the unity between men and women that permeates the Bible. We do not deny the concept of creation order if it is understood in such a way that God created order out of chaos, but this does not mean that there is no room for diversity. On the contrary, unity and diversity are both important themes throughout the Bible. It is about recognizing the variation that exists between male and female in all its imperfection. We are aware that our modern society has a number of different normative narratives regarding gender and sexuality that help to determine the way we read the Bible. The categories generally used are: male or female, straight or gay. In chapter 3, we have shown that there are difficult questions to ask regarding the birth of children without, for example, clear male or female genitals. We need to take

110. Dunning, *Oxford Handbook*, introduction.

111. We do not dispute the fact that there may have been a connection in antiquity.

this reality into account without immediately dismissing it as sinful or imperfect, and without exalting male-female marriage, even though heterosexual relationships are in the majority.

Everything in this world is broken and we must be careful not to apply that to just a few things. Furthermore, we find it important to stand up for vulnerable minorities, because the Bible asks us to do so.

5. It goes without saying that a large number of texts that have already been reviewed betray strongly patriarchal forms of sexuality. As we have seen, these forms and attitudes are closely linked to the cultural, religious, and social context of the ancient Near East. This applies to marital relations (the woman being to a large extent the property of the man), procreation (the man's sperm is crucial in connection with the continuing male line; there is no mention anywhere of a woman's ovum), and many other matters. These are the dominant stories, but there are also so-called *understories*.[112] These are the stories and the texts in which, although they take the relationships of the time into account, a counter-script is provided. In a Roman world where sexuality was an expression of power (from the high to the low, from men to women, see also chapter 2), Paul writes in 1 Cor 7:4: "The wife does not have authority over her own body but yields it to her husband. In the same way, the husband does not have authority over his own body but yields it to his wife." Men were seen as the stronger part of the gender spectrum, and women as the weaker part, as imperfect men with inwardly turned sexual organs. So, we can consider this text as revolutionary.

6. The Hebrew Bible and New Testament passages that generally play a role in the discussion of homosexuality are not separate from the sexual protocols that existed in the Old and New Testament worlds.[113] Status and gender, in the Hebrew Bible, and certainly also in the New Testament thought-world, functioned as the dominant social structure in which the interactions of bodies had their place. There was a clear dichotomy between active/penetrating and passive/receiving role patterns. There was a sexual taxonomy: adult male citizens, who were mainly defined as "unpenetrable," were at the top of the pyramid, with the potentially "penetrable" bodies

112. Dyer, *Jesus and Sex.*
113. Dunning, *Oxford Handbook*; Dyer, *Jesus and Sex.*

having a lower status.[114] Homosexuality was therefore described in that Roman and Greek world as a relationship of inequality, in which older men, in particular, penetrated younger men, often before or during puberty.[115]

Needless to say, these relationships were exploitative in nature. Homosexual relationships of equal value were not openly known, in all likelihood because of the embarrassment of the penetrated party, who would immediately be considered weak. For the free Roman man, it was important to avoid forced penetration (*stuprum*).[116] The public face of "homosexuality" and also of (for the Jews) pagan immoral behavior was *pederasty*: the frequent exploitation of young males (often slaves) by rich and powerful men. Clearly, when slaves were involved, this practice could go on unseen without anyone being worried about it.[117] This is the background against which we must read the following texts of the apostle Paul.

Although in this part of the chapter we concentrate mainly on New Testament texts, we must also look at Gen 18–19 and Lev 18 and 20 because of the importance of these Hebrew Bible texts.

The Story of Sodom—Genesis 18–19

For centuries, the story of Sodom, which begins in Genesis 18, has dominated many of the interpretations concerning homosexuality.[118] Abraham receives a visit from God, and three men (Gen 18:22 and 19:1 refer to "two men" and "two angels" respectively) are welcomed by Abraham (Gen 18:3–8). The promise to Sarah and Abraham is poignant: they will have a son in their old age. God chooses, according to the author, not to keep his plans secret (Gen 18:17) and he shares with Abraham his intention to investigate the iniquity of Sodom and Gomorrah, and to see whether the inhabitants of both cities have brought destruction upon themselves (Gen 18:20–21). God goes out to investigate, but the decision does not seem to be made yet, and Abraham starts his plea for the innocent (Gen 18:23–33). The negotiations with God end when God promises not to destroy the cities for the sake of ten innocents (Gen 18:33).

114. Dunning, *Oxford Handbook*.
115. Dyer, *Jesus and Sex*.
116. Dunning, *Oxford Handbook*.
117. Williams, *Roman Homosexuality*.
118. Jennings, "Same-Sex Relations," 83.

Lot receives the two angels and also offers them a hospitable shelter (Gen 19:1–3). It is not long before "all the men from every part of the city of Sodom" (19:4) are gathering at Lot's house; their intention is to "take" Lot's guests and have sex with them. Lot does not intend to go along with this and in order to assuage the crowd he offers them his two daughters. The offer is refused and the group wants to enter Lot's house by force. The two guests save the situation and afflict the crowd with blindness (19:11). Lot and his family are saved, which means God keeps his promise to Abraham to spare the innocent in the city. God wipes out Sodom and Gomorrah, but allows Lot to escape (19:29). The conclusion is that Lot proved his righteousness by the way he treated his guests, although this did not include—strangely enough—the way he treated his daughters.[119]

The question is: what exactly was the sin of Sodom? A key to a plausible answer to this question is found in the Jewish scripture known as the "Wisdom of Solomon" (first century BC). In this writing, reference is made to Sodom as the city that refused hospitality to strangers and enslaved them (Wis 19:14; the book is apocryphal and part of the Bible for Roman Catholic and Eastern Orthodox Christians). The violation of the guest law was, according to the writer of this scripture, the sin of Sodom. The men of Sodom wanted to rape their guests in their own city.[120] That attempt is an example of Sodom's immorality. This violence that would be used against vulnerable strangers is contrary to the call to welcome travelers, foreigners, and immigrants that we find elsewhere in the Bible (cf. Exod 22:21; Lev 19:34; Heb 13:2), and often in connection with other forms of social and societal injustice.[121] The parallels between the story of Sodom and Judg 19 are interesting, however, in Gen 19, the guest right (or law) of hospitality is at stake and violated. Moreover, it appears from Ezek 16 that the violation of the right of hospitality was not the only sin of Sodom. The inhabitants of Sodom were characterized by pride and a lack of commitment to the poor and powerless (Ezek 16:49). Based on this reading of Gen 18 and 19, it becomes clear that homosexuality is not a core theme and there is a serious lack of evidence to suggest that homosexuality was Sodom's specific sin.[122] However, we do point out that both Philo of Alexandria and Josephus reinterpret the Jewish tradition of Genesis 19 to align with Plato's later view of homosexuality (i.e.,

---

119. Coogan, *God and Sex.*

120. Coogan, *God and Sex.*

121. Jennings, "Same-Sex Relations," 206–21; Coogan, *God and Sex*, 88.

122. Jennings, "Same-Sex Relations," 206–21.

homophobia). Until late in the fifth century, theologians such as Augustine read the story as a violation of guest law.[123]

The Texts from Leviticus

Other texts in the Hebrew Bible that play a major role in discussions about homosexuality are Lev 18:22 and 20:13. In both texts we read:

> Do not have sexual relationships with a man as one does with a woman; that is detestable. (18:22)

> If a man has sexual relationships with a man as one does with a woman, both of them have done what is detestable. They are to be put to death; their blood will be on their own hands. (20:13)

Both texts are included in the so-called "holiness code" and are, in fact, the only texts that refer to sexual activity between people of the same sex in an explicitly negative way.[124] There is, however, no explicit reference to women in these texts. According to Richard Hays, these texts form the foundation of a more general rejection of homosexuality within Judaism.[125] The key question, of course, is whether these regulations are as valid for the church today as they were for Israel. According to Hays, who represents the more conservative view, there is an affirmation of the Hebrew Bible regulations in Leviticus by Paul in 1 Cor 6. The Greek term *arsenokoitai* (those who lie with a man) is thought to be a translation of the Hebrew *mishkav zakur* and thus directly related to Lev 18:22 and 20:13.[126]

The difficulty in interpreting and applying these texts is that they immediately lead to selective text use. If we are to assume that we must apply this text to our modern context, what do we do with a number of other texts: mating animals, sowing different crops, wearing clothes woven from two kinds of thread (Lev 19:19), eating blood (Lev 17:12), eating certain foods (Lev 11), and the birth of children (Lev 12)? How do we evaluate these and other texts in the light of the New Testament?[127] Which ones are still normative and which are not (anymore) or which

---

123. Jennings, "Same-Sex Relations," 206–21.

124. Dyer, *Jesus and Sex*.

125. Hays, *Moral Vision*, 381.

126. Hays, *Moral Vision*, 382.

127. Dyer, *Jesus and Sex*, 15.

should be applied in a different way?[128] What exactly do these two texts prohibit? Is it primarily a prohibition against mixing different kinds of bodily fluids (semen, blood, anal fluid)? Or is it more about wasting human seed and thus about nonreproductive sexuality?[129] Jennings points to prohibitions related to the cult of neighboring pagan peoples, that are specifically about rape. He suggests that the texts may point to a prohibition of sexual intercourse between two men where one of them assumes the role of a woman.[130] Verses such as Lev 18:24–25 suggest there could be a connection with the necessary contrast between the covenant people of Israel and the neighboring Canaanite nations: "Do not defile yourselves in any of these ways, because this is how the nations that I am going to drive out before you became defiled. Even the land was defiled; so I punished it for its sin, and the land vomited out its inhabitants."[131]

A Jewish commentator points out the underlying importance of reproduction, in favor of the argument for a stable family life as a reason for the ban.[132] If this interpretation is plausible—a prohibition on homosexuality for the reason that there is no procreation—we must then note that this is not confirmed in the New Testament. Procreation and a stable family life do not stand as commandments in New Testament ethics, as we encounter a much more radical view of what made a family (Mark 10:29–30).

Three Frequently Discussed New Testament Texts—1 Cor 6:9–10; 1 Tim 1:9–10; and Rom 1:18–32

The best-known texts in the New Testament that have been associated with homosexuality are 1 Cor 6:9–10; 1 Tim 1:9–10; and Rom 1:18–32. The Greek terms used in particular in 1 Cor 6:9 and 1 Tim 1:10, *malachoi* and *arsenokoitai*, are not unambiguous.[133] Hays, however, is of the opinion that there is indeed a direct connection between these terms and the texts from Leviticus (see above). According to him, Paul's use of the terminology in these texts confirms the prohibition of homosexual acts

128. Jennings, "Same-Sex Relations," 206–21.

129. Dyer, *Jesus and Sex*, 16.

130. Jennings, "Same-Sex Relations," 206–21.

131. Coogan, *God and Sex*, 91.

132. Dyer, *Jesus and Sex*, 16–17.

133. Dyer, *Jesus and Sex*, 18; and Jennings, "Same-Sex Relations."

in the Hebrew Bible. We have already addressed the difficulty of the selective use of texts, which arises from this.

However, Hays argues that Paul simply assumes that his readers share his conviction that those who engage in homosexual activity are not righteous.[134] Jennings, however, believes that the term *malachoi*, both in the New Testament and in Hellenistic literature, refers to the softness of those who lead a life of luxury. It would therefore refer to the self-indulgence of the rich. He refers to verses such as Matt 11:8 and Luke 7:25, in which the term is used in relation to Herod's court.[135] Dyer follows this explanation and confirms the emphasis on what is soft and feminine in connection with prostitution: the term is then mainly used as slang for a passive homosexual partner. Paul would thus be addressing homosexual activity in which there is abuse and exploitation: male prostitution and older men abusing (young) boys.[136]

The term "*arsenokoitai*" is not known in other literature of Paul's contemporaries.[137] Jennings connects it to one of the most famous rapes in the ancient Greek world, the rape of Ganymedes by Zeus, drawing attention to culture of rape in the Roman world, with which Paul's hearers would have been all too familiar.[138] According to Jennings, this is also apparent in the context of 1 Tim 1:9–10, where the term is associated with other forms of extreme violence: the killing of parents, etc.

Yet it is Romans 1 that often gets the most attention in the debate. Verses 26–27 form the core:

> Because of this, God gave them over to shameful lusts. Even their women exchanged natural sexual relations for unnatural ones. In the same way men (*arsenes*) also abandoned natural relations with women and were inflamed with lust for one another. Men committed shameful acts with other men (*arsenes*), and received in themselves the due penalty for their error (Rom 1:26–27).

Dale Martin has offered a complete overview of all possible interpretive frameworks through which this text can be interpreted.[139] We will not

---

134. Hays, *Moral Vision*, 383.
135. Jennings, "Same-Sex Relations."
136. Dyer, *Jesus and Sex*, 18–19.
137. Jennings, "Same-Sex Relations," 206–21.
138. Jennings, "Same-Sex Relations," 206–21.
139. Martin, *Sex and the Single Savior*.

discuss these frames here, but we will note, along with Dunning, that many of the starting points have the same problem: we seem to think that Paul speaks of "homosexuality" in the same way as we do now.[140] In addition, we often assume that there is such a thing as an unequivocal, singular, and stable phenomenon across all cultures, which we call homosexuality. Hays concludes, with a reasonable degree of nuance, by stating that, in his opinion, the text from Romans 1 is not aimed at teaching a Christian sexual code of conduct. Although, he does argue that Romans 1 is the most crucial text for Christian ethics, because this passage (as he sees it) is the only one in the New Testament that explicitly rejects homosexual behavior.[141]

Dunning's view, that the whole concept of "homosexuality" as we now know it cannot be imposed on this text, urges us to be cautious. We should also take a much broader and more general view of "sexuality," with room for a so-called historicizing approach. The phenomenon of human sexuality must be viewed from the perspective of the culturally specific concepts and power dynamics that influence it.[142] A reading of Romans 1 with an interpretation that transcends culture and history does not fit into such an approach. To be specific: if in Rom 1:26–27 there is a mention of abandoning natural intercourse, then the interpretation of what is considered "natural" in this text should not be seen in isolation from the cultural and historical context in which it is read. In that context, and in Roman and Greek thought, this had to do with men being active and penetrating, and women being passive and penetrated. Every sexual act therefore assumed a male penetrating party and a female penetrated party, regardless of the physical anatomy of both partners. Sexual acts between two people of the same sex (and class) thus automatically become misguided expressions of a gender hierarchy.[143]

Paul is addressing homosexual activity in which there is abuse and exploitation.[144] Jennings gives an interesting contextual interpretation of Romans 1. According to him, the reference in the text to "men (*arsenes*) also abandoned natural relations with women and were inflamed with lust for one another" should be understood primarily as an indication of the sexual misdeeds of the ruling class. In this context, Jennings points to

140. Jennings, "Same-Sex Relations," 206–21.

141. Hays, *Moral Vision*, 383.

142. Dunning, *Oxford Handbook*.

143. Dunning, *Oxford Handbook*.

144. *Contra* Loader, *Sexuality in the New Testament*, 15–43.

emperors such as Tiberius, Caligula, and Nero. Caligula was stabbed by members of his own guard, who had presumably been raped by him or whose wives had been raped by him. Caligula received a punishment in his body that suited his crimes: he was also "penetrated," namely by knife stabs. According to Jennings, this explanation is confirmed by Paul's argument in the first chapters of the letter to the Romans, in which he criticizes the Roman Empire and its order.[145]

Finally, a brief further reflection is appropriate here. The complexity of the debate is well expressed by Halperin, who gets to the heart of the matter: how can we retrieve the terminology with which the erotic experiences of people from past societies were expressed, and how can we compare this terminology—in a careful way—with the way we look at these experiences today? And how can we then better understand ourselves and our experiences?[146] It is clear by now that we need to keep all of this in mind when applying the Bible to today's practices.[147]

Briefly Back to Some Pauline Texts with New Perspectives

At the beginning of this chapter, we referred to some of Paul's texts and the work of Colleen Conway has already been mentioned. She points to the influence of theorists such as Foucault, Butler, and Sedgwick, who

---

145. Jennings, "Same-Sex Relations," 206–21.

146. See Halperin, *How to Do the History*, 63.

147. Jennings refers to a number of texts in which homosexuality plays a role in some way, and not just to texts in the New Testament. He points to the relationship between Ruth and Naomi (Ruth 1:16–17). According to Jennings, both women have to hide their relationship in a patriarchal society and therefore Ruth has no other option than securing her life by entering in a relationship with Boaz. Interesting is the comment in 4:14. Ruth sleeps with Boaz, is pregnant and gives birth to a son. We then read: "The women said to Naomi: 'Praise be to the Lord, who this day has not left you without a guardian-redeemer. May he become famous throughout Israel! He will renew your life and sustain you in your old age. For your daughter-in-law, who loves you and who is better to you than seven sons, has given him birth.'" The joy about the birth of the son is not so much aimed at Boaz, but focused on the idea that Naomi has received a son! This is a very interesting comment in the text. Jennings's interpretation is challenging and requires further reflection. Subsequently, the relationship between David and Jonathan (1 and 2 Samuel) is referred to, the centurion who asks Jesus to heal his unwell servant (Matthew 8), and the story of the Ethiopian eunuch (Acts 8:26–39). Jennings also points to a possible queer reading of texts regarding the relationship between God and Israel. Jennings contends that it is crucial to see the impact of the feminization of the relationship by the prophets Amos, Hosea, Jeremiah, and Ezekiel. Very often God is the jealous husband who has to deal with an adulterous Israel.

have drawn attention to various "queer" readings of biblical texts. A queer reading of the Bible means, above all, that we pay attention to those categories related to gender and sexuality where there is explicit abuse of power and control.[148] This increasingly raises questions of ethnicity, race, and social class, which play a role in the interpretation of texts. With these frames in the background, Conway discusses various aspects of New Testament texts in which gender plays a role. We follow her briefly in her argument, especially in relation to the letters of Paul and a small number of texts we have taken a look at.

How are gender and sexuality discussed in Paul? In what way does Paul use language to make clear to his readers what he means? Conway refers here to the work of Maud Gleason, who argues that Paul made use of specific rhetorical methods to present himself in certain ways.[149] For example, when he writes in 2 Cor 11 about his own weakness, does this mean that by doing so he is resisting normative concepts of masculinity? But elsewhere he does speak out against his opponents in a way that is in line with the cultural Greco-Roman norms. And what about the well-known text from Gal 3:28, where he writes that in Christ there is "no male or female"? Should we speak of a greater ambiguity in Paul with regard to gender compared to other authors? After all, elsewhere believers are called upon to put on their usual armor (Rom 13:12; Eph 6; 1 Thess 5:1–11): weapons of light, the armor of faith and love, the helmet of hope. Paul writes about weapons of righteousness and sees himself as an athlete in training, a boxer, and a marathon runner, who works hard on himself and practices self-control (1 Cor 9:24–27). Those who could not control themselves were irrevocably seen as less than manly.[150]

Another interesting study, by Stanley Stowers, shows how the letter to the church at Rome can also be read through the lens of self-control.[151] According to Stowers, we should see Paul's conceptualization of righteousness and justice in Christ as an attempt to characterize salvation primarily as the restoration of an essentially masculine trait. Much of this textual material provides evidence for Paul's acceptance, or at least shows a rhetorical use, of a culturally dominant view of masculinity. Conway notes that it is actually only in the correspondence with the church at Corinth that Paul's own weakness and his embrace of that weakness is

148. Conway, "Masculinity Studies."

149. Gleason, *Making Men*.

150. Conway, *Behold the Man*.

151. Stowers, *Rereading of Romans*.

mentioned (2 Cor 12). Paul uses his weakness there in defense against a group of super-apostles. They attacked him, apparently suggesting that he writes weighty letters and impresses, but his personal appearance is not strong, so what he says has little meaning (2 Cor 10:10). Harrill argues that because of this criticism, especially of his physical appearance, Paul may have been seen as unmanly. Paul does not defend himself (against the common views of the sophists and followers of Socrates) with weakness, but he does put physical appearance into perspective as the only means of coming across as convincing.[152] Why would he undermine his own authority for the sake of communicating the Gospel? Moreover, it is important to note that he also makes use of female metaphors and is thus certainly not stuck in using male imagery. In Gal 4:19 he writes: "My dear children, for whom I am again in the pains of childbirth until Christ is formed in you." And in 1 Thess 2:7 Paul uses similar imagery: "even though as apostles of Christ we could have asserted our authority. Instead, we were like young children among you. Just as a nursing mother cares for her children." Is there a form of "de-centering" hegemonic masculinity active here after all? For the time being, we get the impression that Paul's theology is a work in progress, and that an over-systematization would not be wise. Another interesting Pauline theologian is Cynthia Long-Westfall. She points out the function of Paul's use of language and cultural imagery and argues that although he uses culturally appropriate language and imagery, at the same time he regularly breaks through gender stereotyping.[153]

Two other central texts deserve attention in this last part of the chapter: Gal 3:28 and 1 Cor 11:2–16. In the first, Paul (according to Conway) seems to solve a number of social problems at once with a few strokes of his pen. The text comes up in many discussions and is often seen as the *locus classicus* for the proof of gender equality.[154] Wayne Meeks's interpretation of this text is still authoritative: it would concern the ideal of unification of opposing groups, especially in connection with the existence of an androgynous being, a kind of myth of primitive man.[155] In the first century, the two creation stories were often read through the lens of this myth. When Paul claims that in Christ there is no man or woman, according to Meeks, he would claim that in Christ there is a reunion of the

152. Harrill, *Slaves in the New Testament*.
153. Long-Westfall, *Paul and Gender*.
154. Conway, "Masculinity Studies."
155. Meeks, "Image of the Androgyne," 165–208.

two parts of humanity: man and woman. Others point out that although there is equality, this can be understood in different ways, especially in view of gender and sexuality. Equivalence and equality are two distinct issues.[156] Others point out that androgyny (as the ideal) was not always understood in terms of equality/equivalence in ancient times.[157] Perhaps the text offers room for an interpretation in the sense of putting a binary approach into a more relativizing perspective. Galatians 3 will be discussed again in the next chapter.

Conway asks of 1 Cor 11:2–16 whether there is a different view on gender roles here than the one that was prevalent in Paul's time. There may be several readings of this text, but we will pay attention to two here. Long-Westfall believes that Paul's instruction to women to wear a veil was beneficial to women and also went against the dominant cultural norms.[158] The veil represented a woman's honor and her status, but also offered protection. Paul develops his argument through the cultural norms and values of the time regarding a woman's relationship to the *pater familias*, but at the same time addressing the equality of man and woman and their mutual dependence. Although the woman came from the man, the man also came from the woman (1 Cor 11:12). According to Long-Westfall, Paul is not focused on an increase in masculine authority over women, but rather on honoring God.[159] Gillian Townsley approaches the text differently. On the basis of Butler's gender theory and the aforementioned work by Meeks, she suggests that the myth of the androgynous man is in the background. She argues it is possible that in Corinth, based on knowledge of Paul's view, people had decided to represent the reunion of mankind in a symbolic way.[160] This attitude led to the blurring of gender boundaries, and that is what Paul is questioning. This form of ritual *cross-dressing* would have its precedent in Dionysian rituals practised in Corinth.

---

156. Økland, "Pauline Letters," 315–32.

157. Martin, *Sex and the Single Savior*; Boyarin, *Radical Jew*.

158. Long-Westfall, *Paul and Gender*, 42–43.

159. Long-Westfall, *Paul and Gender*, 42–43.

160. Townsley, "Gender Trouble in Corinth."

Looking Back and Forward: Theology Needed (On the Journey toward Chapter 5)

In this chapter, we have started to look at a number of different approaches to the Bible with regard to thinking about gender and sexuality. In doing so, we have made a deliberate choice: We don't want to use the Bible as a manual, or as a collection of dated writings that have no meaning for today. We have focused on the Bible as a *narrative of desire*. As explained, from beginning to end, the Bible expresses relationships: relationships with God, relationships among people, relationships with creation, and so on. The Bible brings these stories of various relationships to our attention, and the core of these stories is always formed by desire. God desires to share his life, love, and grace with us and that is indivisible from gender, sexuality, and physicality. In the many stories in this chapter, it became evident that there is enormous diversity. We read very complicated texts about purity and virginity, but we also gained more insight into the complexity of male-female relationships and the way in which ancient cultures looked at what determined being men and women. Many texts leave no doubt that sexuality is a beautiful gift (think of Song of Songs) and that desire is good. Other texts warn strongly against abusing that gift, for example the stories of David and Bathsheba (2 Sam 11) and Judah and Tamar (Gen 38), where misdirected desire, and its subsequent appalling actions, have major consequences.

The Bible is extremely honest and open. It is striking that in many places, the existing norms are broken. We see this in Jesus, whose interactions with women subverted cultural expectations. We also see it in Paul, who does not shy away from addressing the consequences of following Jesus, especially when it comes to male-female relationships. In many ways, the Bible is diametrically opposed to the dominant culture, which is all about pleasure and power. In the Bible, there is a constant search for relationship with the God who longs for connection with his people and for connection between people. We do not see any attempt to abolish gender and sexuality, or to make them bigger than they are, but neither do we see any attempt to erase them as something that does not matter at all. Rather, time and again, we witness a God whose desire for his creation creates space. In this context, the story of the Ethiopian eunuch in Acts 8 is touching and bewildering at the same time. What happens to the eunuch is illustrative of the way in which God's desire to connect with all people manifests itself. The transforming power of the gospel becomes visible.

In the next chapter, the theme of desire will become even more central as we attempt to present a broader theological and transformative framework. A chapter on the Bible is not enough, it must also be connected with—and applied to—the way we deal with the diversity of gender and sexuality today. The framework of desire both requires further reflection from us and can also provide this connection and application. The biblical texts discussed here will have their own place within this framework, but it is important to continue our theological reflections in order to give direction to discussions about sexuality today.

Questions for Discussion

- What questions does this chapter raise for you when you consider the three approaches we describe? Which approach do you feel most comfortable with?

- We looked in detail at the relationship between Jesus and gender. Themes concerning what is seen as "male" and "female" are regularly discussed. How does this relate to your own ideas and what could this mean for relationships in church and society?

- Halperin focuses on how we translate the concepts and experiences of people then and there into the experiences of people here and now. How do you see the challenge expressed by Halperin and taken up at the end of the discussion on homosexuality?

- What questions does this chapter raise for you about purity and virginity?

- Megan DeFranza points to the position of eunuchs in the early church and earlier. What do you think of her view in relation to people with intersex conditions?

5

"Desire" as a Theological Framework for Gender and Sexuality

Introduction

IN CHAPTER 1, WE briefly explored the connections between theology and sexuality. We outlined our starting point, which is that there are many connections between God, faith, theology, and sexuality on which to reflect. We illustrated this by referring to Rowan Williams's essay on the theme of sexual desire. Williams characterizes this desire as *embodied grace*. In the previous chapter (chapter 4), we discussed how we can use "desire" as a framework within which the Bible can be read. In this chapter, we want to elaborate on the questions of how we can find theological depth through the theme of desire, and how we can connect this with what we have discussed so far.

We have seen that the church has had a fragile and uneasy relationship with sexuality throughout history. In early Christianity, there was sometimes a negative view of the human body, and therefore sexuality, marriage, and family did not always stand in a positive light. Does this discomfort stem from the complex and diverse teaching in the New Testament, as we discussed in the previous chapter? We have certainly seen evidence for this in many texts in the Old and New Testaments. To some extent, we can say that our apprehension toward human sexuality has roots in the classical Christian writings themselves.

In the Bible, we find culturally determined stories that show how important faith and love are, but also how complicated they can be. We have seen how visions of sexuality are contextually determined and that there is much sexual diversity, which often receives minimal attention within Christian circles. And we have demonstrated that sexuality can be viewed from different perspectives, each with its own valuable contribution and connected practice.

When we bring all this information together, an important next step is to look for the theological reflections that can serve as building blocks for a normative framework (see the introduction). We do this following on from the previous chapter and in the perspective of that same normative task. We are looking for a point of orientation that will enable us to better handle the important themes. We believe that this point of orientation is strongly connected to the narrative of desire, which we will explore here.

Four Pathways for Theological Reflection

In an attempt to bring some order to the plethora of views on the relationship between theology and sexuality, we dialogue with British theologian Elizabeth Stuart. She offers us four distinct pathways to think about gender and sexuality in a theological sense.[1] Stuart observes that theological reflection on sexuality is a relatively new phenomenon linked to modernity. Until that time, possibly until the second half of the nineteenth century, the focus was mainly on sexual acts and their moral or immoral character. Reflection on the relationship between sexual acts and the person's self, or rather the insight these acts gave about the person, was very limited.

The emergence of a more direct link is probably due to the changes in family structures, caused, among other things, by the rise of capitalism.[2] Undoubtedly, as we saw earlier, the advance of medical and anatomical knowledge has also played a major role. Scholars generally agree that the developments in thought on sexual differentiation in the past century (homosexuality, heterosexuality, and bisexuality) have led to people being characterized—and self-expressing and self-identifying—more on the basis of their sexual preference or orientation. Be that as it may, Stuart

1. Stuart, "Theological Study of Sexuality," 18–31.
2. Stuart, "Theological Study of Sexuality," 18–31.

rightly points out the rather short development of theological reflection, and uses four distinct paths to categorize the different approaches to thinking theologically about sexuality. She labels them the *via positiva*, *via negativa*, *via creativa*, and *via transformativa*, after a distinction made by the well-known and late-medieval theologian, philosopher, and mystic Meister Eckhart.[3]

Via Positiva

According to Stuart, the first route is one that is primarily taken by both conservative and liberal theologians. Those who take the *via positiva* place particular emphasis on the differentiation of men and women (and with that, the binary character of gender and sexuality). Male and female are seen as theological categories that are directly related to redemption and liberation. Representatives of this approach include Karl Barth and Hans Urs von Balthasar along with Dietrich Bonhoeffer and John Paul II.[4] For Barth, marriage between a man and a woman is a reflection of the Trinity, wherein the relationship between husband and wife should mirror the relationship between Christ and the church. The critical point here is that Barth believes human existence finds its deepest fulfillment as the image of God only in a heterosexual relationship between man and woman. Barth's contribution has made the relationship between both male and female as God's image-bearers more theologically equal than in the past.[5] However, homosexual relationships did not fit into his schema: homosexuals engage in idolatry. This, of course, also raises questions for people who are not in a relationship.[6]

A dominant Christian discourse is that men and women should *complement* each other and therefore have different needs, qualities, and roles. Swiss theologian Hans Urs von Balthasar characterizes femininity mainly by receptivity and masculinity by leadership. For von Balthasar, divine qualities are attributed to a man and a woman is subordinate to him.[7] For John Paul II, the doctrine of God also plays a central role, but in a more nuanced sense. He explains that whoever believes in a God who

---

3. Stuart, "Theological Study of Sexuality," 18–31.
4. Stuart, "Theological Study of Sexuality," 18–31.
5. Leene, *Triniteit, antropologie en ecclesiologie*, 90–91.
6. Barth, *Church Dogmatics*, 165–66.
7. Thatcher, *Redeeming Gender*, 106; Beattie, "Queen of Heaven," 138.

gives himself away in love and opens himself up to humanity, cannot help but see this openness and self-reproduction as the core of the marital relationship. Any form of nonmarital sexuality is thus excluded. Contemporary theologian Adrian Thatcher, in a striking analysis of classical documents, shows how the "complementarian" vision is deeply rooted in a theological reflection in which there is no room for sexual expressions other than those resulting from a binary positioning of male and female.[8]

Stuart points out that liberal theologians often have the same starting point on the *via positiva* as conservative theologians, but come to very different conclusions. As an example, she mentions theologians like James Nelson, who want to take an approach that focuses on a more lived sexuality. Although Nelson is prepared to see sexuality at the heart of humanity, he refuses to start from a normative ideal. The human experience of sexuality is central. It is not gender that is essential, but the question of whether or not those who have a sexual relationship show something of the values of God's reign in Christ. Here the emphasis is on faithfulness and loyalty in the relationships that people have entered into. In this way, marriage can still be seen as a sacrament, but it is opened up to different (other than heterosexual) forms of relationships. Hence, to refer back to Stuart's four pathways, the representatives of the *via positiva* see gender and sexuality mostly from an essentialist perspective, and that they represent the order that God created.[9]

Via Negativa

Those who take the *via negativa* choose a very different approach. The divine not only becomes the object of desire, but also disappears into it. Medieval mysticism is well known for its use of erotic language to describe God and the divine. In a way, God and the erotic were identified with each other. Stuart shows how this approach was adopted, in particular, by feminist-lesbian theologians who defined God as an erotic power that calls people into relationship, based on reciprocity.[10] The principle of reciprocity becomes central and serves to bring God/god into human relationships, with courage, vulnerability, and compassion as core values.

8. Thatcher, *Redeeming Gender,* 84–92.

9. Compare our explanation in chapter 1.

10. Stuart, "Theological Study of Sexuality," 18–31.

For Heyward and Isherwood, the emphasis—especially where sexuality is concerned—is on living in a just relationship, in which patriarchal bonds must be broken.[11] Transcendental aspects that refer to God here dissolve, as it were, in the immanent manifestation of the quality of the love relationship. The ethics and virtues that belong to the sexual relationship take precedence. God is above all *erotic power* and just relationship. The question Stuart rightly asks is what the norm for these relationships and sexuality is, as there may be a very strong privatization of sexuality.

Via Creativa

The *via creativa* travels along a road that intentionally focuses on an eschatological perspective. People participate in the process by which God brings about the new creation. This new creation is initiated by Christ and participation is realized through baptism. Christian identity, as given in baptism, is eschatological in nature, focusing on the completion of all life, thereby stripping sexuality and gender of their ultimate status (Gal 3:28). In fact, this is where queer theology begins: any notion of a fixed sexual identity is relativized or denied. Those who think "queerly" about gender and sexuality will want to challenge the existing dominant positions about them.[12] Gender is primarily a learned "performance" based on cultural scripts, but this can lead to rejecting the existence of stable forms of gender and sexuality. It is one thing to state that gender and sexuality should not have an absolute status, but it is quite another to do away with any form of necessary stability.

However, the *via creativa* leads us to interesting insights. For example, ethicist Kathy Rudy contends that it is baptism that brings people into Christian communities and into the people of God, and not their biological predisposition.[13] Gender and sexuality therefore do not need to be categorized, since Christianity and the church are about conversion, repentance and, by extension, hospitality. From this point of view, sexuality is part of discipleship and should therefore be judged on the

---

11. Stuart refers to the publications of Heyward, *Touching Our Strength*. Also Isherwood, "Sex and Body Politics," 20–34.

12. Stuart, "Theological Study of Sexuality," 18–31.

13. Rudy, *Sex and the Church*. Compare also Bennett's *Water Is Thicker than Blood*. Bennett shows the ways in which a normative theology of marriage potentially damages the ecclesiology. She contends that eschatological insights are necessary in this context.

basis of its ability to contribute to hospitable communities.[14] Tina Beattie points out the importance of a certain "queer space."[15] According
to Beattie, the Virgin Mary is the first to benefit from the redemption
of humankind through her own Son. The announcement of the birth of
Jesus to Mary is an example of a nonsexual conception and, in this way, a
possible overvaluation of sexuality is destabilized and made impossible.
The virgin who becomes a mother moves the discussion beyond binary
gender and offers space where we would otherwise experience complexity. Humanity, then, is to be understood, above all, as free from the cycle
of sexuality, birth, and death.

Via Transformativa

Finally, Stuart explores the transformative pathway. She prefers this
path and, from here, wonders about the future of theological reflection
on sexuality.[16] For Stuart, a key question is what impact faith in the
resurrection has on gender and sexuality and, quite rightly, she thinks
theologians should be more concerned about this. Moreover, the church
has the task of dealing with sexuality on the basis of core values such as
justice and equality. Theologians have the task of reflecting deeply on the
ordering and channeling of human (sexual) desire—if one thinks this has
something to do with God—not in the moralistic framework determined
by an emphasis on heterosexual marriage, but in coming from a deep
spiritual connection. The question of faithfulness in relation to sexuality
and how sexual desire plays a role in relationships is therefore becoming
increasingly important.

Stuart refers to Sarah Coakley who emphasizes the importance of a
new asceticism, similarly focusing on the place of desire, but as a component of Christian discipleship.[17] The aim of such an approach is, on the
one hand, to escape from the unbridled freedom we find in contemporary
culture and, on the other, to escape from the unbalanced suppression of
desire.[18] Heleen Zorgdrager elaborates on Coakley's analysis and proposal:

---

14. Rudy, *Sex and the Church.*

15. Beattie, "Queen of Heaven," 138.

16. Stuart, "Theological Study of Sexuality," 18–31.

17. In this chapter we frequently return to Coakley and her scholarly work: Coakley, *God, Sexuality, and the Self.* Also Coakley, *New Asceticism.*

18. Stuart, "Theological Study of Sexuality," 18–31.

The deeper problem, Sarah Coakley argues, is that we do not know how to relate to our desires, to sexual and other desires such as food, drink, recognition, power, money, wealth. The question is how we can live a life of balance and moderation in such a way that desire really contributes to human well-being. As modern people, we have individualized and sexualized desire, whereas erotic desire in early Christianity was physical as well as spiritual and social, community-oriented. Transformation of desire is needed, not eradication. Coakley proposes a "new asceticism." In the confusing multiplicity of good and bad urges, the challenge is to move from the "corrupt" to the "very excellent," through contemplative practices of prayer, ritual, practical exercise, which bring God into focus as the source and goal of all desires. The controlling subject, the "fat self," is destabilized. Real relationship is established through a subtle sacrifice of surrender, a form of willed "vulnerability" that opens one's consciousness to the other. I also find it important that Coakley does not speak of Spirit only in terms of a fusion. The Spirit brings people together in intimate relationships, but also intervenes as a guardian of human integrity. It breaks the desire to possess, control, and abuse.[19]

The key concepts emerging here regarding sexuality are: moderation, contribution to human welfare, community orientation, and, last but not least, God as the goal of all desires. Coakley contributes to a transformative approach through promoting a deeper grounding of gender and sexuality in forms of Christian faith. In this way, the shadowy and dark side of desire—the fact that for so many people sexuality equals exploitation, abuse, and violence—can be addressed. Faith, sexuality, and eroticism are not simply linked to, but are embedded in, a discourse of shalom (peace, well-being, wholeness) and justice. The transformative path looks at the practice of the sexual relationship in parallel with the practice of the love of God, together in an existential spirituality that wants to stimulate and form a way of life and attitude to life, and therefore does not settle for less.

According to Zorgdrager, this approach demands humility and modesty, the development of a kind of sensitivity and respect, which makes it possible to love each other reciprocally in words, images, looks, and touch.[20] We are not, at heart, "freelancers in love," with our own au-

---

19. Zorgdrager, *Tussen Hooglied en #MeToo*, 17–18; translated by the authors.
20. Zorgdrager, *Tussen Hooglied en #MeToo*, 22.

tonomy at the center. In essence, this means that we must do something with the way in which we have individualized sexuality.

Contours of Our Approach: Desire as a Transformative Framework

It may have become clear from the previous paragraphs that we see the transformative pathway as the most theologically balanced. It does justice to the connection between faith, God, and sexuality. In chapter 4 we have chosen a clear starting point: the Bible as a narrative of desire. Compared to the other approaches mentioned, this starting point forms an alternative approach in which God's desire to connect with us and our desire to connect with God and others are central.[21] Sexuality is one of the dimensions that expresses the desire for relationship and communion with the other. The critical question that can—and in fact must—be asked is how desire—especially sexual desire—can be expressed in a way that is not in conflict with the other and remains in balance. Or rather, how does it remain a sacred desire? It is about its orientation and order. Not every desire is by definition a desire for the good. To discuss this further, we can use two well-known Greek concepts: *eros* and *agape*.

Eros and Agape

David Jensen points out that, in our culture, desire plays a major role when it comes to sexuality. He argues that the right form of desire is disturbed when possession of the other is sought. Desire needs space. Many people are never satisfied with one relationship because of these desires, but almost automatically and excitedly look for the next new one. If this type of desire only finds expression in sexuality, then the search for sex becomes restless.[22] In popular scientific circles, one often hears the view that men compulsively look for their next sex partner because they have a deep and innate urge to reproduce, which they can only satisfy by spreading their own genetic material everywhere. Both men and women seem to be caught up in this "game."

---

21. See the beginning of chapter 4 and our approach that we have taken from Jensen, *God, Desire, and a Theology of Human Desire*.

22. Jensen, *God, Desire, and a Theology of Human Desire*, 19.

Here again, we see the tension between biological-genetic explanations of sexual behavior on the one hand, and explanations that characterize that same behavior from a more social-constructivist viewpoint on the other. The popular view of a constantly wandering desire can be found in many places in society. Just think of magazines like *Playboy* and *Men's Health*. The idea is quite simple: only a variety of sex partners can satisfy this restless desire.

Of course, according to Jensen, men are not the only ones who suffer from these restless desires, women seem to have them too. Just look at *Sex and the City* or other series, films, and television programs in which relationships and sexuality play a major role. At the other end of the spectrum, we find almost the opposite, what we may call for the sake of convenience "frozen desire." In this view, sex can only take place within marriage; in all other instances, sexual intercourse would be damaging and dehumanizing. The problem with this view of desire is that it gives the impression that sex within marriage is a singularly sacred and straightforward experience, which, as we now know, can cause a lot of pressure in relationships. This seems to be a very limited vision of what sexuality is. Here I quote the definition of sexuality used by the Evangelical Lutheran Church in America as a representative example:

> Sexuality especially involves the powers or capacities to form deep and lasting bonds, to give and receive pleasure, and to conceive and bear children. Sexuality can be integral to the desire to commit oneself to life with another, to touch and be touched, to love and be loved. Such powers are complex and ambiguous. They can be used well or badly. They can bring astonishing joy and delight. Such powers can serve God and serve the neighbor. They also can hurt self or the neighbor. Sexuality finds expression at the extreme ends of human experience: in love, care and security, or lust, cold indifference and exploitation. Sexuality consists of a rich and diverse combination of relational, emotional and physical interactions and possibilities. It surely does not consist solely of erotic desire.[23]

Sex does not liberate or save, says Jensen; the good news is that God in Christ saves our body, soul, and spirit, and sex is part of what God saves.[24] Some would argue that marriage is the foundation of a good society but, from a Christian perspective, Christ is the foundation.

23. See Evangelical Lutheran Church in America, "Statement," 10–11.

24. Jensen, *God, Desire, and a Theology of Human Desire*, 21.

Many of these discussions seem to be trapped in either an undervalua-
tion or an overvaluation of sexuality and eroticism. At the center, is the
demonstrable tension between *agape* and *eros*. Agape is then presented
as the self-giving and sacrificial love, the Christian love of Jesus in the
New Testament, while eros stands for selfish love, eroticism, and lust.
Agape love must then be safeguarded above all, with no contamination
from the eros virus. Eros is like a wide river that very easily overflows its
banks; agape is the small stream that sometimes dissolves in the larger,
wider river of eros.[25]

In a fascinating essay, Wim ter Horst put his finger on the sore spot
thirty years ago: our aim should be "restoring the honour of love."[26] Ter
Horst's work accords with Jensen's image of men and women hunting,
wandering around with an "eros without depth." He therefore wonders
what eros has to do with true love and discusses the impact that the
"ancient god" Eros has had. Eros went through his own development
from the powerful god who creates order in chaos to the son of Ares and
Aphrodite (Venus), the goddess of fertility. Eros is often depicted as the
companion of his mother Venus and as the "little guy shooting arrows."
Ter Horst wrote:

> His mother is the eternal sweetheart, the object of lust, who is
> also the goddess of fertility. His father is the god of violence.
> Eroticism here is a game for hard, ruthless ("real!") men, who
> puts a quick end to (temple) whores.[27]

Typical ter Horst, we could say, but here we see the problem at its root:
eros is primarily about sensuality, lust, and possible pleasure. More could
be said about this (also about Narcissus as the prototype of the consumer)
than is possible in this context, but the history of eros shows that concerns about him were sometimes justified, for example, when we think of
the excesses, perversity, and the abuses of power surrounding boys' love.
Eros fit into the Greco-Roman, world where male and female were characterized by a strong dualism (see also chapter 2). Ter Horst rightly states
that the church had and has great difficulty with eros. He is looking again
for eros, but not for eros without depth ("eros w.d." is a hunter, a decent or
an indecent one), or in other words: eroticism without deep connections,
bonding, and authentic desire. Eroticism with such connections will be

25. Coakley, *God, Sexuality, and the Self*, 30.
26. Ter Horst, *Eerherstel van de liefde*, 69–70; translated by the authors.
27. Ter Horst, *Eerherstel van de liefde*, 70; translated by the authors.

broader and deeper: physical touch, eyes searching each other, and hands gently caressing at breakfast. It only becomes real, according to ter Horst, when the "I" and the "heart" are moved and joined.[28]

Desire has a dark side. Not every desire is, by definition, a desire for the good. Thatcher gives some good insight into the various theological and ethical aspects of this shadow side.[29] Lust and desire are discussed in connection with each other. He draws our attention to the fact that the question of definition cannot be avoided. What exactly are we talking about? It is not difficult, for example, to find opposing definitions of lust. Lust can be defined, on the one hand, as twisted desire, directed toward selfish sexual pleasure and, on the other, as spirited desire, directed toward sexual activity. In the first definition, lust is suspect and morally reprehensible. In the other, a more value-neutral and perhaps more positive approach is discussed. Thatcher believes this ambiguity (lust with two conflicting faces) is illustrated in the well-known biblical narrative of David and Bathsheba (cf. 2 Sam 11). Central to this story is the abuse of power that manifests itself in an apparently uncontrollable lust, ending with the murder of Uriah, Bathsheba's husband. The story shows that sexual desire in the form of uncontrollable lust has a destructive character.

A positive view of sexual desire begins with a realistic view of the destructive forces that can be associated with lust. The Christian tradition is therefore well placed (think, for example, of lust as one of the classic deadly sins) to keep pointing this out. It does not do so from an arrogant position, but precisely in order to help us make choices around and about lust. (See also later in this chapter). It is therefore necessary to distinguish between creative sexual desire and destructive forms of desire. Thatcher shows that we must not separate sexual desire from our cultural context and society, in which all sorts of desires play a role. Think of greed, for example, and of the way in which economic systems stimulate and fuel this greed. Not everything a person desires is necessarily good for him or her and their loved ones. In many places, in both the Old and New Testaments, we can find warnings against this (cf., e.g., Exod 20; Luke 12:15; Matt 6:24).

As a positive counterpoint, Thatcher raises the texts of Song of Songs 7 and 8.[30] Those who delve into the Song discover pure love poetry. Though these texts are often spiritualized (thereby almost denying

---

28. Ter Horst, *Eerherstel van de liefde*, 80.

29. Thatcher, *God, Sex, and Gender*, 57–65.

30. Thatcher, *God, Sex, and Gender*, 69–81.

physical love) they show that deep, abiding sexual love and the appreciation of goodness, fertility, beauty, and attention to God's creation are inextricably linked. Profound sexual love and the appreciation of goodness can be understood as interconnected forms of our innate longing for the God who bestows them both. Thatcher makes a practical connection between sexual desire, love, doing good, and the desire for God. Becoming more familiar with texts like the Song of Songs creates clear and responsible interpretations that do justice to the deep connections between sensuality and spirituality.

A thorough reading of Song of Songs 7 opens our discussion on how to better deal with our desires, our experience of sexuality, and even our thinking about it. The lovers practiced waiting. When she decides to give herself completely to him, they decide to make love to each other outside, among all the beauty of God's creation; flowers, fruit, and so on. Their love play is to be surrounded by the most sensual and joy-giving fruit and so they commit themselves to a song of praise for their God, whose love is reflected in the love between people. The Song of Songs is unique in the canon in many ways, including when we speak of gender equality. At the very least, it gives equal space to the woman's desire for her husband and to his desire for her. There is no lust for power in these stories, no domination, no submission, no call for a man to be the head of a woman, no call for obedience to the woman. There is also no reference to having children as a justification for making love. Song of Songs points to a powerful, loving union that has nothing to do with subordination or rank. In this way, sexuality and intimacy come closer to their original purpose, so that sexual desire and creative lust have their place in equality, without falling into cheap and flat eroticism. Desire thus becomes a creative force, stripped of one-sided binary thinking. This comes close to what theologian Frank Bosman calls *frui* sex.[31] He refers to the distinction that Augustine makes between *uti* (use) and *frui* (enjoy). The first word is about enjoying in an instrumental sense, while the second, *frui*, stands for enjoying for the sake of enjoying. *Frui* is fitting in reference to God, according to Bosman, but also for people and aligns with eroticism. This theological vision of eroticism has a double critical message for the church and society. He points out that the church has often focused on sex as an instrument: to control lust or to have children, through marriage. However, sex to enjoy becomes a mirror according to Bosman,

31. Bosman, *God houdt van seks*, 64.

as it is the only moment that persons can fully surrender to their own humanity: naked, without reservation, embracing his own finiteness and imperfection. The concept of *frui* also criticizes modern society in which sex is put to use (*uti*) for money, human trafficking, or a medical problem to be solved.

In the context of further discussions on the right ordering of desire, the approach proposed by Margaret Farley may be of significance.[32] Farley develops a framework for sexual ethics. She proposes seven norms that should contribute to sexual justice: (1) sex should not harm anyone, (2) sex should take place on the basis of mutual consent, (3) the principle of reciprocity should be applied, (4) equality as a principle is crucial, (5) devotion and loyalty are at the core, (6) joy and finally (7) social justice are involved. Of course, much depends on how these standards are put into practice, but there is no doubt that it is right to address them.

Returning to Jensen's work on *eros*, *agape*, and the right form—or right ordering—of desire, we can learn to move away from individualized desire. The concern of theologians such as Barth and Anders Nygren was that in *eros* there is too much emphasis on the human being who loves rather than on God who loves humankind first and foremost.[33] The result is that *eros* has been isolated from its connection to God and hardly has meaning anymore for the life of a Christian, while at the same time, in parts of the Christian tradition, longing for God is central—after all, humans were created to long for God and to live in his love and light. However, there is an example of more nuanced thinking on eros. Susannah Cornwall shows that in Pope Benedict XVI's first encyclical, *Deus Caritas Est* (God is Love), he revisits early Christian traditions in which God and eros were readily identified together.[34] While this integrated understanding of eros helps us to establish desire as a framework for theological reflections on sexuality, it is still the case, according to Jensen, that the starting point for eros is in decidedly one-sided human desire, quite apart from God.

Jensen, like ter Horst, points to the need for balance in our considerations of eros. On one side of the coin, a denial of eros leads to an entrenched problem in modern society: the oppression of women. The identification of the feminine (particularly female bodies) with eros, earth, and flesh (as counterparts of agape, heaven, and spirit) leaves a

32. Farley, *Just Love*, 216–32.

33. Jensen, *God, Desire, and a Theology of Human Desire*, 24.

34. Cornwall, *Theology and Sexuality*, 31.

huge patriarchal mark on women. On the other side of the same coin, overemphasis of eros also does not help. Eros becomes a consumer product with which one tries to fulfill the (false) promises of a consumer society, in which women (and their bodies) are objects to be owned. The way out of this conundrum is not easy. Undoubtedly, eros must remain within a relational framework if it is to truly contribute to people's well-being and to a flourishing life. In doing so, we cannot ignore the shadow of abuse and violence, because that is where the greatest risk lies in a society in which sexuality and violence merge all too easily.[35] Jensen's answer lies in a reevaluation of the Christian mystics, who he is convinced illustrate for us how immersion in pleasure (also physical pleasure and the *bonding* that is locked up in it) and the renunciation of pleasure keep each other in check. It is in this fragile balance that eros and eroticism find their place. The parallel is this: just as in the life of a Christian the deep experience of grace and contact with God alternate with *dark nights of the soul*, so our sexual life is also characterized by both the presence and absence of lovers.[36] Just as the way to God is characterized by desire—longing—for God, and sustained through encounters with God in everyday life, this takes place just as much in the dark times as it does in times of joy.

The experience of sexuality, nourished by the longing of one human being for another, takes place in ordinary everyday life. Our (human) desire is a derivative: we desire in response to the God who first desires us. Goodness and beauty, according to Jensen, are directly connected to both these desires (for God and humans); they cannot be obtained separately.

God's longing is, as it were, the force that draws us closer to him, and this takes place in ordinary, everyday life. The longing of one human being for another is derived from this force. It has a centripetal and centrifugal dynamic, pushing lovers toward each other (centripetal) and from there the relationship opens up again, making room to share life and love with others—with God and with the world around them (centrifugal). Desire is strong, increasing through focus and discipline— especially in relationships—but it can also decrease, because the reality is people in different life stages can differ in their actions, feelings, and well-being. Jensen writes:

> Whereas the consumer narrative of sex fosters an indefatigable quest of doing it all night long, all the time (more, longer, and

35. Jensen, *God, Desire, and a Theology of Human Desire*, 26.
36. Jensen, *God, Desire, and a Theology of Human Desire*, 28.

bigger are always better), Christian narratives juxtapose the pursuit of pleasure with its accompanying rest. Making love, in this regard, is not synonymous with physical acts that lead to orgasm, but in the broad scope of coming to know, coming to touch, coming to pleasure, coming into each other's arms, and falling asleep side-by-side. The intensification of desire also leads to the peace that surpasses all understanding, given by God.[37]

In this way, eros and agape keep each other in balance, because longing has its deepest home in God.[38] Paul Lakeland analyzes this coherence in an impressive essay in which he pays specific attention to ecclesiology and states:

> We can perhaps say, with reasonable accuracy, that the erotic depends upon the dialectic of absence and presence, of anticipation and realization, of promise and fulfillment. The challenge of eros is that it is fueled by absence, by lack of possession, by an imagination that is feeding on what is not yet or what has been, but its drive toward satisfaction requires presence that will temporarily erase eros itself. Eros is not satisfied with presence, only with possession. In its turn, however, possession is the anteroom to further absence, the fulfillment that portends renewed wanting, the presence becomes absence again, the little death out of which eros may again be kindled, but which is in itself at least the temporary end of wanting. In this complex process, the desire may be as delicious as the enjoyment, the anticipation indeed more pleasurable than the capture.[39]

To summarize Lakeland, the erotic depends on the dialectic of absence and presence. As one part of desire, it is nourished by absence, promise, and fulfilment. But in order to achieve the fulfillment of desire, presence is needed: the lovers must be in each other's presence. Eros that is more than lust seeks to be in the presence of the beloved, to know the other in a way that transcends a sexual union. And to end this paragraph, we fittingly (and tellingly) reorient these reflections toward God: in sexual desire, we do not find God completely, rather, God finds us in that desire, as he surrounds our lives. Thus our sexuality, even our imperfect desire, is included in a deep process of transformation in God's direction.

37. Jensen, *God, Desire, and a Theology of Human Desire,* 34.
38. Cornwall, *Theology and Sexuality,* 21–37.
39. Lakeland, "Ecclesiology, Desire, and the Erotic," 251.

Desire in an Eschatological Perspective

For Jensen, this process of transformation is related to our ability to make a connection between sexual desire and the resurrection of Jesus. The first reaction to this question is probably a new one: what does the resurrection have to do with sexuality? This is a legitimate question for those who follow Jesus's statement in Matt 22:30: "At the resurrection people will neither marry nor be given in marriage, they will be like the angels in heaven." The quick conclusion based on this text could be that the resurrection body is a body without sex; the changing power of the resurrection transforms our "earthly" desires and then sexuality plays no more part. We need not spend much space dealing with this traditional view, since it has too many issues to discuss here, and because Patricia Beattie Jung has already thoroughly addressed them in her exploration of desire from an eschatological perspective.[40]

Instead, we ask how sexuality might be transformed just as our resurrection bodies will be transformed.

In this alternative interpretation, the body of the risen Jesus becomes the focal point of God's nearness. In the union of the church—the body of Christ—with this resurrected body of Jesus, our physical bodies too will one day change. Jensen points to the significance of the body and the physical and makes it clear that the church and her tradition have not always connected the consequences of the resurrection to the whole body.[41] Hands, feet, eyes, and head are quickly referred to as the hands, feet, eyes, and head of Christ, and we do not hear much about the rest of the body. He wonders if we have also admitted the risen Lord into our sexual bodies, precisely because the Christian faith is a faith in which the body plays such an important role. Think of the incarnation: God enters the world in a human body and leaves it also with a body, albeit renewed, with the signs of the crucifixion still visible.[42]

Jensen's question is an honest question about the impact of the resurrection on concrete life, with all of its desires. If sex is about a loving touch, about an expression of the greatest possible closeness, about making room and giving space to each other, then it must make a difference in the light of the resurrection. And it must also make a difference in the here and

40. Beattie Jung, *Sex on Earth*, 1–40.

41. Jensen, *God, Desire, and a Theology of Human Desire*, 43.

42. Jensen, *God, Desire, and a Theology of Human Desire*, 43; and Cornwall, *Theology and Sexuality*, 21.

now, because God commits to us in the midst of life with a *violated* body that heals our lives at the same time. The risen Jesus who disarmed the alleged imperial power as a slaughtered Lamb (Rev 5:19, 21) puts an end to all violence in his body and emphasizes that our bodies do not belong to ourselves. Therefore, we are called to live out a new reality with our bodies. Our sexual desire is embraced in this new reality and finds a home there. This does not diminish the difficulties of balancing eros and desire, as we discussed, and nor does it erase life's imperfections: There is no such thing as perfect sex. Sex does not redeem but, by God's grace, sex becomes graceful. Desire then takes the shape of embodied grace.

Desire in a Trinitarian Perspective

Until now, we have tried to delineate sexual desire mainly around concepts such as eros and agape. This was necessary in order to set boundaries. We have also linked this desire to christological and eschatological notions concerning the resurrection, following Jensen. To do justice to the broader framework, we now place desire in a trinitarian perspective. In doing so, we are actually going a step further than Jensen and connecting human sexual desire more deeply with faith in our God who reveals himself in a threefold manner: Father, Son, and Spirit. The steps we take here are directly related to our goal: to use "desire" as a theological framework for reflecting on gender and sexuality, and in which desire can be fulfilled through constructive connection with God and others. To do this, we follow the work of Sarah Coakley, as she has a broader perspective and anchors her starting point more in gender expression than in sexuality.[43] Coakley has made the notion of desire the core concept of her theology, which she links to the Trinity. In particular, she helps us to see that belief in Father, Son, and Spirit (the Trinity) has everything to do with desire and thus also with sexual desire. Coakley writes in her introduction:

> Further . . . this book is written in the fundamental conviction that no cogent answer to the contemporary Christian question of the trinitarian God can be given without charting the necessary and *intrinsic* entanglement of human sexuality and spirituality in such a quest: the questions of right contemplation of God, the right speech about God and the right ordering of desire all hang together. . . . Thus the problem of the Trinity cannot be solved

---

43. Coakley, *God, Sexuality, and the Self,* 1–2.

without addressing the very questions that seem least to do with it, questions which press on the contemporary churches with such devastating and often destructive force: questions of sexual justice, questions of the meaning and stability of gender roles, questions of the final theo-logical significance of sexual desire.[44]

In short, in thinking about God, who reveals himself as Father, Son, and Spirit, there must be room for the critical questions that arise in relation to sexuality, gender, and the theological meaning of sexual desire. Coakley rightly observes that these questions often have a destructive force in many communities, and are often the cause of division within the church. We need only to recall the upheaval over the Nashville Declaration (2019), which we discussed earlier in the introduction.

According to Coakley, the Trinity should be at the center of our discussions about desire, and precisely because of the necessary connection between God and people. In this respect, she proposes a different order: desire has priority over sex, gender, and sexuality. Both God's desire for his creation and the human desire for God are points of orientation. Coakley does not want to allow herself to be seduced into a discussion that only deals with the so-called "problem" of, for example, homosexuality. According to her, there is a deeper issue at stake: the longing for God must be above all other longings, and it is the lens through which all other longings are evaluated. In order to make this possible, Coakley searches for a way of thinking about Father, Son, and Spirit, which characterizes a different approach to sexuality and gender in relation to current social issues. For this, she draws on texts by one of the Cappadocian fathers, Gregory of Nyssa.

Coakley's aim is to develop a vision of the "self" in which who we are is transformed only through participation in God's love as manifested in Father, Son, and Spirit. This reformation of the "self" leads to a radical purification of misguided desires. Desire, in this view, is the determining factor for who we are as human beings. In fact, we need to rediscover these roots and this requires rethinking both our assumptions and deeply held beliefs about sexuality, gender, and the "self." In short, it is her hope that a better understanding of God and of God's desire for his creation will make it possible to deal with human desire in a more balanced way. This sounds fairly idealistic, and perhaps vague to begin with, but it is a

---

44. Coakley, *God, Sexuality, and the Self,* 1–2.

theology of desire that builds on a trinitarian perspective. So, what does that look like?

This more balanced approach to human desire will, in turn, have a positive effect on complex debates in the church over gender and sexuality. Thinking about gender must be subordinated to thinking about desire.[45] Gender refers to a person's differentiated and embodied relationship with God and others.[46] An important question here is what being made in the image of God means. Human desire is thus placed in perspective with creation, sin, and redemption. This may seem self-evident, but it has not been. The starting point may be creation, but viewpoints on gender and its related complexities vary enormously.

Timothy Tennent, for example, advocates for a gender binary by starting at the creation of man and woman, arguing that since the whole story of creation is designed around God-ordained binary elements (light and darkness, day and night, water and air, sun and moon), this also applies to human gender. He blames modern gender theory for erasing the God-ordained binary character of sexuality and with it the initial moral framework within which relationships should be formed.[47] According to Tennent, this theory of creation and its implications have lost a great deal of significance, resulting in an increase in Gnostic visions of the body: the inner self is autonomous and somewhat disconnected from the body. Tennent begins to undermine his own argument by claiming that these elements of creation cannot be presented as simply or merely binary. By implication, one element of the binary may be quickly labelled as negative, for example darkness versus light. However, the creation of the moon and the stars is not so much opposed to the creation of the sun as it is for light and dark, along with other examples. Tennent also contradicts himself when, on the one hand, he wants to give the body a central role on the basis of his doctrine of creation, but at the same time he moralizes about male and female identity being primarily concerned with man and woman as moral image-bearers of God in this world.[48]

The way we think about body, soul, and spirit are in need of review from a trinitarian perspective, instead of a one-sided embedding in Greco-Roman dualistic concepts. Gender and desire are imperfect and need perfecting and completing. From creation, it is clear that every human

---

45. Coakley, *God, Sexuality, and the Self,* 53–54.
46. Coakley, *God, Sexuality, and the Self,* 53.
47. Tennent, *For the Body,* 20.
48. Tennent, *For the Body,* 19.

being, however different from others, is an image of God. And people are created in that image, even after the fall.

What is "fallen" can be redeemed and sanctified through participation in Christ.[49] Gender can thus be seen as a potential vehicle for embodied salvation: God is at work in it. This way of theologizing about gender is in some ways different from what we are used to. This is because of its focus on and sensitivity to the flow of God's desire to love people. It is about a different kind of logic and about openness to growth in the image of Christ. This fundamental openness to change and a willingness to reflect on the essence of what gender is seems essential: the embodied differentiation and variation (of gender) do not need to be erased, but they deserve to be changed and transformed. This perspective applies to the whole spectrum of gender and sexuality, as well as relationships. Only God is able to recreate and perfect gender as an *embodied difference* in the image of his Son.[50]

Desire in a Pneumatological Perspective

Coakley pays particular attention to the work of the Spirit within her transformational and trinitarian thinking. Coakley's analysis of Rom 8:26 (NIV) exemplifies this for us:

> In the same way, the Spirit helps us in our weakness. We do not know what we ought to pray for, but the Spirit himself intercedes for us through wordless groans.

It is this text that strongly determines Coakley's understanding of the function and role of prayer when it comes to the influence of the triune God on human desire. The experience of powerlessness in prayer is overcome by the fact that God prays in us and for us in the person of the Spirit. There is a permanent pendulum movement that the Spirit makes between us and God the Father, between God the Father and us. It is the Spirit who transmits to each of us God's desire to love us. It is the Spirit who transfers to God our desire to love God. This is an endless tenderness and also a frequent interruption and testing of our own desires, if we are open to that interruption and testing.[51] And it is a permanent invitation

---

49. Coakley, *God, Sexuality, and the Self,* 53.

50. Coakley, *God, Sexuality, and the Self,* 55.

51. Coakley, *God, Sexuality, and the Self,* 55–57.

to continue to participate in life in and with God, in order to experience fulfillment of desire in connectedness with God and others. If life is a continuous invitation to partake of and participate in life in and with this triune God, then the binary thinking around gender must be abandoned, because participation in this life has a transcendent character that gives concrete meaning to the transformative and recreative work of God.

The triune character of God must impact debates over gender and sexuality; after all, we are created in the image of God (the image of Father, Son, and Spirit). This interrupting activity of the Spirit is crucial for human gender. The fixed gender differences in this world are incorporated by the Spirit of God in a movement of purification and change. It may not be the right term, of course, but "two-ness," we could say, is constantly under attack by the life of the "trinity." God in his plural love (God is the Triune God) breaks through the binary thinking that is so dominant in our world, and at the same time shows us how important being relational is. Relationship with God, with people, and with the whole of creation is central to the search for connection. As Coakley writes:

> So this irreducible threeness in God cannot be insignificant for the matter of gendered twoness, since the human is precisely made "in God's (trinitarian) image," and destined to be restored to that image. It must be, then, that in this fallen world, one lives, in some sense, between twoness and its transfiguring interruption; so one is not, as in secular gender theory, endlessly and ever subject to the debilitating falseness of fallen gender, fallen twoness. In fact, in Christ, I meet the human One who, precisely in the Spirit, has effected that interruptive transfiguration of twoness. He has done so by crossing the boundary between another "twoness" more fundamental even than the twoness of gender: the ontological twoness of the transcendent God and the created world.[52]

In fact, Coakley, like Jensen, refers in this citation to the meaning of the resurrection of Jesus. It is the Spirit of Jesus who continues his transformative work and unites what is divided. Then it is not about the numbers of two or three or five, but about the *relationship*. Gender remains important, but it is placed in a different framework. It is the Spirit who, in our praying, "breaks open" the human heart, as it were, and who provides the much needed testing and cleansing of human desire. For Coakley, one thing is crystal clear: a theology that grapples with power, gender, and

---

52. Coakley, *God, Sexuality, and the Self,* 56–57.

sexuality will have to be reconsidered in light of this trinitarian approach. The dominant binary thinking is thus broken, because it fails to appreciate the unity and diversity of God's creation.

In a follow-up publication, *The New Asceticism: Sexuality, Gender and the Quest for God,* Coakley further elaborates on her trinitarian thinking on desire, gender, and sexuality.[53] Church and society need a new theology of desire, precisely because of all the conflicting visions that so often cling to Christian and secular practices. The confusion inherent in, and over right-ordering of, desire needs to be analyzed, especially from a theological perspective. Coakley searches for a form of ascetic life that can also be respected in a post-Christian world.[54] The journey to this form of life is not easy because theories of power and gender, such as those of Foucault and Freud, cannot be ignored. In their analyses, whether we appreciate them or not, they brought attention to the Christian tradition's poor handling of sexuality. The relationship between power, abuse, and sexuality must therefore be taken seriously, especially because the connections between power and abuse were—and are—so often the subject of institutional church debates.

Coakley shows that, sadly, oppression can be front of mind when thinking about the relationship between God and sexuality, but there was actually hardly any openness to a positive view of the relationship between God and sexuality. Coakley frames conversation about the relationship between desire and a form of ascetic life with three paradoxes. First, she points to a preoccupation with the body and physicality, while at the same time all kinds of popular magazines call for a strong degree of control over "flesh and body," which is precisely the opposite of paying too much attention to the body. The question that arises from this is one of equivalence between self and body. Am I only a body or is there something else going on?

A second paradox is related to this: is physical sexual desire so directly linked to physical satisfaction that rejecting it could lead to a threat to one's health? Or can we say that a certain degree of restraint is culturally important and healthy?

Coakley sees a third and final paradox in relation to food. Self-indulgence on the one hand and strict forms of self-imposed dieting on the other play a role. In a way, even fasting can then imply a form

53. Coakley, *New Asceticism,* 1–40.
54. Coakley, *New Asceticism,* 1–50.

of self-indulgence. For Coakley, these paradoxes are a sign of the enormous shifts in relation to thinking about physicality. She points to the evidence for this in things like addiction treatments, imposed treatments for obesity, etc. These three examples illustrate a need for balance, and it is precisely these reflections that can help us to prevent an overvaluation of sexuality and stay away from an eroticization of God.[55]

Adrian Thatcher moves in the same direction as Coakley, although within his trinitarian approach he emphasizes a christological perspective.[56] In his impressive work *Redeeming Gender*, he seeks to resolve a number of fundamental problems that he sees in three possible views on sex and gender. In chapter 1, we already sketched the background to his thinking on these three views. We saw (1) the singular continuum: men are hot, more rational, and more perfect than women; (2) the two-sex model that developed in the seventeenth and eighteenth centuries: male and female are unequal; and (3) male and female as two equal genders. Thatcher shows that the first position above all helps us to understand where our modern ideas about gender and sexuality come from. A positive of this view is that male and female are seen from a kind of unity: a unity in diversity, admittedly, but still a unity. At the same time, however, this approach leads to what Thatcher calls a *gender slide*, a kind of gender shift-mechanism in which relationships are organized hierarchically (and vertically).[57]

According to Thatcher, the second view does not receive much attention within contemporary theology. The third, however, is almost the standard view in the modern West. It seems to be the best understanding and for many churches it is the preferred approach. Thatcher, however, is not convinced of the solidity of this third option. He believes that theology can propose a better way, but also—and we share this view—he traces the impact of this viewpoint in the lives of too many men and women: it remains a binary model that continues to lead to the struggle between the sexes. Another important argument is the overvaluation of biological sex that comes with this view. Thatcher does not deny biological diversity, but calls attention to diversity within the sexes.[58] The differences between women and men are probably as great as the differences between the two sexes. Moreover, as we have already seen, the so-called

55. Cornwall, *Theology and Sexuality*, 21–37; Thatcher, *Marriage After Modernity*.
56. Thatcher, *Redeeming Gender*, 137–60.
57. Thatcher, *Redeeming Gender*, 138.
58. Thatcher, *Redeeming Gender*, 139.

discovery (see chapter 3) of two incomparable sexes led to a kind of heteronormativity: the expectation that everyone would be in a male or female body. This development in turn reinforced binary thinking on homosexuality versus heterosexuality.

Thatcher embraces a singular continuum that accepts diversity as a given, but not only sexual diversity. *In abstracto*, the name for this continuum is human, humanity, persons.[59] However abstract it may be, this must, by definition, precede sexual diversity. He grounds this idea not in creation (on the basis of Genesis 1 and 2), but on the meaning of Jesus as the new creation, the second Adam. The two key texts that play a role in this for Thatcher are 2 Cor 4:4 and Col 1:15. Christ has priority over Adam. He is the image of God, the image of the invisible God, first-born of all creation (Col 1:15). Chronologically, Adam may be the first human, but both texts leave no doubt about it: Christ is ontologically the first. Because of Christ, everything has changed.

This representation of the image of God is not a restoration of the existing order, but a totally new order. The theological problem surrounding gender, as Thatcher then contends, is how relationships are transformed when they share in the life of Christ, the new image of God.[60] The new creation in Christ leads to a fourfold reality in which the masculine and the feminine are reshaped: a new kingdom (Col 1:13, "the kingdom of his beloved Son"), a new creation (Col 1:15–17, "in him all things were created"), a new body (Col 1:18, "he is the head of the body, the church"), and a new humanity (Col 3:9–15, "and have put on the new man"). It is interesting to note that in Col 3:9–15, the words of verse 10b are, theologically speaking, the leading edge: the new human who is constantly being renewed in the *image of their Creator*. Recreated humanity is involved in a *continuous* process of recreation as image-bearers of God. Christ opens this fourfold reality and liberates humankind from sin, but also from the sin that hides itself in improper gender differentiation, e.g., holding on to binary thinking.[61]

Coakley goes a step further than Jensen when she insists on subordinating thinking about gender, in a theological sense, to thinking about desire. The way in which she presents desire means sexual desire and the desire for God are no longer at odds, but are related to each other: sexual

---

59. Thatcher, *Redeeming Gender*, 141.

60. Thatcher, *Redeeming Gender*, 147.

61. Thatcher, *Redeeming Gender*, 202.

desire can be normalized and balanced by the desire for God.[62] Questions of gender remain relevant because it is on this point that opinions and perceptions both in broader society and in Christian circles diverge sharply. For secular theorists of gender issues, gender is still a symbol of rigid and oppressive binary thinking. For Christians with more conservative views, the discussion leads to a certain heteronormativity that is seen as biblical, with little or no room for gender variation, at least not in practice. Biblical texts that deal with relationships and sexuality are therefore invariably read and explained through the same binary lens. Thinking about gender is important, because it has direct consequences for practice. The gender spectrum we discussed in chapter 1 illustrated this well. Most of the attention in Christian discussions is paid to a person's sexual orientation, but not to the underlying gender identity that forms and guides this orientation.

Coakley shows that sexuality, gender, and spirituality are very closely related. She does this, among other things, by seeing gender primarily as the differentiated and embodied relationship of a person with self and others, but also with God. It is precisely at this point that the question of the meaning of the human being as an image-bearer of God (*imago Dei*) becomes operantly crucial, but with openness to diversity (*imago Trinitatis*).[63] The appeal of Coakley's analysis lies primarily in its positive approach to desire. Though, Coakley touches minimally on practical matters and on "hot topics," as we will call them in the next chapter. The question we are left with is what this theological framework means for all kinds of issues under discussion. The meaning of her thinking must be sought primarily in a derived sense, it's application is not so self-evident.

Desire as Embodied Grace

We referred to Rowan Williams's "The Body's Grace" in chapter 1. The importance of this essay may now perhaps be clearer. The theme at the center of this chapter—desire—is beautifully presented in all its depth in that essay. In this chapter, we have looked for theological language to deepen our reflections on sexuality, and we have done this through the key concept of desire. We took a journey through the various possible approaches, focusing on the transformative approach. The main argument

---

62. Coakley, *New Asceticism*, 1–40.

63. Leene, *Triniteit, antropologie en ecclesiologie*, 90–91.

was that the connection between desire and transformation puts sexuality in a balanced framework. Sexuality is one of the dimensions that expresses the desire for relationship and communion with the other person we love. This transformative approach makes it possible to keep the experience of sexuality close to the ordinary daily reality of life, characterized by highs and lows. *Eros* and *agape* are both allowed to be part of that; they are not played off against each other, but are given their place in the longing and desire for God. This transformative approach also characterizes how we deal with questions concerning gender; embodied diversity acquires new depth and meaning as we are renewed and recreated in the image of the beloved Son, Jesus. Differences between men and women are not eliminated, but are normed by the primacy of Christ who affirms unity in diversity in his body. Sexual desire and sexuality are thus given the form of embodied grace.

In "The Body's Grace," Williams similarly establishes what Coakley and Thatcher have both already offered: the relationship between our human and sexual desire and God's desire for us.[64] For Williams, this begins with the language of grace. It is crucial that we realize we are loved by God, and that we can identify ourselves as children of God. There is a connection between loving, being loved, and experiencing this. Without this threefold, interconnected experience, it will be difficult to feel love, including in a physical sense.

The first embodiment of love takes place in being incorporated into the body of Christ through the Spirit. From this starting point, Williams brings the fundamental principle of reciprocity into our conversation about sexuality and desire. According to Williams, the experience of being able to love each other in return must be seen as embodied grace. Every real experience of desire puts us in the position of not being able to satisfy our own needs without distorting them. If I want to be the cause of joy with my body, I will need to be there with my body for the other, so that I can be perceived, accepted, and nurtured, and experience this deep connection.

When I am focused on the joy and longing of the other, my surrender becomes a loving surrender. Longing for my joy means longing for the joy of the one for whom I long. In such surrender there is grace, the grace of the body. An important spiritual connection can also be seen in this. Isn't believing in the triune God about profound surrender, just as mutual

64. Williams, "Body's Grace," 309–21.

surrender in the context of sexuality is also the deepest form of experiencing pleasure and connection? This embodied grace requires time to be discovered and to unfold, because I am not just on my own, it is precisely because of the reciprocity involved. As lovers, we are not passive instruments of each other, but we learn in the daily rhythm of our relationship, in conversation, touch, and cooperation. This is not without risk, because our perceptions of each other change and differ so often. At the same time, these perceptions, what we see in each other, are crucial for nurturing the relationship, including our sexuality. As ter Horst has already shown: it only becomes real when the "I" and the "heart" are also moved.[65]

In another, more recent publication, Williams points out the importance of the other in the perception of our own physicality.[66] In an attempt to describe what it means that we *have* a body and also *are* a body, he quotes the philosopher Edith Stein, who remarked that it is interesting to reflect on the fact that we as humans cannot see the back of our heads. If we really want to have a three-dimensional image of our body, of our "being," then we need other people to help us. There is always something the other person knows that I absolutely cannot know. This, according to Williams, does not only apply to our heads. I can't invent a language for myself, I have to be spoken to first. I cannot form a picture of myself without someone else forming a picture of me.

These different forms of identification lead me to one of the most fundamental truths: I am only myself thanks to the other. This certainly applies to sexuality and desire, because it requires deep reciprocity. Connectedness, desire, and intimacy have a profound bodily expression. This revaluation of the body is of great importance in view of the binary and dualistic views that the church in general has long practiced, in which body and spirit were so often played off against each other. God chose to reveal himself through a human being with a specific human body (that of Christ). The interaction between this one human being with his body and other human bodies opened the way to liberation and wholeness for the whole of creation. Physicality matters: it is fundamental in the incarnation of God in Jesus, and thus touches all other dimensions of physicality in human existence.

---

65. Ter Horst, *Eerherstel van de liefde*, 80.
66. Williams, *Being Human*, 12–18.

Questions for Discussion

- In which of the four outlined paths of theological reflection on gender and sexuality do you feel most at home? Why is this the case?

- In conversations about sex, attention to the role and meaning of eroticism, pleasure, and lust often remains in the background or unmentioned. How could you reflect more about this on the basis of this chapter?

- Many publications focus on the overvaluation of sexuality in peoples' lives. To what extent can a conversation about the ordering of our desires, and therefore of our sexual desires, help us with this?

- How do you see the attention to physicality in our culture? To what extent does that require a correction along the lines of Sarah Coakley's plea for a new form of restraint?

- We make a case for seeing sexual desire as *embodied grace* (think about Rowan Williams). What do you think of that?

6

Hot Issues

Introduction

DIFFERENT THEOLOGICAL PERSPECTIVES ON gender, sexuality, and desire require a concrete connection to real practices; without that connection our theological reflection would not be valid. With this in mind, we need to, once more, take a step back to the beginning, to the descriptive task from our preface, and ask the key question: what is going on? We will describe a number of issues or phenomena that are at play in society and then connect them to our normative framework from chapter 5. We do this because we are aware this is precisely where the rubber hits the road and our reflections about God, faith, and sexuality meet with real people in the real world. And that often brings tension.[1] Quick answers here will not suffice. Our challenge, therefore, is to connect these fundamental theological values with how people are living today.

Our aim with this chapter is to move further toward that necessary connection between lived reality and the theological lens and transformative framework of desire. Needless to say, this is quite a challenge! Some of the lived experiences that come to mind are polyamory, virginity and purity, passion and bonding, sexuality in relation to illness and disability, prostitution, pornography, and sexual abuse. Sexuality, power, and violence and their impact are also discussed. The recent *#MeToo* disclosures,

---

1. Compare chapter 5 and specifically the input into our discourse by Sarah Coakley.

the resulting lawsuits, and the subsequent public uproar all force us to look at the relationship between sex and the abuse of power and take it seriously. Does theology have anything to say in this space? Can it bring something meaningful to conversations about passion or prostitution or purity? We, of course, believe that theology has something good to say here. Throughout this book, we have been peeling back the different layers of the phenomenon that is human sexuality. In this chapter, we take a closer look at some representative and more concrete examples, commenting on them, and connecting them to God's desire for us. In our next and final chapter, we give a short summary of these examples, and we take stock and briefly reflect on the other layers of human sexuality and gender we've explored throughout this book. But first, let's peel back a tricky layer: polyamory.

Polyamory

As our reader, you may be wondering, why do we need to talk about polyamory? A first response might be: "This does not happen here!" An understandable response, but as we already noted, the Bible (see chapter 4) has quite a few examples of polygyny (one man with several "wives," married or not). In addition, what many of us have undoubtedly experienced, is that men and women cheat and separate. This tends to raise the question of whether people are made for a lifelong relationship with one person. This makes discussion of polyamory important. What is polyamory? Let's approach this a little differently. Suppose you have an intimate relationship with someone; do you insist that your partner is monogamous? For many people, the answer is a heartfelt "yes"! This is not only true for heterosexual couples. It seems that gay couples are even more likely to want monogamy than straight partners.[2] Researcher Nathan Rambukkana (Wilfrid Laurier University, Canada) describes the history of polyamory and points out that it is only very recently that the attention it gets has increased. Monogamy is the norm in western thinking about sexuality. Polyamory questions this norm and is based on the idea that it is possible to love several people at the same time. In this kind of nonmonogamous relationship, one has several consensual (sexual) relationships with different partners.

2. Rambukkana, "Open Non-monogamies," 236–52.

It is estimated that in the US more than half a million families are open about their polyamorous relationships. According to Janell Carroll, there are at least three basic forms of polyamory: 1) one primary partner plus other secondary partners; 2) a triad; 3) an individual with several primary partners. In the first form, there is one primary or main partner relationship, which remains the most important, alongside other relationships. In the second form, three people are involved in an intimate relationship and all three are equal, without any primary or main relationship. Finally, the third form involves one person having separate but equal relationships with (at least) two others who have no relationship with each other.[3] In general, people who are polyamorous should be distinguished from *swingers*, who openly have an intimate relationship with other people at specially designated events where they change sex partners. Clearly swinging needs to be differentiated from openly entering into "responsible nonmonogamous" (*consensual*) long-term relationships, as that is the common definition of polyamory. Rambukkana raises a series of critical questions about polyamory based on existing and recent research. They range from the way a romantic relationship between more than two people looks, to the effects of polyamory (and possibly polygamy) on (women) raising children, and finally also to the ways in which the dynamics of the relationships are experienced in a psychological sense. A frequent question is how do people in polyamorous relationships deal with feelings of jealousy.

In a recent publication, Mimi Schippers (professor of sociology, gender, and sexuality in the US) discusses polyamory.[4] She begins her description with a number of concrete practical examples. We present them here because they show that polyamory is not just about theory, but about the stories and experiences of real people.

> A man and a woman have an open relationship. At the start of their relationship, they agreed that having sexual relations outside their own relationship was allowed. One evening, when her partner is in another city for work, the woman has sex with her partner's best friend.

> A woman has an affair with a man other than her husband for twelve years. During those years, she refuses to leave her husband, despite her lover's request to do so: she loves both men.

3. Carroll, *Sexuality Now*.

4. Schippers, *Beyond Monogamy*. Schippers works at the Tulane University in the US and is an expert on polyamory.

One evening, her husband listens to voicemail messages on her phone. One of the messages is from the lover, saying that he needs her and cannot live without her, he wants to see her.

A married man tells his friend that he and his wife had a three-some with another woman. He proudly says that this is "every man's dream" and that he really enjoyed it. When his friend asks him if he has ever had a threesome with his wife and another man, he answers with disgust: "Absolutely not! I am not gay!"

Schippers wonders what these stories have in common. Nonmonoga-mous relationships are at play in each. For Schippers, it remains undecid-ed if there is only one interpretation of these experiences and therefore also only one outcome: emotional trauma and the end of respective re-lationships. She contends that this would be a typical heteronormative reading, which is imposed by the prevailing culture. She states that one of the things given to us by heterosexual culture is the "monogamous couple." The predominant thinking is that to live a good life with sexual and emotional intimacy, we must turn away from other lovers.[5] Could the man in the first story accept that his wife has a relationship with his best friend? And is it conceivable that the man whose wife has been in a relationship with another man for so many years could accept him as part of the family? What would it be like if having multiple long-term partners were possible for both men and women? And what would it take for that to happen?

Schippers answers these, her own, questions very clearly: a new structuring of relationships is needed, breaking through all races and classes. She believes it is necessary to give more room to "poly-sexual-ities" and polyamorous relationships. As a consequence, "compulsory monogamy," as it has been called as the normative paradigm, must be abandoned. Schippers builds on the work of Adrienne Rich, who strongly opposed "compulsory heterosexuality."[6] Rich defines this as a network of social beliefs, customs, and practices that force women into intimate relationships with men. Schippers is not the only one to focus on this element and, in particular, she wants to emphasize the importance of nonmonogamous relationships.

5. Schippers, *Beyond Monogamy*, 3.

6. Rich, "Compulsory Heterosexuality."

Monogamy as a one-sided expression of social structures is called into question and Schippers frames this as "mononormativity."[7] Schippers approaches compulsory monogamy as the institutionalized provision that forces people into this monogamous reality. She states that for many people it is an unspoken assumption that their relationship has a monogamous character. According to her, many people think that couples who do not behave monogamously will "calm down" sooner or later—but, in fact, this assumption functions as a dismissal of nonmonogamous relationships as immature and belonging to a transitional phase.[8]

Schippers approaches the phenomenon of polyamory in a specific way because of her own theoretical interests. She uses the so-called FMM-relationship as a starting point, where one woman has a relationship with two men. This is in contrast to the MFF-relationship, in which one man has a relationship with two women. According to Schippers, her choice offers the possibility of illustrating how compulsory monogamy and entrenched notions of what is masculine and feminine can be broken.[9] The Dutch national newspaper *Trouw* reports that since 2005 the Netherlands has had a foundation called *Polyamory*. The newspaper quotes writer Simone van Saarloos and her pamphlet "The Monogamous Drama" [translation by authors]. Van Saarloos moves in the same direction as Schippers. She affirms the necessarily open character of polyamorous relationships. They are not always linear in nature (ever onwards and upwards), but the character of these relationships can be, for example, continuous and playful.[10]

From a theology of desire, and transformational framework, it may help to reflect on polyamory. Polyamory, we believe, may lead to a separation of *eros* and *agape* and that is not preferable. On the contrary, we would like to see them kept together very closely. Approaching desire from a theological perspective has something *exclusive* about it, because it requires connectedness and surrender. And, as many of us know, this is already very complicated between two people, let alone between several. It makes sense to keep emphasizing, from a reality-based point of view, that pure desire, real connection, and complete surrender do not come naturally. Expecting relationships to be perfect, especially in the area of sexuality, is risky because desire can then be used as an excuse

7. Schippers, *Beyond Monogamy*, 12.
8. Schippers, *Beyond Monogamy*, 13.
9. Schippers, *Beyond Monogamy*, 32.
10. Van Saarloos, "Monogame drama."

to enter into other relationships. While Schippers perceives the nature of monogamy as obligatory, this can be experienced differently through transformation, over time, because the relationship then stems from a deep desire in which the physical and spiritual coincide. The fact that for many people a monogamous relationship is an unspoken assumption may also point to this type of relationship being the most desirable. Although of a different nature, the polygynous relationships we read about in chapter 4 caused plenty of problems, not only on a personal level but also in the political and administrative spheres. Think of Hannah, Elkanah, and Peninnah (1 Sam 1) and David and Solomon.

Purity and Virginity

Purity and virginity are dominant themes in sexuality, as we noted in our first chapter. They still play a major role in religious communities in many countries and communities, and they are still taboo in many places. The question we want to ask is: what is the function of purity and virginity in our current context? At this point, we will not dive too deep into specific biblical-theological arguments, but we will focus on the ways in which people think about purity and virginity in some (Christian) circles and reframe this thinking toward a theology of desire. The Christian tradition has always paid much attention to purity. A whole range of concepts and themes play a major role here: whether or not to live a celibate life, whether or not to have sex before marriage, virginity, and so on.

We can generally say, though with some caution, that the church has a love-hate relationship with each of these concepts. Frank Bosman is correct when he writes: "Sexuality, often in combination with concepts such as physicality and femininity, was and is associated with sinfulness, and sometimes even with more anthropological categories such as filth or uncleanness."[11] In a lecture entitled "Why Do Christians Always Fuss about Sex?" which he presented at the University of the Netherlands, Bosman discusses the conflict that exists in relation to sexuality and the concepts mentioned.[12] Although critical voices about the role of the church can be heard throughout the centuries, it is clear that taboo and conflicting ideas are not only to be found in Christian circles. According to Bosman, what is lacking is language that helps to discuss the beautiful

11. Universiteit van Nederland. "Waarom doen christenen."
12. Universiteit van Nederland. "Waarom doen christenen."

and the darker sides of human sexuality at the same time, in a caring and nonanxious way. Themes such as connectedness and (self-)surrender can then be discussed (cf. chapter 5). In his lecture, Bosman points out the extent to which virginity and celibacy were seen as ideal, often on the basis of a one-sided reading of biblical texts such as Matt 19 and 1 Cor 7. Along with Bosman, we see and acknowledge the complex and dark side of sexuality. At the same time, we think we should take an honest look at the extent to which concepts such as purity and virginity form a part of oppressive patterns.

A few years ago, so-called purity balls, specially organized chastity galas in the US, attracted a lot of media attention. The newspaper *Trouw* reported about it in 2007. An example is US Pastor Randy Wilson and his wife, who organized ceremonies in which fathers take vows with their daughters in front of everyone:

> I, (daughter's name)'s father, choose before God to cover my daughter as her authority and protection in the area of purity. I will be pure in my own life as a man, husband and father. I will be a man of integrity and accountability as I lead, guide and pray over my daughter and my family as the high priest in my home. This covering will be used by God to influence generations to come.[13]

The ceremony has wedding-like features, and it is striking that the daughters promise God and their father that they will remain virgins until after their (church) wedding. There is a party, purity rings are exchanged, and, says Bosman, "an intriguing detail is of course that this purity is expressed almost exclusively in physiological terms: the daughter must remain a virgin until marriage. Her body does not belong to herself, but to God the Creator, who—for the sake of convenience—is represented by her father and—later—by her husband."[14]

Like Bosman, we feel this practice is problematic, and indeed it is "difficult to say which is a bigger problem: the pseudo-incestuous language or the old-fashioned notion that fathers own their daughters and their sexuality."[15] And another important question: how is purity defined here? Where does this definition come from? Are there perhaps values other than purity that should be imparted to young women so that they

---

13. http://www.generationsoflight.com/; cf. "Kuisheidsbals nieuwe rage in VS."
14. Bosman, *God houdt van seks*, 15–16.
15. Valenti, *Purity Myth*, 69.

can grow up to be independent, mature, and moral people? Doesn't this mean that sexuality is once again labelled as dirty? Is it possible to have a more positive view of female sexuality? This practice reeks of a one-sided and unnecessary sexualization of young women. Why does this ceremony not exist for men? The whole pattern of binary thinking and the affirmation of predetermined gender norms is joined in with this practice.

We see that long-standing definitions of what is masculine and feminine have an enormous influence on what is meant by "purity." Purity and virginity are therefore not separate issues in this discussion. It would be interesting to do further research into the way in which, for example, purity and virginity are discussed and experienced within Christian student associations.

In another article in the Dutch newspaper *Trouw*, gynecologist Ineke van Seumeren writes about the ways in which women's virginity is considered in different cultures.[16] Under the heading "Virginity Is Not Medically Demonstrable," she discusses reports about female demonstrators who were "virginity tested" on Tahrir Square in Egypt because people wanted to prevent soldiers from being falsely accused of rape. According to the authorities, the fact that the women who were "tested" had camped on the notorious square was sufficient reason to assume that they were no longer virgins, and so the authorities could prosecute them for prostitution.

Van Seumeren opens up a debate about what she calls "the myth of virginity" and refers to similar incidents in India, where young women were "tested" to prove their virginity after reporting rape. Van Seumeren writes that the women had to undergo a so-called "finger test": a gynecologist would insert two fingers (the size of a penis) in a woman's vagina to assess whether she had already had sex. The women in whom two fingers were easily inserted were considered to have provoked the rape themselves because it had now been "proven" that they had been sexually active.

Van Seumeren explains that the idea that virginity is medically demonstrable is still alive and well in the wider public. Even in the Netherlands, many people are convinced of this. From a medical point of view, however, it is a different matter: "the hymen is not a dense membrane. In most cases it is a small flexible rim, sometimes hard and rigid, sometimes jagged or crescent-shaped. It varies from woman to woman and says nothing about virginity. A vagina is made to let a baby through, it

---

16. Van Seumeren, "Maagdelijkheid is niet medisch aantoonbaar."

is an illusion to think that a vagina stretches from something as small as a penis."[17] These horrific and traumatic incidents, and the thinking that underpins them, are a means to restrict and oppress women. Of course, cultural patterns of values and norms elicit such incidents and Van Seumeren states that this can involve serious violations of human rights.

Jessica Valenti makes similar points to Van Seumeren when she discusses the way virginity is defined.[18] Valenti also argues that although virginity has been discussed with great authority for thousands of years, there is still no single workable medical definition. She wonders what exactly do we mean when we try define it, for example, as the situation in which a man or woman has not yet had sex with a partner. If this definition refers only to sex in a heterosexual relationship, what does it mean for other sexual relationships? Moreover, this definition narrows the definition of sex, because it limits it to penetrative sexual intercourse. We then arrive at the same point that Van Seumeren warns against: why must we determine whether penetration has taken place? What do we know then? Of course, discussion about virginity tends to focus mainly on women. Here too, the debate over what is normative with regard to "male" and "female" plays a major role.

Valenti shows that in American culture the desirable virgin is young, white, and skinny. She is usually a cheerleader, a babysitter, and is almost never disabled. Many conservative schools work to confirm this image and do their best to educate students that virginity is the standard and desirable. For example, students (and it is almost always only the female students) are given vouchers, a sort of credit card, with writing such as: "Don't accept the lie, save sex for marriage." Or they are given a pin in the shape of a rose, with a card that says: "You are like this rose. Every time you have sex before your marriage, a petal will fall off the rose. Make sure that your future husband is not just holding a bare stem."

Valenti generously admits that many of these practices are not unrelated to the ubiquity of pornography. The virginity movement acts as a kind of contrast, often defined in opposition to pornography, and is seen as an antidote to it. The leaders of the virginity movement seem to need pornography in order to make a solid case for their purity campaigns. And rather than have nuanced conversations, it is easier to say that almost everything is of a pornographic nature. Others point out that

17. Van Seumeren, "Maagdelijkheid is niet medisch aantoonbaar," para. 3.
18. Valenti, *Purity Myth*, 19–22.

these practices reveal a deeper problem: *femiphobia*, the difficulty that people, especially men, have with anyone who presents themself as too feminine.[19] Masculinity is said to be hard-won and must therefore also be defended in a strongly binary-oriented culture. Stephen Ducat makes it clear when he names the related fear that being more reciprocal in relationships blurs the boundaries between what is masculine and feminine, making them more permeable.[20] In other words, gender fluidity is a problem and is particularly undesirable in cultures with rigid gender roles and hierarchies.

It is important to pay attention to the importance of gender from a framework of desire and transformation. Purity balls, and their relationship between father and daughter, are reminiscent of Old Testament practices where possession was central. Transformation in Christ and by the Spirit, in which there is redemption and freedom, serves as a necessary perspective for how we look at masculinity and femininity. There is no room for owning or controlling the other or for double standards.

It makes sense to think about virginity from the perspective of Mary's virgin conception. Mary's virginity is associated with being pregnant and this is extraordinary. It functions as a paradox to make clear that Jesus was God's Son and that no man was needed for this: it is entirely God's initiative. At the same time, there are many women in Jesus's genealogical line who were also in extraordinary (in one way or another) relationships, at God's initiative, and who God used to bring about change and breakthrough. Tamar was childless (in Gen 38) and sought out her father-in-law to become pregnant. Rahab did something remarkable by hiding scouts as a prostitute in Jericho. And Ruth lay down with Boaz in the middle of the night while he slept.

Throughout church history, Mary's virginity has been valued differently—as an ideal, but also as a sign of God's intervention in this world. The latter seems the most theologically correct. Mary cannot be held up as an example for all women when it comes to virginity: men and women are to go forth and multiply. Thus, even Calvin denied the relationship between virginity, purity, and holiness.[21]

We can also comment on this from an ecclesiological and eschatological point of view. Metaphorically speaking, men are also the bride of Christ. When the unity of husband and wife in marriage is used as

19. Valenti, *Purity Myth*, 168–70.

20. Ducat, *Wimp Factor*.

21. Huijgen, *Maria*, 325.

a metaphor for the mystery between Christ and the church, it is not so much the gender roles that are decisive, but the unity and connectedness (within community). In the Old Testament, but also in other places, we see that God compares God's relationship with the people of Israel with that of a man and a woman. Another example is 2 Cor 11:2: "I am watching over you as God watches over you. I have married you to one man, Christ, and I want to give you to him as a chaste bride." Chaste can also be translated as "virginal" and Paul seems to use the Hebrew cultural idea that a father is responsible for his daughter. Of course, in this case it is not about sexual virginity, but about a life focused on the bridegroom, on following Christ. The congregation is the "property" of Christ and therein lies great security. This security, however, goes far beyond a transaction, like the transition of property from father to husband. This security comes from God's love and from the fact that God is the Creator, who made us in God's own image. This is why we must be careful in our understanding of metaphorical language and pay attention to other metaphors for the congregation, for example, the body of Christ.

Finally, from a reading of Revelation 21 we can understand that this bride of God is coming; she is presented in this chapter of Revelation as the new Jerusalem (verse 2) and as the woman of the Lamb (verse 9). It is also striking how differently these metaphors are used; they are intermingled without any difficulty. After all, there is no mention of the bride with the bridegroom, but of the bride and the lamb. This discussion shows that we must be careful not to elevate virginity above all other matters and that we cannot link in gender in such a way that it only concerns women. We think Sarah Coakley's pneumatological insights (see chapter 5) are helpful to consider here. And, finally, these metaphors speak to our transformational framework and God's desire for all humans. The gender (roles) of the bride and groom are not the focus; we are all one in Christ Jesus—we are all the bride.

Disability, Illness, and Sexuality

I (René) remember a conversation, in the context of the appointment of a new colleague, about a study into the meaning of illness and disability. The soon to be colleague had applied for a job and, as an interview committee, we were impressed by the way biblical texts on disability and impairment were considered in her presentation. The interpretation of a text like Mark 2:1–5, about the paralyzed man who was brought to Jesus by his four friends, was challenging. The focus is on the man who has been sick and limited for such a long time. And, in a way, that determines the interpretation of the text. However, the colleague pointed out to us that we are all really only temporarily limited. Of course, she was referring to a very specific physical disability, but we are all limited people. We are all, at best, temporarily disabled. In fact, this changes the way we talk about (physical) disability and illness.

In her analysis, Deborah Beth Creamer illustrates that different people are confronted with (a severe) disability in different ways.[22] When it comes to sexuality, there are many challenges similar to those faced by people who do not have (the same) disabilities. There are single people who struggle with, for example, severe physical disabilities, as well as married couples, and so on. According to Creamer, many people will have unique problems that others simply do not face: specific obstacles or difficulties that hinder meaningful sexual expression. In an attempt to define disability and limitation, Creamer reviews a number of models, starting with a somewhat stricter medical model.[23] This medical approach to disability actually has as its ideal the "normal" and "healthy" body; body parts or functions or the *persons* that deviate from this are then considered "impaired" or "disabled." There is a strong focus on trying to normalize or eliminate that disability. Seen in this way, a disability functions as a problem in or around the body and this should be avoided wherever possible.

We should perceive it immediately: this model does not tell the whole story, no matter how hard we try, and even though it serves as a core model in our society. It is fair to say that it is a one-sided model that it does not do justice to the experiences of people living with (severe) disabilities. Creamer shows that the medical model is particularly suspect because the so-called problem of being "limited" or "disabled" is not so much to be found within individual bodies and individual people as in the responses (or lack of response) and systemic patterns of how we react to disability in society. Think, for example, of the emphasis (or lack of emphasis) on making buildings wheelchair accessible.[24]

Creamer sees another approach in the social model of disability. In this model, limitations and impairments are mainly seen as a social

22. Creamer, "Disabled People," 676.

23. Creamer, "Disabled People," 676–79; Iantaffi and Mize, "Disability," 408–21.

24. Creamer, "Disabled People."

problem and less as a physical or medical problem. It is interesting to see that social constructivist thinking also plays a role here, as we saw before in views on gender (see chapters 2 and 3).[25] Restriction and what constitutes restriction is primarily a social construct, and it moves along on the waves of culture and the norms and values that people ascribe to it. And indeed, one must admit that the labels people are given, or use to self-describe, differ and shifts may occur as medical and social knowledges are combined; just think, for example, of the difference between the way we think about autism spectrum disorders today and the way autism was thought about twenty years ago.

Creamer refers to the example of leprosy to illustrate the difference between past and present approaches.[26] An approach that is within the social approach category is the model of disability that is mainly seen from a minority perspective. The emphasis is on the concept that people with disabilities have been minoritized and marginalized; disabled people have been oppressed, excluded, and often discriminated against. In this sense, we could speak of similar problems as we see in racism and sexism. For example, people have less opportunity to find a good job and employers are not, or hardly, willing to provide adapted facilities, reasonable adjustments, supports, etc. Although many supports and services are well organized in some countries, this remains a subject of attention for the government and many social organizations.[27]

Another classical model can be found in the so-called moral model. In this model, a restriction, limitation, or impairment was primarily a sign of a curse resting on someone. It was often seen as the result of disbelief or even of certain sins that someone may have committed. In fact, a moral value is attributed to the restriction (created or present).[28]

Finally, Creamer refers to the boundary model, which is in line with the interview presentation of the aforementioned colleague. This model points to the fact that no one lives without limitations and boundaries; limitations are a normal part of our human existence. As we grow older, the chance that we will experience some form of physical, mental, or psychological impairment increases. One person may need glasses to be able to write this text, another to read it, and another may need support with

25. Liddiard, "Theorising Disabled," 37–52.

26. Creamer, "Disabled People," 677.

27. See the website of the Dutch Government, "Rechten van mensen met een beperking."

28. Creamer, "Disabled People," 678.

their hearing, and so on. Many tools are fortunately there to assist us and nobody can do without them; independence is an illusion! Creamer argues that from this perspective, thinking about disability with respect to other models becomes arbitrary because it gives the false impression that people can be divided into two groups: those who live with a disability and those who are not hindered by a disability.

What does this mean for the experience of sexuality? Creamer follows Mollow and McRuer in their analysis. They conclude, on the basis of a large study in the US, that "whenever sex and disability are linked in American culture, this usually leads to marginalization or astonishment; the sexuality of people with disabilities is usually portrayed in terms of 'defective' or 'freaky and extreme.'"[29] The cultural norm—not surprisingly—is: the sexiest people are young, fit, and active. So, there is clearly an interaction between moral notions about disability and moral notions about sexuality.

In the previous chapter, we concentrated on the importance of sexual desire and its theological significance. The question that can rightly be asked, then, is how sexual desire relates to limitations. If sex is aimed at desire and limitations are seen as undesirable, what do we do with that? If we see sexuality as a "normal" physical expression (even if there is more to it than just physicality) and people with disabilities as physically "abnormal," this could lead to the conclusion that sexuality is not relevant for people with (severe) disabilities.[30]

However, this possible conclusion is unjustified and harmful. It does not do justice to what is really going on. Creamer points out that the history of the relationship between sex and disability is a complicated one, with legal, political, and relational dimensions in which people with disabilities have often been wronged.[31] Research also shows that people with disabilities experience domestic and sexual violence more often than the average. This concerns not only people with physical disabilities, but also those who have to contend with other mental health, developmental, or cognitive limitations. Creamer is right in saying that we must be careful not to pathologize limitations, especially where sexuality is concerned. She points to the many good examples in art, literature, manuals, and research, which show that sexuality and disability can be highlighted in a positive and truthful way. Central to this is creativity for what is possible

29. Creamer, "Disabled People," 679; McRuer, *Crip Theory*.

30. Liddiard, "Theorising Disabled," 39.

31. Creamer, "Disabled People," 680.

and attention to the ways in which people with a (serious) disability or a damaged body, for example, can have a positive experience of sexuality.

It also shows that in this broken world, sexuality is always limited. What is clear is that illness, in whatever form and in a general sense, has an impact on people's sexuality, either temporarily or for a longer period of time. Alex Iantaffi and Sara Mize point out that too often people with disabilities are not seen as sexual beings, especially by health professionals, and the complexities surrounding gender, sexual orientation, ethnicity, and socioeconomic status are not sufficiently considered.[32]

The stories, and especially the prejudices, about people with disabilities who choose to invite professional sex workers to help them with their sexual needs are legion.[33] At the same time, these stories show that there are real problems regarding people with intellectual disabilities and how this relates to their own individual sexual choices.

As we saw in chapter 4, the themes of the body and physicality are discussed in the Bible. We can even say that limitation is also discussed in the many stories in the Old and New Testaments; just think back, for example, to the story from Mark 2 at the beginning of this section. The issue of physical limitation also arises in theological discussions about the body. The early Christian discussions about the nature of Jesus, and about his physicality—particularly his incarnation—have had a great influence on our thinking. Researchers have increasingly made room for other interpretations of disability and sexuality, whether based on a different understanding of the image of God or on deeper reflections on the theological meaning of, for example, dementia, Down syndrome, or cognitive impairment.[34]

The core in all of this is always that God is on the side of what is broken and violated, and that Jesus was broken and violated, and is so close to us in our hurt. Desire as embodied grace, and the imperfection of desire throughout the course of life, can be seen exactly where there is limitation and (severe) disability (cf. chapter 5). The contradictions of life and precisely the imperfections and vulnerabilities visible in it matter for human sexuality too. In this sense, sex is much more than the ability to achieve an orgasm. There is no such thing as perfect sex. Sex does not redeem, but by God's grace it becomes grace-filled.

32. Liddiard, "Theorising Disabled," 41.

33. Iantaffi and Mize, "Disability," 414–15; Wotton, "Paid Sexual Services," 433–49.

34. Eiesland, *Disabled God*. Eiesland, "Encountering the Disabled God," 10–15; Lewis, *Deaf Liberation Theology*; Swinton, *Dementia*.

Desire takes on the form of embodied grace. A human being is more than his or her limitations, in whatever sense. Physical, intellectual, or any other kind of limitation does not define the way sexuality is expressed. Sexuality has a place in the relationships between people where it can, in all its limitations, even when those limitations are severe. For those who guide and support in a caring role, this requires tact, sensitivity, and the ability to take time to offer space for people to experience intimacy.

Sex in the Marketplace—Love and Sex Online

There is no doubt that major changes are taking place to do with sexuality and relationships.[35] Earlier in this book, we pointed out some of the trends that can clearly be observed: sex is increasingly becoming a consumer product, different relationship models are developing, (sexual) violence and abuse are becoming more visible in large sections of society, and, together with Heleen Zorgdrager, we wondered whether the impact of the sexual revolution has been sufficiently digested. Within these trends, we find the themes of "sex in the marketplace" and "sexuality online." Here we refer to a wide range of radical changes, but especially to the fact that sex (and love) is increasingly available through (the anonymity of) the internet. The Israeli philosopher Aaron Ben-Ze'ev, a leading expert in the field of emotion research, points to the social space that has been created by the development of cyberspace, the virtual space that has gradually taken over more and more of our lives in recent decades.[36] Millions of people are surfing this virtual space at the same time and are experiencing romantic relationships, sex, etc. There is enormous attraction in all these possibilities. People immerse themselves in a space of seduction.

Research shows that it is an intense experience in this seemingly imaginary world. Ben-Ze'ev wonders if we can speak of new types of emotions and new forms of romantic relationships. Can online and offline relationships be compared? What kind of relationships is this computer- or television-based communication presupposing or developing? We see one-on-one relationships, of course, but also group relationships, people who make contact with characters who, as it turns out, are created from fantasy, anonymous relationships, and so on. The forms are multiple: text, video, audio, or combinations thereof. Contact via e-mail,

35. Zorgdrager, *Tussen Hooglied en #MeToo;* Erwich, "Practical Theology."
36. Ben-Ze'ev, *Love Online.*

SMS, or other text-based messaging systems are among the most common, often without revealing the true identity of the parties involved.[37]

According to Ben-Ze'ev, we should not see cyberspace as opposed to visible reality; according to him, it is fully part of our reality.

The interactive nature of this online reality reinforces its social and psychological dynamics. Ben-Ze'ev rightly states that the movement made from a passive imaginary reality to an interactive virtual reality is of a different and more radical nature than the movement from photos to film. In fact, this is correct because in online spaces there is human interaction, quite apart from the question of the *quality* of that interaction. In all sorts of ways, the boundaries of reality are becoming blurred. All kinds of forms of fantasy are accessible at the click of a mouse and the lure of this is great, as are the risks involved.[38]

"Cyberlove," the experience of a romantic relationship based on computer-mediated communication, is no longer the exception. Although your virtual partner is not physically present, and may be anonymous, the intensity of the experience is characterized as being just as intense as an "offline" relationship. Ben-Ze'ev uses a narrower definition than cyberlove when defining "cybersex." He describes cybersex as the social interaction between at least two people who send live digital messages to each other with the aim of sexual arousal. People send erotic messages to each other that can lead to orgasm.[39] According to Ben-Ze'ev, the attraction to cybersex lies mainly in the freedom of imagination, the interactive nature, the availability, and certainly also the anonymity. Research shows that people feel freer and the anonymity, in particular, makes them feel they are taking fewer risks and facing fewer undesirable consequences. We also observe a fear of long-term commitment, but people are keen to give space to their passions. Research seems to indicate that people are prepared to open up more online than in offline relationships.[40] Cyberspace relationships are characterized by a number of aspects that, in many ways, seem opposite to those of offline relationships. According to Ben-Ze'ev: distance and immediacy, specific and rich communication, anonymity and self-disclosure, sincerity and disappointment, continuity and discontinuity, low physical investment, and considerable mental

37. Ben-Ze'ev, *Love Online*, 1.
38. Ben-Ze'ev, *Love Online*, 93.
39. Ben-Ze'ev, *Love Online*, 5.
40. Ben-Ze'ev, *Love Online*, 18–20.

investment are all at play.[41] Undoubtedly, it would be interesting to look at this phenomenon from more and different research perspectives.

The reality of online love, sex, and romance is a fact, no matter what we think of it. It forms the background against which many other developments are taking place. Sex and romance are for sale and a billion-dollar industry has developed around them. The arrival of the internet has unmistakably led to an enormous shift in how we experience sex and love.[42] Ronald Weitzer (a professor of sociology in the US) discusses this shift in detail. In 2006 alone, Americans spent $13.3 billion on erotic magazines, live sex shows, strip clubs, erotic films, and pornographic material via cable TV and internet connections, and telephone sex. Between 1995 and 2005, the number of pornographic films made doubled: from 5,700 to just under 14,000. Weitzer claims that the figures for Europe are not much different, for example, when it comes to the use of paid sex. In Europe, the percentage of men who paid for sex in a specific period seems to be around 15 percent, according to Weitzer, but according to other sources, it was at a lower level. Related to a program on national radio, Ine Vanwesenbeeck, professor of sexual development at the University of Utrecht, stated:

> The number of questions asked in the census about people paying for sex is steadily decreasing. In 2011, people were still asked, but mainly about paying for sexual intercourse, and that really doesn't cover it all. And back then, 2.3 percent (1 in 43 men) of men aged between 19 and 69 said they had done so.[43]

An earlier study revealed other figures.[44] To the two questions asked about paying for sex, 21 percent of men between the ages of fifteen and seventy answered "yes." To a follow-up question of whether they had done so in the previous year, 4.2 percent replied that they had. In that case, it could be one in twenty-four men.

Weitzer also points to the increased privatization of sexual services and products. Porn has moved from the film booths or small cinemas to the living room. The advent of stable internet connections and, certainly more recently, fiber internet, has only confirmed this move.

---

41. Ben-Ze'ev, *Love Online*, 27.
42. Weitzer, *Sex for Sale*.
43. Cf. Radio EenVandaag, "Feit of fictie."
44. Vanwesenbeeck, Bakker, and Gesell, "Sexual Health in the Netherlands."

The internet has not only caused the relocation of pornography but it has also given a new dimension to the work of sex workers.[45] However, the image of the sex work has not changed very much; it is still often seen as a dark business that one should stay away from. It is interesting to see that the social sciences are linked to two almost contradictory positions when it comes to sex work: condemnation versus normalization and regulation.

In addition to the group that is condemning sex workers—often also from a Christian background—there is a group that characterizes sex work as being under the strong influence of patriarchal gender relations. Sex work is then identical with exploitation, oppression, and violence against women, in whatever context. The verdict on pornography, strippers, and other commercial forms within the sex industry is then similar. The only solution is the eradication of the entire sex industry. Additional prejudices also abound. It is still common to think that all sex workers were sexually abused as children, or forced into the industry at the age of thirteen or fourteen, and so on. Weitzer shows that language plays an important role in how we think about the sex industry: sexual slavery, paid rape, survivors, etc. Clients are then portrayed (as a counter-image) as sexual predators. We will come back to these characterizations and their value, especially when it comes to the complexity of research on this theme, and for now we note that the research is often anecdotal in nature, generalizations are commonplace, and counter-evidence is often ignored.

At the other end of the social sciences spectrum, there is usually more support and confirmation.[46] Here, the emphasis is on the way in which sex work is—and is allowed to be—real work, based on clear employment frameworks and protections. The central idea underlying this is that sex work can, in principle, be organized in a way that is safe and careful for all parties involved and can thus, in fact, be seen as any other economic transaction. In this view, violence and coercion are not seen as core aspects of the work. According to Weitzer, both perspectives are limited because they are too one-dimensional: there is simply much more variation than can be locked into two paradigms. He would rather view the whole phenomenon from a more varied model. He introduces a series of variables that one should want to look at, with the aim of better mapping out what is actually happening.[47] We will now zoom in on two

45. Weitzer, *Sex for Sale*, 1–2.
46. Weitzer, *Sex for Sale*, 5–6.
47. Weitzer, *Sex for Sale*, 5–6.

important phenomena that are concrete examples of sex in the marketplace: prostitution and pornography.

Prostitution

If you pick up any dictionary, you will find different definitions of prostitution. Wikipedia gives the following: "Prostitution" is derived from the Latin words for *pro* (= in front) and *stature* (= to place, set down).[48] A literal meaning would therefore be: to display, to put in front, to put on show. Janell Carroll defines prostitution slightly differently: "The act of a male or female engaging in sexual activity in exchange for money or other material goods."[49] Weitzer categorizes different kinds of prostitution (call girl, escort, brothel worker, massage salon worker, bar-club or casino worker, street worker) and connects various contextual details (location of work, price, exploitation levels) and risks (violence and threats) to the types of prostitution.

The limitation of the data presented in Weitzer's research is that it only refers to female sex workers. Furthermore, he notes that the group of sex workers active in brothels and massage parlors does not include workers who are victims of human trafficking, and others who are working in prostitution against their will. With regard to the term "exploitation," Weitzer assumes that there is a third party who gains financially from the work. The overview makes it clear that prostitution has many faces and does not only take place on the street. We have no figures or evidence to check this, but Weitzer claims that, compared to street workers, sex workers who are active indoors are less likely to have abuse, incest, and/or violence in their background. They are also less likely to engage in risky behavior.[50] A British comparative study among two groups of prostitutes (street workers and workers in saunas) showed that street workers were more often beaten, robbed, threatened with weapons, kidnapped, or raped. In most cases, the street workers were much more likely to experience these forms of violence and abuse.[51]

---

48. Wikipedia, s.v. "Prostitution," accessed June 14, 2024, https://en.wikipedia.org/wiki/Prostitution.

49. Carroll, *Sexuality Now,* 524.

50. Weitzer, *Sex for Sale,* 9–10.

51. Weitzer, *Sex for Sale,* 9–10.

Who becomes a prostitute? What motivates men and women to work as sex workers? Carroll wonders how much this has to do with money. Or is there some other necessity? According to Carroll and others, the majority of those working in the sex industry seem to be motivated by financial gain.[52] The idea that it is mainly women who end up in prostitution because they love sex or are addicted to it is a myth. Research shows that the majority of women who are sex workers do not really enjoy their work. Moreover, a study from 2003 shows that about 89 percent would consider leaving.[53] Carroll shows that the majority of female prostitutes live in groups with each other, with the group functioning as a pseudo-family.[54] Carroll points to research that shows starting out as a sex worker is usually a gradual process.[55] Interestingly, however, the common factor is often a background of poverty.

Carroll puts this into perspective, explaining that many studies focus too one-sidedly on women from a low socioeconomic background and this would lead to a somewhat distorted picture. Frequent sexual contact in superficial relationships at a young age also seems to be a factor, as does inter-familial violence and abuse. Black women who have a history of being emotionally and physically abused also appear more likely to become involved in prostitution than white women. Another important group who are more likely to try prostitution are children who have been abused and run away from home. Carroll emphasizes that these factors lead to higher risk factors, but do not automatically turn women into sex workers.

Weitzer goes into detail about policy in the US, which in recent years has been more strongly aimed at confronting those who visit prostitutes rather than the prostitutes themselves. The age-old debate of criminalization versus legalization remains at the center of policy discussions, although in the US (and elsewhere) it clearly seems that the trend toward criminalization is at the forefront. Anti-prostitution groups and organizations are aimed at putting an end to paid sex.[56] Perhaps the best-known example is the Swedish system, in which legislation was developed that focused unilaterally on punishing the visitors to sex workers. Since its introduction in Sweden, many other countries have also considered

---

52. Carroll, *Sexuality Now*, 525–28.

53. Farley, "Prostitution," 247–80.

54. Romenesko and Miller, "Second Step in Double Jeopardy," 109–35; Carroll, *Sexuality Now*.

55. Carroll, *Sexuality Now*.

56. Weitzer, *Sex for Sale*, 30.

adopting this approach. The motivations of the predominantly male visitors to prostitutes are manifold: availability of sex workers, knowledge of the location, the relative anonymity, the desire for specific sexual acts, emotional intimacy, and seeing sex as a commodity. There are no unambiguous reasons, and it is certainly not the case that the majority of visitors are out to mistreat women.

Weitzer reports that motivations also differ by social background. Men with a university education seem more inclined to succumb to the excitement of illicit sex. Married men tend to seek sexual behavior that cannot be experienced with their spouse, while unmarried men report the difficulty of finding regular and traditional relationships as a reason. Although these insights are not really surprising, more research could help. Especially if the possible relationship between perceptions of masculinity and sexuality on the one hand, and a possible future search for sex workers on the other, is better mapped out.[57]

A much bigger problem is, of course, international human trafficking, which certainly cannot be seen in isolation from the worldwide context. Fortunately, much progress has been made in combating it. According to some, the great evil behind trafficking women is prostitution alone, and this is what keeps it going. Related to this is the ever-present debate over legalization versus criminalization.

Weitzer tries to take a nuanced position when he states the importance of paying attention to careful, targeted interventions that help women who have been forced into sex work, whether or not in the context of trafficking. He does not shy away from criticizing what he calls the "moral crusades" used by some organizations. Fortunately, there are examples of many good and careful practices, also in our own country. The good work done in the Netherlands by the *Scarlet Cord* has been impressive. This national organization is part of a larger Christian foundation offering all kinds of social services. Its work among women who are active as sex workers focuses on specific preventions and resilience. From a Christian perspective, staff work to support those who are coerced into working in the sex industry. The *Scarlet Cord* opposes the idea that sex work is only ever just work. It points to experiences of violence, the development of a negative self-image, and psychological disorders, and states that 60 percent of all victims of trafficking end up in prostitution.[58]

57. Weitzer, *Sex for Sale.*

58. See Scharlaken koord.

Weitzer's claim that the majority of sex workers do not experience their work as positive is confirmed by this organization. They focus on dignity and justice and do not judge the sex workers or ask them to stop working. On the website, stories and experiences of (former) sex workers can be read. Some of the broader debate is presented on the website under the heading "opinion." This section takes a closer look at the crucial concept of "coercion," but also delves into recent research on prostitution and violence. Questions of protection, compulsory education, the effects on the environment, etc. are raised. The contrast with the more economic approaches seems to be that of social responsibility. Here, as we saw with Weitzer, the role of the client, visitor, or sex buyer is examined.

Dutch government policy is geared toward the safe and healthy exercise of the profession. On the government website, this is emphatically addressed.[59] Unsafe sex, unhygienic working conditions, forced sex work, and exploitation, violence, and prejudice hinder this. There are references to exit programs and also to the regulations and conditions for working in the prostitution sector. You can find brochures with information and there are references to the Coordination Centre for Human Trafficking (CoMensha). The Regulation of Sex Work Act is in the process of finalization, but it has yet to be put to the vote in Parliament. The draft law contains an impressive amount of background description, not only with respect to the realization of the law, but also concerning other important background information and research.[60]

In chapter 2, we wrote that prostitution was often permitted throughout church history because it was seen as less terrible than wasting seed through masturbation, since the male seed was thought to have potential life in it. One-sided interpretations of Genesis 38 undoubtedly played a role in this. Onan interrupted sexual intercourse with his brother's wife, which was not actually about masturbation. Prostitution does not have a positive ring to it, especially when power, abuse, and human trafficking are involved. From a framework (presented in chapter 5) of desire, reciprocity, and embodied grace, it is justified to ask critical questions about prostitution. Contrary to much of (church) history, masturbation, then, can have a positive meaning (precisely for this reason, that is, not visiting a prostitute) as long as the masturbation does not take place in public, and will not cause any damage to another person, or to the one

59. "Beleid voor een veilige en gezonde seksbranche." This website is run by the Dutch Government.

60. "Memorie van Toelichting Wet regulering sekswerk."

who masturbates (as, for example, when it becomes an addiction). Even in the context of connectedness and reciprocity, masturbation can play a significant role in knowing one's own desire (with a view to one's partner) and knowing one's partner's desire. This will be different for people who have been single for a long time or do not have a partner at all. It would be strange to assume that they do not (or no longer) have any sexual desires.

Pornography

There is nothing new under the sun and since the dawn of mankind, people have made images of themselves and their surroundings. Think of painted naked figures in caves and of the many representations that could be deemed as explicitly erotic.[61] The fascination with what was naked and/ or erotic, as depicted on papyri or walls, has always been strong. From the earliest history, Carroll argues, erotic art aimed to excite the viewer. But was this already pornography? According to Carroll, we can only speak of pornography as a separate category from the mid-eighteenth century. As discussed earlier, until that time, sexuality was much more embedded in the religious and moral context and was not designated as a separate area of attention. Before the beginning of the nineteenth century, overt sexual depictions were rare. This is not to say that there were no overt allusions to erotic acts.

The discovery of Pompeii made it clear that the public nature of sexuality and erotic depictions and symbology was a fact. Carroll points to the ubiquitous phallus symbols on every street corner, including the numerous erotic frescoes in houses.[62] And one only has to look at some of Shakespeare's plays to see that they are teeming with allusions to sex. Much like we have discussed the advent of the internet, the invention of the printing press, and then the wide availability of printed text (and images), certainly contributed to the development of pornography.

One of the best-known early pornographic works is *Memoirs of a Woman of Pleasure* (John Cleland, 1748), also known as *Fanny Hill*. The aim of the book was clear: to provide the reader with excitement. The BBC adapted this controversial book into two filmic episodes around 2007 and brought it to a wide audience. *Fanny Hill* tells the story of a young country girl who is lured into prostitution in London. Carroll rightly argues

---

61. Carroll, *Sexuality Now*, 510–11.
62. Carroll, *Sexuality Now*, 510–11.

that this story (and probably others) shows that the meaning of the term "pornography" must be seen within a specific discourse. The story of pornography is not only about the publication of erotic material, but also about the struggle between those who produce it and want to distribute it and those who try to stop its production and distribution.[63] This dynamic largely determines whether material is seen as *erotica* or as *pornography*: what is erotica to one person is porn to another. The central question remains, of course, what role both play in, for instance, the experience of one's own sexuality. It is interesting to note, as Carroll does, that one group of people opposed to the production and distribution of pornography may include radical left-wing feminist scientists and right-wing fundamentalist preachers working together. And just as unlikely bedfellows work together to defend pornography, often under the guise of the limitation of free speech! Thus, pornography is defined by some as "sexually oriented material made for the conscious and active arousal of the viewer" and with a negative assessment of it, and (some) pornography is defined by others as "sexually oriented media that are judged by the viewer and society as being within the bounds of what is acceptable."[64]

In what follows, we position pornography against the background of a strongly developing digital world. We pay attention to various forms of pornography, but also to the two extreme polarities in the debate about the function and meaning of pornography (and the related appreciation of it). We conclude with a brief consideration of the role of the porn industry itself and with the not unimportant debates over the damages of consumption (the effects of watching porn regularly or even frequently) and production damage (the damages caused to those who make porn). We are aware that we are mainly guided by debates in the US. Nevertheless, we think that there is a lot of comparative material that can help conversations about pornography in (other) Christian circles.

Pornography has evolved rapidly: from telephone sex to video rental, from cable television to the freely available pornography based on an ever-developing (high-speed) internet. In their writing on pornography, Matthew Hall (a researcher at Ulster University, UK) and Jeff Hearn (senior lecturer in gender studies, UK) pay attention to the shift in our understanding of sexuality to a much broader conception of sexuality as identity (cf. Stuart in chapter 5).[65] They echo researchers who link the

---

63. Carroll, *Sexuality Now*, 510.
64. Carroll, *Sexuality Now*, 510–11.
65. Hall and Hearn, *Revenge Pornography*.

development and availability of pornography mainly to freedom of expression and sexual liberation.[66] Terms such as "mainstreamification" and "pornography" take center stage together. With these terms, they point to a western society in which pornography increasingly permeates the culture. The fact that pornography has increasingly become a common good is evidenced by the fact that pornographers publish books, and give advice in lifestyle magazines (think of *LINDA*), for both men and women. Porn is visible, in art and on TV, in music and in advertisements.[67]

Phenomena such as "Brazilian waxing," in which men and women have their pubic hair completely removed, and *sexting* (distributing self-made sexually oriented photos) have each increased. The corresponding level of acceptance is now high and seems to have largely been normalized. The shift that has taken place is from a social censorship of porn to an informed consumer culture.[68] The availability of pornography is ubiquitous, partly due to increased technological possibilities. Porn consumption now takes place in the anonymity of one's own living room. The well-known "tube" and "hub" websites, referring to variants of the well-known YouTube streaming service, have grown exponentially. And now there is also the advent of abusive categories such as *revenge porn*.

Although different definitions are offered (the online dissemination of sexually explicit images, without the consent of the person depicted, by one of the ex-partners in a broken relationship, with the aim of taking revenge for experienced or perceived injustice), the core of revenge porn seems to be the deliberate intention to cause damage to someone with whom an intimate relationship has existed. Hall and Hearn point out that people can become victims of this while they themselves have never actively, and with permission, participated in the production of the explicit visual material.[69] This also brings up the importance of including the experiences of victims in the definition of revenge porn. They therefore define revenge porn as follows: the online and offline distribution of real or fake explicit images, without a person's consent, by ex-partners, partners, or third parties such as hackers, with the aim of revenge, entertainment, or for political purposes. Of course, it is extremely problematic that all kinds of websites (Cliphunter, Xvideos, etc.) contain this type of material, and there are even websites that have very explicit references

66. Hall and Hearn, *Revenge Pornography*, 44.
67. Hall and Hearn, *Revenge Pornography*, 44.
68. Attwood, *Mainstreaming Sex*.
69. Hall and Hearn, *Revenge Pornography*, 16.

to revenge porn in their name. For that matter, social media platforms such as Facebook also appear to contain this material. The distribution of explicit images is extensive and reports of companies such as McAfee (virus software company) show that (at least in the US) more than 50 percent of adults shared sexually explicit material via a mobile phone. Also, 50 percent of the group surveyed reported storing images online and 16 percent claimed to have shared explicit material with strangers. These figures are telling and betray a certain popularity. Hall and Hearn highlight the enormous impact that sexting and revenge porn have on victims. Fortunately, there is increasing legislation in this area, which can guarantee better protections.

There is no doubt that the production of pornography has become an industry in its own right. Andrew Altman and Lori Watson (both professors of philosophy in the US) estimate that the industry, in the US alone, is worth about 13 to 14 billion dollars a year.[70] Porn is made for entertainment and profit. They also point out that the various components of this commercial industry—stripping, porn, and prostitution—are strongly intertwined and that those who participate in them often move back and forth between these different forms of work.[71] The very large annual turnover does not have a commensurate impact on the earnings of those who work in this industry. The idea that everyone in porn is rich is a persistent myth. A 2016 survey found that the average amount earned from a traditional sex scene is between $800 and $1,000.[72] Some "stars" receive between $1,500 and $2,000, but this is definitely not the case for the vast majority.

Altman and Watson also point to the wide variety of different types of sex videos produced and viewed. Tellingly, the most common search terms in the US are "lesbian," "teenager," and "ebony." The relationship of pornography to vulnerable, marginalized, and minoritized groups of women and teenagers, and especially to racism, is clearly evident here.[73] Watson explains that the popularity of these and other themes in the choice of pornography undoubtedly leads to the eroticization of inequality, between races (black and white), between mothers and children,

70. Altman and Watson, *Debating Pornography*, 207.
71. Altman and Watson, *Debating Pornography*, 209.
72. Altman and Watson, *Debating Pornography*, 201.
73. Altman and Watson, *Debating Pornography*, 212.

between young and old, etc. What is "sexy" is determined by inequality, and inequality is transformed into (exploitative) sex.[74]

The argument that Altman and Watson construct in their book (*Debating Pornography*) is interesting and worth following, because it provides a good picture of the various sides of the debate. One of the key questions they raise is whether there is such a thing as a fundamental right of access to pornography, and whether and to what extent pornography is harmful to people. For them, the starting point must be that there is a fundamental equality between men and women. However, Altman and Watson have almost opposing views on pornography. Let us take a closer look at their respective arguments. Altman believes that there is a moral right to sexual autonomy. This right exists for every adult human being, and this *includes* the right to buy and sell pornography produced by adults who have consented to its production.[75] According to Altman, the current discussions about pornography have mainly developed out of the social and intellectual debates surrounding the sexual revolution of the 1960s. These, of course, revolve around individual sexual autonomy and the related idea that human sexuality should be restricted by all kinds of legislation and norms. Opposition to such legislation and norms was at the heart of the resistance. In his part of the book, Altman mainly examines evidence for the idea that pornography is harmful to women and maintains a social system in which women are second-class citizens. He finds that this evidence is largely lacking.[76] The weight of sexual autonomy is so great for Altman that there must be more weighty empirical evidence than, for example, the use of alcohol. According to him, there is insufficient evidence that pornography causes a serious increase in violence and harm toward women; rather, there seems to be evidence for the opposite, namely, that there is a decrease in violence and harm toward women.[77]

The importance of a careful interpretation of research data thus seems to be emphasized. We will certainly come back to this later, but first we will continue here with our exploration of Altman's position and the problems connected to it. The question is whether Altman's definition of "sexual autonomy" is not too narrow. In cases of sexual violence, sexual autonomy appears to be under threat.

74. Altman and Watson, *Debating Pornography*, 212–13.
75. Altman and Watson, *Debating Pornography*, 2.
76. Altman and Watson, *Debating Pornography*, 3.
77. Altman and Watson, *Debating Pornography*, 4.

Watson sees the big problem emerging here: pornography that is the result of eroticized inequality.[78] Watson argues in response that it seems to boil down to this: men who use porn for sexual arousal and gratification seem to (think they) have the right to use whole groups of systematically disadvantaged women for their own masturbation. Watson believes that Altman has a pessimistic view of humanity, where there are privileged people who have the power to seek excitement and sexual release at the expense of groups of vulnerable women. That one group uses pornography on the basis of sexual autonomy of the individual is possible (to a certain extent) because of the restriction of the sexual autonomy of the group (who are exploited through being part of) making the pornography. Watson's view, in response to Altman, is most clear when she writes:

> The eroticization of inequality is nowhere more apparent than in pornography. In addition to the inequality between men and women, any social inequality you can think of has a subgenre of pornography devoted to it. Racial inequality is sexualized in white-master/black-slave genres, in Asian-themed subgenres drawing on stereotypes about submissive Asian women and geishas, and in depictions of Latina women as "oversexed" and "hot and fiery." Age inequality is sexualized in teen-porn genres, with depictions of school-aged girls as virgins having their first "encounter" with older men. Child pornography eroticizes the vulnerability of children, as does pornography of small women said to be over the age of majority but presented as if they are children eager for male sexual attention. Incest porn is a popular subgenre, capturing both the inequality of youth and of the parent/child relationship. Age inequality is also sexualized through subgenres, where older women are made into grandma porn. Physical disability and inequality are sexualized in genres of pornography that depict persons (largely women) with physical disabilities, including missing limbs and dwarfism. Obesity is an inequality that is sexualized in "fat porn." Nazi/Jew pornography exists, sometimes presenting Jewish women eager to enter concentration camps for sexual purposes. The inequality between nonhuman animals and humans is sexualized in bestiality and "crush" videos where women in high heels crush small rodents, puppies, and kittens to death by stepping on them as they shriek. For any social inequality and hierarchy that exists,

---

78. Altman and Watson, *Debating Pornography*, 278–81.

you can count on finding a subgenre of pornography that sexu-
alizes that particular form of inequality.[79]

Porn eroticizes inequality; that is the core of the argument for Watson. The
various forms of inequality that are eroticized are discussed in the above
quotation: age, racial inequality, physical limitation, human and animal,
etc. They correspond to the various forms of pornography produced.
Watson bases her argument on the work of MacKinnon and Dworkin,
dating from the 1980s.[80] For them, too, pornography was increasingly
becoming a social practice that undermined the equal status of women.

Watson concludes, on the basis of decades of research, that pornography should be directly associated with sexual violence, including
rape, and that pornography actually encourages violence against women.
The frequently used arguments given in defense of the production and
consumption of pornography, freedom of speech, the pro-porn position
(originating in feminist circles), and sexual autonomy, are no longer de-
fensible, in her opinion. Especially arguments for freedom of speech and
opinion, she thinks, are no longer valid because it places the "rights" and
speech of one powerful group above that of a mostly vulnerable group.[81]
Watson elaborates on the work of Langton who, on the basis of Austin's
philosophy of language, shows that pornography assumes or encourages
an inappropriate role for women.[82] Watson quotes Langton:

> Just as the speech of the umpire is authoritative within a certain
> domain—the game of tennis, so pornographic speech is author-
> itative within a certain domain—the game of sex. The authors of
> pornographic speech are not mere bystanders to the game; they
> are speakers whose verdict counts. Pornography tells its hearers
> what women are worth: it ranks women as things, as objects, as
> prey. Pornography tells its hearers which moves are appropriate
> and permissible: if it tells them that certain moves are appropri-
> ate because women want to be raped, it legitimizes violence.[83]

In the same publication, Altman and Watson discuss the possible physical
and emotional damage caused. A distinction is made between consumption damage and production damage. Altman and Watson let former

---

79. Altman and Watson, *Debating Pornography*, 169–70.
80. Altman and Watson, *Debating Pornography*, 5.
81. Altman and Watson, *Debating Pornography*, 5–8.
82. Altman and Watson, *Debating Pornography*, 187–88; Langton, *Sexual Solipsism*.
83. Altman and Watson, *Debating Pornography*, 193–94.

porn star Jenna Jameson speak for herself; she relays her own experience of production damage. According to Jameson, there is a great deal of emotional damage caused to actors, especially in the early stages of their work. Emotional production damage is a constituent part of the industry.[84] Women become a product to be bought and sold. The health risks are often unknown, but frequent viral infections and STIs, with short or long-term effects, are the order of the day. The discussions regarding consumption harm are complex and multilayered. Early studies among men in the 1970s pointed to a possible increase in aggression, especially when viewing aggressive or violent pornography. Milder forms of pornography led to a significantly lower level of aggression. In a later phase of research, more attention was paid to other variables: an increase in insensitivity to sexual violence, an increase in sexist beliefs and associated behavior, a possible increase in demand for violent material, damage to family relationships, and physical consequences such as erectile dysfunction.[85] According to Watson, there is compelling evidence for the role and impact of pornography in many forms of sexual violence: the more violent the pornography, the greater and more negative the impact on the viewer.[86]

Yet not all researchers in this field agree with Watson. In a fairly recent publication, we come across an analysis that questions the obvious relationship between violence and the viewing of pornography.[87] Ronald Weitzer enters into the discussion on the basis of a careful analysis of recent research and presents four interesting findings that outline the various critical positions that exist on the connections between violence and pornography.

The first finding is that pornography is actually an open door: the viewing of porn can have a positive impact on men and women. The second finding is that although the anti-porn literature focuses on specific terminology around "dehumanization" and "lack of empathy among viewers," these concepts are not elaborated and are therefore open to all kinds of interpretations. The third point concerns the difficulty Weitzer encounters with respect to empirical research: people claim to know everything already. Watson, quoted earlier, also joins the ranks of these critics and does not expect too much from empirical data. This is somewhat surprising. Much of the evidence cited appears to be primarily of

84. Altman and Watson, *Debating Pornography*, 193–94.
85. Altman and Watson, *Debating Pornography*, 218–19.
86. Altman and Watson, *Debating Pornography*, 221–23.
87. Weitzer, "Interpreting the Data."

an anecdotal nature, and contains little background information. Finally, critics have little to say about a number of specific categories of porn: homoerotic male porn, lesbian porn, porn made by women, feminist porn, etc. Weitzer discusses the two main opposing camps and provides insight into the various studies conducted in recent years. It appears that the presentation of concepts and the methods used are lacking, the sample size is too small/response rate is too low, results are generalized too easily, conclusions do not always match the findings, the levels of sexual violence claimed did not appear to be present or appeared to be present to a very small extent, etc. It is clear that the discussion is certainly not over, and that thorough research is needed into this complex and layered phenomenon. According to Weitzer, research does not provide an unambiguous picture of the effects of seeing porn: men become desensitized and look for more extreme pornography to satisfy their needs; a causal relationship between media presentation and its reception by the viewing public and porn seems to be rather imposed.[88]

A crucial question is how this debate relates to the theological framework that we described in the previous chapter, namely that of sexuality as embodied desire. Anyone who connects this framework with the issues of pornography will ask themself the question whether pornography fits with a theology of desire. In a certain sense, pornography shows how far desire can go and that many people are prepared to go very far in satisfying these desires. Without wanting to provide a strict ethical framework, a question that remains is to what extent sexuality can be seen as a consumer product. As we saw in chapter 5, there is little room for this.

It is also important to place sexuality in a relational framework, where sexuality is supposed to nurture a relationship, especially if it is the vehicle of reciprocal intimacy. This is where things get difficult and where there are no simple answers. Or can we offer space to those forms of porn and erotica which (under the condition that they are not based on power imbalance and abuse) can breathe new life into a long-term relationship? Would that be possible in a Christian context and under those conditions? In any case, there is no room for inequality, not for racist expressions, and not for any form of violence. It would be good to discuss the impact of pornography in Christian circles in the light of the broader discussion about sexuality as embodied grace. The attention

---

88. Weitzer "Interpreting the Data," 257–67.

and space we give to that which is visual in our culture should also be addressed here. Perhaps the excessive attention to visualization can be exchanged for healthy imagination.

Sex, Sexism, Power, and Violence

The recent #MeToo revelations have once more shown that sex and the abuse of power are related. Sex seems to be a fixed ingredient of power or power is an integral part of sexual relationships. When that power is shared in a healthy relationship, things can be good and right, but we sense that this is not the whole story. Power can be abused, and games of seduction can turn into forced sex and rape. There are too many stories in which (mostly) women are forced into sex, and too many stories of physical and psychological violence, sometimes continuing for many years. Incidentally, we talk about sexism, not everyone will immediately think of rape, but again and again we see that all kinds of sexism drive violence against women, including sexual violence and rape. In 2021, Aliene Boele conducted research into sexism experienced by female pastors. The study showed that nine out of ten female ministers experience a form of sexism. This includes expressions aimed at the competence of the pastor, unwanted remarks about her appearance, her marriage, or the fact that she is single, etc.[89] It is a worrying reality that demands attention and change. It is therefore not only about violence against women, or even sexual violence in particular, but about the much broader societal problem of gender inequality and sexism that allows violence and abuse to take place.

The statistics on rape, by the way, do not lie. Men with more power abuse women with less or no power and force them into sexual relationships. Carroll shows that the US has the highest rate of registered rape in the western world, four times that of Germany, twelve times that of the UK, and twenty times that of Japan.[90]

It should also be noted that rape is among the crimes that are the hardest to be registered, because not all victims (in fact, very few) report it. Also problematic is the context where women are blamed for, or accused of lying about, their rape, precisely because of the gender inequality that contributed to the rape in the first place. The idea behind this is quite

89. Boele, *Seksisme in de kerk.*
90. Carroll, *Sexuality Now*, 480.

clear: victims are said to make themselves vulnerable to abuse by wearing certain clothes, displaying certain behaviors, etc. Women who—according to certain groups of men—dress suggestively and drink alcohol are seen by that group of men as having a greater degree of sexual intent than women who dress "neutrally" and do not drink.[91]

Feminist researchers point out that, in their view, the social, economic, and political separation of the sexes (binary in particular) has only encouraged sexually transgressive behavior. The whole discussion, of course, circles around the ways in which this is an expression of unequal power in society. Men overpowering women functions as an attempt to maintain or regain male control (in their own lives). Although, rightly, much attention is paid to the abuse of women, men are also among abuse victims, although this is to a lesser extent. Rape, sexual violence against, and abuse of men is perpetrated by both men and women.

Research data shows that rape and other forms of abuse in prisons affect not only men (men who rape or assault men), but also women. In addition, figures show that rapes of women are mostly related to prison staff.[92] Lehmiller deliberately uses a broader definition of sexual assault, providing examples such as: situations in which a person touches another person in a sexual manner against his or her will, or when a person forces another person to perform a sexual act.[93] The gender of the person in question does not matter here. In fact, Lehmiller provides a scale on which any form of unwanted touch of a sexual nature should be rejected, but also on which the severity increases the more coercion is involved (e.g., whether or not the victim was under the influence of drugs like Rohypnol, which is known as a "date-rape" drug, or alcohol). As a part of this whole discussion, sexual intimidation and sexual harassment should also be mentioned. Here too, especially in the workplace, power is a key factor. An example is when a promotion depends on whether or not a person in a higher (decision-making) position's advances or unwanted touching are accepted. Another related issue, is that (inappropriate) sexual intimacy between colleagues or in the workplace can create an unsafe atmosphere in which people feel severely hampered in their autonomous functioning.

---

91. Carroll, *Sexuality Now*; Maurer and Robinson, "Effects of Attire," 423–34.
92. Struckman-Johnson and Struckman-Johnson, "Sexual Coercion," 217–27.
93. Lehmiller, *Psychology of Human Sexuality*, 354.

Sexual Abuse and Incest

This subject requires much more in-depth study and deserves more atten-tion than is possible in the scope of this book. Nonetheless, it is impor-tant to mention here because abuse, sexual assault, and rape are serious examples of aberrant sexuality and lead to untold suffering and trauma. Unfortunately and shockingly, more children are the victims of sex abuse than adults. In recent years, we have had several encounters in our pasto-ral practice with young people, men and women, who had been abused by a family member, relative (incest), or acquaintance, and it is often the case that they suffered this abuse for a protracted period of time. Many of them have survived the abuse, but carry the scars of what happened to them and live with severe trauma and long-term psychological problems. In the practice of caring for people in a church community, it is necessary to provide a safe space for survivors to tell their stories and for them to find or be referred to good help. Situations in which religious aspects play a role, where the victim is abused using specific religious language, religious authority, or theological concepts, are extremely complex and require careful handling. Such abuses of power and injustices must be stopped.

Intersex and Transgender

In chapter 3, we discussed sex difference and people who are intersex, as well as terms such as gender dysphoria and people who are transgender. We discussed this in detail and from different scientific perspectives. We showed how gender and also gender variations were thought about in different time periods and described the shift in the naming of issues associated with gender.[94] In the following chapter, DeFranza gave us some food for thought based on her analysis of the position and role of eunuchs and the possible relation of this ancient category to modern intersex conditions. Though DeFranza's work is helpful, it is certainly not the final word because, for many people, questions about people who are intersex or transgender remain.

Without repeating here what was discussed in the previous chapters on the subject, we would like to offer some theological reflections on the issues associated with being transgender or intersex. As we covered in chapter 3, intersexuality describes a number of conditions that are all

94. Van Heesch in chapter 3.

atypical in relation to the physical (internal and external) sex organs. Intersex conditions are not the same as being transgender. Transgender people often experience a mismatch between their biological sex as assigned at birth and their gender identity, for example, a person with a biologically female body, who strongly experiences themself as a man. Devastatingly, sometimes intersex and transgender people have been told that their condition or their gender identity is a result of the fall, or directly a result of their (or someone else's) sin, but certainly not a part of God's creation. This, as we stated before, has everything to do with the current dominant binary thinking: there are two genders, male and female, and that is how it was created by God. The evangelical theologian Dennis Hollinger states that intersex conditions are so rare that they do not break the normative male-and-female pattern. If the statistics are correct, this (theological) position already has problems, because one out of every 2,500 people is born with an intersex condition.[95]

Susannah Cornwall explores the pastoral needs of people who live with an intersex condition. In quite a few cases, they have undergone major surgery/s in childhood, without their consent, often even without knowledge of what is involved in the operation/s, and have problems with their gender identity later in life. Others have great difficulty in visiting a doctor and asking for help. In addition to the many practical problems people have, intersex conditions pose questions for theology.[96] The difficult question to be asked is whether an intersex condition can be part of God's good creation. For people of faith who are intersex, this question may culminate in the question of the meaning of Psalm 139:13–16 for their lives.

In relation to the framework we developed in chapter 5, the conversation about intersex and transgender people takes on another dimension. With Coakley, we see room for a different understanding. Starting from a more trinitarian theological frame, transgender and intersex people are included in the same transformative work of God in Christ and by the Spirit. Christ has broken through binary thinking once and for all. Because of Christ, everything has changed and there is one humanity. We noted this in chapter 5 and repeat it here: chronologically, Adam may be the first man, but both related and crucial verses (2 Cor 4:4 and Col 1:15) leave no room for doubt: ontologically, Christ is the first. The masculine

95. Cornwall, *Intersex, Identity and Disability.*
96. Cornwall, *Intersex Conditions.*

and the feminine receive their final destination in Christ. We believe that this way of thinking, this theology, is significant because time and again intersex and transgender people are stigmatized, for example, as people with a serious (physical and/or psychological) imbalance, while what is actually at issue (see chapter 3), namely sex difference or sex change, is not taken seriously.

The existence of all kinds of gender variations challenges us to think again about the meaning of gender and sexuality. In chapter 3, we stated that biological and sociological matters both play a role in our view of gender. We should not play them off against each other, not even from a theological perspective. Therefore, we could even say that we should not see sex and gender variations as problematic but, in fact, they could lead to deeper theological reflection, holding a mirror up to us all and taking us further in our theological anthropology; further in our thinking on what it means for God to desire each one of us.

Questions for Discussion

- Our analysis of purity and virginity gives a somewhat more nuanced picture than is often espoused. How do you view these two concepts and in what way do they play a role in conversations in the church?

- The complexities of disability and sexuality may not get enough attention. How can you give this more space in a culture where everything that is young and healthy is placed on a pedestal? We stated: "it is only for a short time in our existence that we are not living with disabilities." What could we do to break the taboos that exist?

- How can we best have a conversation about a difficult topic like sex online?

- How do you feel about the discussion of pornography in this chapter and what questions does the analysis raise for you? What advice do you give to someone who says they struggle with it and what is your advice based on?

- Abuse in relationships and transgressive behavior have had a huge impact on the lives of many people. What do you think can help prevent this in the family, church, and society?

7

Unquenchable Love
Looking Back and What to Do Next?

The Harvest of This Book

WHAT DID OUR SEARCH yield? The aim of this book was to create a space for reflection. We wanted to provide food for thought from a theological perspective, in the hope that it might help in conversations about gender and sexuality. The journey has been multicolored and multifaceted. There were several interlocutors along the way, some of them more scientific and some of them more popular. We started with recent developments in our own Dutch context and discussed some of the confusion surrounding gender and sexuality in the broader context of Christian communities around the world. The contradictions and ambiguities experienced, particularly in Christian circles, means a framework is required within which discussions can be carried out. Of course, to a certain extent, these conversations are about values and norms. However, we have chosen not to present a specific ethical argument; rather, we have engaged with ideas that can help all of us to have a better conversation, where there is room to think, and freedom to look at the matter from different perspectives.

In the second chapter we skimmed through hundreds of years of history. The multitude of different experiences, beliefs, and practices to do with sex and sexuality is certainly worthy of a whole separate book, but for our purposes this chapter's historical excursions were sufficient to show how the views and practices surrounding sexuality moved with the waves of culture—including religious culture—and scientific and philosophical insights. New insights often led to new practices and new practices also led to reactions against them. The lessons of history are manifold, but there are two things that clearly stand out to us. First, it is striking that in our expression of sexuality we are children of our time. Our beliefs and values do influence our patterns of thought on sexuality and at the same time these beliefs and values are also shaped by historical developments. The pendulum regularly swings back and forth. Throughout history, the church has tried to exert power over what people were and were not allowed to do sexually, and we have observed the accompanying double standard throughout history, too.

This double standard is due to the second thing that is clear to us: the inequality between men and women. Gender inequality, and what people think about gender inequality, continues to shape discussions about gender, sex, and sexuality. Much of the literature on sexuality was written by men without adequate reflection on the power differentials involved and the various abuses of that power. It is obvious that this is a major problem and has caused much of the tension and problems that persist in Christian circles.

In chapter three, we concentrated on different scientific perspectives. Here, the question of *nature* versus *nurture* received much attention. No matter what we ultimately think about gender, orientation, and expression, what is striking is the constant tension between more constructivist approaches and more essentialist approaches. And this discussion, we think, has not yet ended. This is, in and of itself, an important finding because it helps us to get a realistic picture of the complexities we are dealing with. New insights from anthropology and from genetics (think of the physical visibility of gender variations), and also from neuroscience, point to a conversation that is anything but simple. Theologically and practically speaking, it is simply not good enough to state, for example, that there is brokenness in creation and that we therefore have to deal with gender variation. The religious and also pastoral-theological questions that this raises are numerous. The different scientific insights, which act as the different lenses through which we see the complexity of the human experience, can lead to greater understanding, for example, for people who struggle with gender dysphoria, or to support new parents who do not know how to raise a child without a visibly discernible gender.

We made it clear in the next chapter (chapter 4) that a more in-depth and contextual reading of the Bible is necessary. What is needed, as we showed, is clarity about our hermeneutic—the ways in which we interpret the Bible—and the biases we bring to that interpretation. In other words, the reading lenses we put on when we read different biblical texts are, without exception, meaningful for how we understand those texts. We chose "desire" as our core metaphor—our hermeneutic—because we feel that it does the most justice to the meaning and function of human sexuality in relation to who God is—a God who desires us and his world. From this perspective, we (re)interpreted a number of crucial texts and fundamental themes in both the Old and New Testaments. In doing so, we did not shy away from some very difficult questions. The way in which the New Testament also reflects gender remains fascinating, especially in relation to the embedding of the many texts that we dealt with.

Our hope is that a careful rereading will highlight the space that is present in many texts for something other than strict binary gender roles and hierarchies, and that this will lead to the Bible once again—or perhaps for the first time—being a serious discussion partner for people today, who have their own struggles and concerns about gender and sexuality. Personally, we are amazed and surprised again and again at the incredible wealth we have found—and there is so much more to discover!

As announced at the beginning of this book, we wanted to propose a theological framework for considering gender and sexuality that was different from the dominant Christian discourse, and we have presented this framework in chapter 5. By definition, constructing a framework is—and remains—a challenge, but we have tried to provide at least some basic building blocks, if not more. The route we eventually chose has echoes of different theological traditions and we like to think of it as a colorful collection of thoughts and voices. This undertaking was by no means easy, and we certainly do not pretend to think we have had the final word. We do think, however, that the characterization of sexual desire and sexuality as embodied grace is a serious attempt to do theological justice to the dynamics of human sexuality. We share Thatcher's view that a balanced approach to gender and sexuality will have to be specifically related to trinitarian thought and, in particular, to the person of Jesus Christ. Following Thatcher, we explained that recreated humanity is involved in a continuous process of transformation as God's image-bearers. Christ opens the fourfold reality and frees humanity from all sin, and that includes the sin that may lie in misdirected passion or improper gender differentiation.[1] Equally important to thinking through gender and sexuality is Coakley's vision of the transformation by the Holy Spirit.

In chapter 6, we return to the diversity of issues and phenomena that are usually associated with gender and sexuality. We have called these "hot issues" without wanting to relegate them to the corner or reject them out of hand. For this reason, we have chosen to write in a descriptive and informative way, rather than a critical or (superficially) judgmental way. Subjects that were discussed included polyamory, virginity, pornography, prostitution, and abuse. As part of this discussion, we tried to discuss how these topics may or may not work within the theological framework explored in chapter 5. This approach was aligned with the overall structure of this book, as outlined in the preface. Each subject gave us food for thought, and plenty more could be written on each topic. It may be the case for many of our readers that this chapter left you with more questions than answers. It is our hope that—from whatever field of enquiry, be it anthropology, biology, philosophy, or theology—new insights, research, and concepts will provide support and opportunity for continued and deepened dialogue.

One thing has become crystal clear, and perhaps this is visible on every page: we have been discussing an endlessly complex subject, and this cannot be captured in the short span of this book. So many things remain a mystery about gender and human sexuality. It cannot all be framed rationally, philosophically, or even theologically. Words often fall short. And that, of course, is part of the complexity. Answers cannot always be given. One reason for this is because it is not theoretical, real people and our emotions are involved: this is not a neutral conversation, and everyone has his, her, or their own experiences. Something of the mystery and the intangible and the sacred, but also of the transformative, comes to the fore in the ambivalences surrounding gender and sexuality is full of contradictions: there is beauty and there is ugliness, light and darkness, passion and selfish lust, reciprocity and self-centeredness, embrace and exclusion, and we could go on, but part of its beauty and mystery is the way the sacred and transformative can coalesce in sexuality. This shows the simultaneously fragile and powerful nature of love. A fire that is indeed unquenchable, with its own secrets and mysteries. We believe that theology is part of that mystery, because the creator of sexuality and everything connected with it reveals something of who the creator is.

1. Thatcher, *Oxford Handbook*, 202–3.

Space to Think and Courage to Act

Throughout this book, we have tried to write in such a way that our readers feel invited to think further, individually or in a group. The latter requires courage because (as we have seen) not everything is so easy to interpret. Crucial for discussion in groups will be that there is a genuinely safe space for dissenters, in whatever direction. It is precisely this topic that often gives rise to all kinds of new conflicts, which benefit no one. There are plenty of manuals available for conducting such conversations, and we encourage you to take a look at them, but we will offer a few pieces of advice here, too.

In the preface, we outlined the approach this book would take. We concentrated on Richard Osmer's four-task model. In each chapter, we worked on one or more tasks as described in this model. We repeat the overview here and provide further explanation for the practical use of this model to stimulate discussions about gender and sexuality.

Task	Key question	Activity	Application
Empirical-descriptive	*What is going on?* Chapter 1 (and also chapter 6)	Examine and discern how themes play a role in society and the church	An investigative and descriptive task: listening and observing
Interpretive	*Why is this happening?* Chapters 2 and 3	In particular, giving space for the various ways of seeing gender and sexuality	An interpretive task: seeking wisdom from different sources
Normative	*What should (ideally) be going on?* Chapters 4 and 5 (and also this chapter)	Especially, looking for the ways in which theological reflection can provide us with a new frame of mind	A normative task: thinking through and developing standards/a framework

Task	Key question	Activity	Application
Pragmatic-strategic	*What are we going to do differently in practice?* Chapters 6 and 7	Particularly, formulating how the issues can be discussed safely and constructively	A practical task: make things practical through applying theory, insights, etc. to real-world topics

Table 5: Osmer's Four Tasks Results

Without wanting to only take "small bites," our aim has been to write in such a way that new or different insights can be put into practice. We chose this model because Osmer is a *practical* theologian. That is, he wants to help groups and communities find new and different ways of doing things to better shape and improve our conversations and practices. This is only possible when we are prepared to go through these four tasks with each other in a thoughtful and respectful way. Often, we walk through these tasks almost automatically (without even knowing it), but the risk with topics like gender and sexuality is that we immediately want to start with the Bible. In and of itself, there is nothing wrong with that, but it can lead to a deadlock in the conversation because we have not yet properly explored the first and second tasks together. If we immediately jump to task three (the normative task), which considers the Bible, our discussion might not progress any further. We first require clarity about the reading glasses we use when we "tackle" the biblical texts (see chapter 4). Each of the tasks has its own meaning and value, and you can categorize a conversation according to these four tasks. The model gives conversation partners clarity about the route that is to be taken. It is even possible to organize a whole group or community discussion or study to progress along with the tasks described above. With issues as complex and important as gender and sexuality, clarity about the path that is taken is important, even if the outcome is not necessarily fixed.

Below, we briefly outline a possible route for a discussion process, using this book—along with other sources as required—as a sort of study/conversation guide and for background information.

1. *The investigative and descriptive task.* Questions with which we start the conversation are often along the lines of:

   - What exactly is going on in our context?

- How can we listen to each other and to the people with whom we want to discuss difficult topics concerning sexuality?

Invite people to join you in conversation; talk *with* them and not *about* them. This avoids unnecessary stigmatization and forming opinions too quickly. The basic attitude for this conversation is one of being present and priestly listening.

People's stories about their struggles with their own sexuality or how they have experienced life with people from an early age are crucial. In chapters 1 and 3, we have paid attention to this.

2. *The interpreting task.* Questions that arise in this task often go like this:

- Why is this happening?
- What explanations can be found in various sources, such as scientific articles, studies, etc.? We then concentrate on how we can better understand the complex phenomena.
- What other sources do we know, from which we would like to draw?

The basic posture of this task is the open search for wisdom that helps people to better shape their lives.

In this book, several scientific insights are discussed in chapter 3. These align well with this second task: Various theories explain the "why." There may be practical guides available within the churches that can help as well.

3. *The normative task.* Questions that arise in this task often look like:

- What should be done?
- What biblical and theological data can we find? And, what ethical aspects of gender and sexuality do we want to address?
- Do we know of other contexts in which things were deliberately done or developed differently that would be helpful to us in this task?

The basic attitude that fits with this task is the willingness to go a little further in thinking through familiar Bible texts and the willingness to take more time for this.

In chapter 4 of this book, we looked at a large number of texts and themes from the Bible. These theological data deserve to be weighed in a careful discussion. The central question is always: how or to what extent can they help us to better work through the challenges we face? So, it is also about thinking through the norms and values we have derived from these Bible verses and passages.

4. *The practical task.* Questions that arise in this task are often things like:

- What can we do now on the basis of these other three tasks that we have worked through?

- How can we create a better environment in our community, group, etc.? How can we give practical shape to the challenges we face?

The basic posture here is the readiness to focus concretely on a pastoral approach that does justice to people in their situation.

What Needs to Be Followed Up?

In a study such as this, there will always be plenty of questions left that need much more time and attention. Much has been written about theology, sex, and gender, but not always from multiple perspectives, as we have done now. We believe that this is necessary in order to continue the conversation in our churches. We are aware of the different positions that are often taken in churches. There is a lot of confusion, embarrassment, and perhaps a lack of good information. Wouldn't it be amazing if more people in churches and religious communities were prepared to share their personal experiences of gender and sexuality? It may not always do justice to the vulnerable situations in which people find themselves, but every attempt that can be made to have a serious and open conversation is important, even if differences of opinion remain. Such an important step was taken by professor Heleen Zorgdrager (PThU) with the publication of *Transgender, Faith and Church.*[2] This is a practical guide for faith communities and pastors who are thinking through gender diversity, or who have transgender people in their congregations, etc. Zorgdrager also published *You Have Made Me Wonderfully: A Guide for Christian*

2. "Transgender, geloof en kerk."

Transgender Persons and Workers in the Church.[3] It is these, and many other publications, that help to start the conversation and hopefully offer more protection within our faith communities. Perhaps the conversation starts with people who are transgender, but a broader, more inclusive discussion about gender and sexuality is crucial as a first step.

3. Title translated by the authors.

Bibliography

Ackerman, Susan. *Warrior, Dancer, Seductress, Queen: Women in Judges and Biblical Israel*. New York: Doubleday, 1998.

Alcoff, Linda M. *Visible Identities: Race, Gender, and the Self*. Oxford: Oxford University Press, 2005.

Allender, Dan B. *Healing the Wounded Heart: The Heartache of Sexual Abuse and the Hope of Transformation*. Grand Rapids: Baker, 2016.

Allender, Dan B., and Tremper Longman III. *God Loves Sex: An Honest Conversation about Sexual Desire and Holiness*. Grand Rapids: Baker, 2014.

Altman, Andrew, and Lori Watson. *Debating Pornography*. Oxford: Oxford University Press, 2019.

Anderson, Irina. "Explaining Negative Rape Victim Perception: Homophobia and the Male Rape Victim." *Current Research in Social Psychology* 10.4 (2004) 43–57.

Angora, Jo, and Judith Baxter, eds. *The Routledge Handbook of Language, Gender, and Sexuality*. London: Routledge, 2021.

Arterburn, Steve, and Fred Stoeker. *Every Young Man's Battle: Strategies for Victory in the Real World of Sexual Temptation*. Colorado Springs: Waterbrook, 2012.

Attwood, Feona. *Mainstreaming Sex: The Sexualisation of Western Sex*. London: Tauris, 2009.

Augustine. *Confessions*. Edited by Albert C. Outler. Library of Christian Classics. Louisville: Westminster John Knox, 2006.

Barth, Karl. *Church Dogmatics*. Vol. III, pt. 4. Edinburgh: T. & T. Clark, 1961.

Beattie, Tina. "Queen of Heaven." In *Queer Theology: Rethinking the Western Body*, edited by Gerard Loughlin, 293–304. Oxford: Blackwell, 2007.

Beattie Jung, Patricia. *Sex on Earth As It Is in Heaven: A Christian Eschatology of Desire*. New York: State University of New York Press, 2017.

Bennett, Jana Marguerite. *Water Is Thicker than Blood: An Augustinian Theology of Marriage and Singleness*. Oxford: Oxford University Press, 2008.

Ben-Ze'ev, Aaron. *Love Online: Emotions on the Internet*. Cambridge: Cambridge University Press, 2004.

Binnie, Jon. *The Globalization of Sexuality*. London: Sage, 2004.

Bloch, Iwan. *Das Sexualleben unserer Zeit in seinen Beziehungen zur modernen Kultur*. Berlin: Marcus, 1907.

Boele, Aliene. *Seksisme in de kerk: Onderzoek naar wat vrouwelijke voorgangers ervaren in hun werk.* Afstudeeronderzoek. Ede: CHE, 2021.

Boer, C. P. de "Genderideologie: heidense religie in postmoderne tijd." *Reformatorisch Dagblad,* May 1, 2021.

Borger, Arjet. *In gesprek over seks: Voor een nieuwe kijk op gezonde seksualiteit.* Heerenveen: Jongbloed, 2013.

Bos, David. *2000 Jaar Nederlanders en hun seksualiteit.* Zwolle: Waanders, 2009.

Bosman, Frank G. *God houdt van seks: Kleine theologie van de erotiek.* Utrecht: Kok, 2015.

Boswell, John. *Christianity, Social Tolerance, and Homosexuality: Gay People in Western Europe from the Beginning of the Christian Era to the Fourteenth Century.* Chicago: University of Chicago Press, 1980.

Botton, Alain de. *How to Think More about Sex.* New York: Picador, 2012.

Boyarin, Daniel. *A Radical Jew: Paul and the Politics of Identity.* Berkeley: UCP, 1994.

Bradley, Harriet. *Gender.* Cambridge: Polity, 2007.

Breevoort, Johanna. *Stomme Zonden: Een waarschuwend woord voor onze jongelieden.* Kok: Kampen, 1916.

Brenot, Philippe, and Laetitia Coryn, eds. *The Story of Sex: From Apes to Robots.* London: Penguin, 2016.

Brooten, Bernadette J. *Love Between Women: Early Christian Responses to Female Homoeroticism.* Chicago: University of Chicago Press, 1996.

———. *Women Leaders in the Ancient Synagogue.* Chico, CA: Scholars, 1982.

Brown, David. *God and Grace of Body: Sacrament in Ordinary.* Oxford: Oxford University Press, 2007.

Brown, Gavin, and Kath Browne, eds. *The Routledge Research Companion to Geographies of Sex and Sexualities.* London: Routledge, 2016.

Brownson, James V. *Bible, Gender, Sexuality: Reframing the Church's Debate on Same-Sex Relationships.* Grand Rapids: Eerdmans, 2013.

Buchbinder, David. *Studying Men and Masculinities.* London: Routledge, 2013.

Burr, Viv, and Jeff Hearn. *Sex, Violence and the Body: The Erotics of Wounding.* New York: Palgrave MacMillan, 2008.

Burrus, Virginia. *The Sex Lives of Saints: An Erotics of Ancient Hagiography.* Philadelphia: University of Philadelphia Press, 2004.

Butler, Judith. *Gender Trouble: Feminism and the Subversion of Identity.* New York: Routledge, 1990.

Callaghan, Brendan. "Contributions from Psychology." In *The Oxford Handbook of Theology, Sexuality, and Gender,* edited by Adrian Thatcher, 88–104. Oxford: Oxford University Press, 2017.

Canning, Maureen. *Lust, Anger, and Love: Understanding Sexual Addiction and the Road to Healthy Intimacy.* Naperville, IL: Sourcebooks, 2008.

Carmichael, Calum. *Sex and Religion in the Bible.* New Haven: Yale University Press, 2010.

Carr, David M. *The Erotic Word: Sexuality, Spirituality, and the Bible.* Oxford: Oxford University Press, 2003.

Carrigan, Mark. "How Do You Know You Don't Like It If You Haven't Tried It? Asexual Agency and the Sexual Assumption." In *Sexual Minority Research in the New Millennium,* edited by T. G. Morrison et al., 3–19. Hauppauge, NY: Nova Science, 2012.

Carroll, Janell L. *Sexuality Now: Embracing Diversity.* 3rd ed. Belmont: Wadsworth, 2010.

———. *Sexuality Now: Embracing Diversity.* 5th ed. Boston: Cengage, 2016.

Chodorow, Nancy J. *Femininities, Masculinities, Sexualities: Freud and Beyond.* Lexington: UPK, 1994.

Cleland, John. *Memoirs of a Woman of Pleasure (Fanny Hill).* London: G. Fenton, 1748.

Clough, Miryam. *Shame, the Church and the Regulation of Female Sexuality.* London: Routledge, 2017.

Coakley, Sarah. *God, Sexuality, and the Self: An Essay "On the Trinity."* Cambridge: Cambridge University Press, 2013.

———. *The New Asceticism: Sexuality, Gender and the Quest for God.* London: Bloomsbury, 2015.

Coleman, Lindsay, and Jacob M. Held. *The Philosophy of Pornography.* Contemporary Perspectives. London: Rowman & Littlefield, 2014.

Comella, Lynn, and Shira Tarrant, eds. *New Views on Pornography: Sexuality, Politics, and the Law.* Oxford: Praeger, 2015.

Connell, Raewyn W. *Masculinities.* Los Angeles: UCP, 2005.

Conway, Colleen M. *Behold the Man: Jesus and Greco-Roman Masculinity.* Oxford: Oxford University Press, 2008.

———. "Masculinity Studies." In *The Oxford Handbook of New Testament, Gender and Sexuality,* edited by Benjamin H. Dunning, 77–93. Oxford: Oxford University Press, 2019.

———. *Sex and Slaughter in the Tent of Jael: A Cultural History of a Biblical Story.* Oxford: Oxford University Press, 2017.

Coogan, Michael. *God and Sex: What the Bible Really Says.* New York: Twelve, 2010.

Cornwall, Susannah. *Intersex Conditions (DSDs) and Pastoral Care: A Guide for Christians.* Manchester: LTI, 2012. Briefing Paper 1.

———. *Intersex, Identity and Disability: Issues for Public Policy, Healthcare and the Church.* Briefing Paper 4. Manchester: LTI, 2012.

———. *Intersex, Theology, and the Bible: Troubling Bodies in Church, Text, and Society.* New York: Palgrave, 2015.

———. *Theology and Sexuality.* London: SCM, 2013.

———. *Un/familiar Theology: Reconceiving Sex, Reproduction and Generativity.* London: Bloomsbury, 2017.

Creamer, Deborah Beth. "Disabled People." In *The Oxford Handbook of Theology, Sexuality, and Gender,* edited by Adrian Thatcher, 676–87. Oxford: Oxford University Press, 2017.

Davidson, Richard M. *Flame of YAHWEH: Sexuality in the Old Testament.* Peabody, MA: Hendrickson, 2007.

D'Avray, David L. *Medieval Marriage: Symbolism and Society.* Oxford: Oxford University Press, 2005.

DeConick, April D. *Holy Misogyny: Why the Sex and Gender Conflicts in the Early Church Still Matter.* New York: Continuum, 2011.

DeFranza, Megan K. *Sex Difference in Christian Theology: Male, Female, and Intersex in the Image of God.* Grand Rapids: Eerdmans, 2015.

Denman, Chess. *Sexuality: A Biopsychosocial Approach.* New York: Palgrave, 2004.

Diamond, Lisa. "Female Bisexuality from Adolescence to Adulthood: Results from a 10-Year Longitudinal Study." *Developmental Psychology* 44.1 (2008) 5–14.

Ditmore, Melissa Hope, ed. *Encyclopedia of Prostitution and Sex Work.* Vols. 1, 2. Westport: Greenwood, 2006.

Donaghue, Chris. *Sex Outside the Lines: Authentic Sexuality in a Sexually Dysfunctional Culture.* Dallas: BenBella, 2015.

Douglas, Mary. *Leviticus as Literature.* London: Oxford University Press, 1999.

———. *Purity and Danger: An Analysis of the Concepts of Pollution and Taboo.* London: Routledge & Kegan, 1966.

Drost-de Wit, Cocky. *Ik wil heel dicht bij je zijn: Een boekje open over beminnen.* Zoetermeer: Boekencentrum, 2016.

Ducat, Stephen J. *The Wimp Factor: Gender Gaps, Holy Wars, and the Politics of Anxious Masculinity.* Boston: Beacon, 2004.

Dunning, Benjamin H. ed. *The Oxford Handbook of New Testament, Gender and Sexuality.* Oxford: Oxford University Press, 2019.

———. *Specters of Paul: Sexual Difference in Early Christian Thought.* Philadelphia: University of Philadelphia Press, 2011.

Dyer, Keith. "A Consistent Biblical Approach to '(Homo)sexuality.'" In *Whose Homosexuality? Which Authority? Homosexual Practice, Marriage, Ordination and the Church,* edited by Brian Edgar and Gordon Preece, 1–21. Adelaide: ATF, 2006.

———. *Jesus and Sex.* Melbourne: Whitley College, 2012.

Eiesland, Nancy. *The Disabled God: Toward a Liberatory Theology of Disability.* Nashville: Abingdon, 1994.

———. "Encountering the Disabled God." *The Other Side* 38.5 (2002) 10–15.

Einstein, Gillian, ed. *Sex and the Brain.* Cambridge: MIT Press, 2007.

Ekins, Richard. *Male Femaling: A Grounded-Theory Approach to Cross-Dressing and Sex-Changing.* London: Routledge, 1997.

Ellens, Harold J. *Sex in the Bible: A New Consideration.* London: Praeger, 2006.

Ellis, Sonja J. "Lesbian Psychology." In *The Palgrave Handbook of the Psychology of Sexuality and Gender,* edited by Christina Richards and Meg John Barker, 109–28. New York: Palgrave, 2015.

Erbele-Kuster, Dorothea. *Body, Gender and Purity in Leviticus 12 and 15.* Library of Hebrew Bible/Old Testament Studies 539. New York: Bloomsbury T. & T. Clark, 2017.

Erwich, René. "Practical Theology as a Practice of Hope: Reflections on a Discipline that Connects." Inaugural lecture, University of Divinity, Whitley College, 2020.

Exum, J. Cheryl. *Song of Songs: A Commentary.* Louisville: Westminster, 2005.

Farley, Margaret A. *Just Love: A Framework for Christian Sexual Ethics.* London: Bloomsbury, 2006.

Farley, Melissa. "Prostitution and the Invisibility of Harm." *Women and Therapy* 26.3–4 (2003) 247–80.

Farvid, Pantéa. "Heterosexuality." In *The Palgrave Handbook of the Psychology of Sexuality and Gender,* edited by Christina Richards and Meg John Barker, 92–108. New York: Palgrave, 2015.

Ferwerda, Rein. *Aristoteles: Over voorplanting.* Groningen: Historische Uitgeverij, 2005.

Feuereisen, Patti. *Invisible Girls: Speaking the Truth About Sexual Abuse.* 3rd ed. New York: Seal, 2018.

Fishbane, Michael. *Song of Songs.* The JPS Bible Commentary. Philadelphia: JPS, 2015.

Fisher, Helen E., et al. "Romantic Love: A Mammalian Brain System for Mate Choice." *Philosophical Transactions of the Royal Society B: Biological Sciences* 361 (2006) 2173–86.

Follow, Anna, and Robert McRuer, eds. *Sex and Disability*. Durham: Durham University Press, 2012.

Foucault, Michel. *Histoire de la Sexualité*. Vol. I, *La Volonté de Savoir*. Paris: Gallimard, 2013.

———. *Histoire de la Sexualité*. Vol. II, *L'usage des Plaisirs*. Paris: Gallimard, 2013.

———. *Histoire de la Sexualité*. Vol. III, *Le Souci de Soi*. Paris: Gallimard, 2013.

Fox, Robin Lane. *Pagans and Christians: In the Mediterranean World from the Second Century AD to the Conversion of Constantine*. London: Penguin, 2006.

Friesen, Steven J. *Imperial Cults and the Apocalypse of John: Reading Revelation in the Ruins*. Oxford: Oxford University Press, 2001.

Frilingos, Christopher A. *Spectacles of Empire: Monsters, Martyrs, and the Book of Revelation*. Philadelphia: UPP, 2004.

Gagnon, John H. *An Interpretation of Desire: Essays in the Study of Sexuality*. Chicago: University of Chicago Press, 2004.

Garton, Stephen. *Histories of Sexuality: Antiquity to Sexual Revolution*. London: Equinox, 2004.

Gerster, Daniel, and Michael Krüggeler, eds. *God's Own Gender?* Würzburg: Ergon, 2018.

Giddens, Anthony. *The Transformation of Intimacy: Sexuality, Love and Eroticism in Modern Societies*. Stanford: Stanford University Press, 1992.

Gleason, Maud. *Making Men: Sophists and Self-Presentation in Ancient Rome*. Princeton: Princeton University Press, 1995.

Grant, Jonathan. *Divine Sex: A Compelling Vision for Christian Relationships in a Hypersexualized Age*. Grand Rapids: Brazos, 2015.

Greenberg, Steven. *Wrestling with God and Men: Homosexuality in the Jewish Tradition*. Madison: University of Wisconsin Press, 2004.

Gregoire, Sheila Wray, et al. *The Great Sex Rescue: The Lies You've Been Taught and How to Recover What God Intended*. Grand Rapids: Baker, 2021.

Grenz, Stanley. *Sexual Ethics: An Evangelical Perspective*. Louisville: Knox, 1990.

Gunasekera, Hasantha, Simon Chapman, and Sharon Campbell. "Sex and Drugs in Popular Movies: An Analysis of the Top 200 Films." In *Journal of the Royal Society of Medicine* 98 (2005) 464–70.

Haeberle, Erwin J. *The Birth of Sexology: A Brief History in Documents*. Indiana: Kinsey, 1983.

Haldeman, Douglas C. "Gay Rights, Patient Rights: The Implications of Sexual Orientation Conversion Therapy." *Professional Psychology: Research and Practice* 33 (2003) 260–64. DOI: 10.1037//0735-7028.33.3.260.

Halík, Tomaš. *De nacht van de biechtvader: Christelijk geloof in een tijd van onzekerheid*. Zoetermeer: Boekencentrum, 2016.

Hall, Matthew, and Jeff Hearn. *Revenge Pornography: Gender, Sexuality and Motivations*. London: Routledge, 2018.

Halperin, David M. *How to Do the History of Homosexuality*. Chicago: University of Chicago Press, 2002.

———. "Is There a History of Sexuality?" *History and Theory* 28.3 (1989) 257–74.

Harper, Kyle. *From Shame to Sin: The Christian Transformation of Sexual Morality in Late Antiquity*. Revealing Antiquity 20. Cambridge: Harvard University Press, 2013.

Harrill, Albert J. *Slaves in the New Testament: Literary, Social, and Moral Dimensions*. Minneapolis: Fortress, 2006.

Harris, Joshua. *I Kissed Dating Goodbye: A New Attitude Towards Romance and Relationships*. Colorado Springs: Multnomah, 1997.

Harrison, Glynn. *A Better Story: God, Sex and Human Flourishing*. London: IVP, 2016.

Harrison, Katherine, and Cassandra A. Ogden, eds. *Pornographies: Critical Positions*. Chester: University of Chester Press, 2018.

Hawkes, Gail. *The Sociology of Sex*. Buckingham: Oxford University Press, 1996.

Hays, Richard B. *The Moral Vision of the New Testament: A Contemporary Introduction to New Testament Ethics*. San Francisco: Harper, 1996.

Heesch, Margriet van. *Ze wisten niet of ik een jongen of een meisje was: kennis, keuze en geslachtsvariaties: Over het leven met en het kennen van intersekse condities in Nederland*. Amsterdam: Amsterdam University Press, 2015.

Herzog, Dagmar. *Sexuality in Europe: A Twentieth-Century History*. Cambridge: Cambridge University Press, 2011.

Heyward, Carter. *Touching Our Strength: The Erotic as Power and Love of God*. San Francisco: Harper & Row, 1989.

Hines, Melissa. *Brain Gender*. Oxford: Oxford University Press, 2004.

Hirsch, Debra. *Redeeming Sex: Naked Conversations about Sexuality and Spirituality*. Downers Grove, IL: IVP, 2015.

Hoff, James. "Why Is There No History of Pornography?" In *For Adult Users Only: The Dilemma of Violent Pornography*, edited by S. Gubar and J. Hoff, 17–46. Bloomington: Indiana University Press, 1989.

Hollinger, Dennis P. *The Meaning of Sex: Christian Ethics and the Moral Life*. Grand Rapids: Baker, 2009.

Horst, Wim ter. *Eerherstel van de liefde*. Kampen: Kok, 1992.

Huber, Lynn R. "Revelation." In *The Oxford Handbook of New Testament, Gender and Sexuality*, edited by Benjamin H. Dunning, 349–69. Oxford: Oxford University Press, 2019.

Huijgen, Arnold. *Maria: Icoon van Genade*. Utrecht: KokBoekencentrum, 2021.

Hunt, Stephen, ed. *Contemporary Christianity and LGBT Sexualities*. Surrey: Ashgate, 2009.

Hunter, David G., ed. *Marriage and Sexuality in Early Christianity*. Minneapolis: Fortress, 2018.

Iantaffi, Alex, and Sara Mize. "Disability." In *The Palgrave Handbook of the Psychology of Sexuality and Gender*, edited by Christina Richards and Meg John Barker, 408–21. New York: Palgrave, 2015.

Isherwood, Lisa. "Sex and Body Politics: Issues for Feminist Theology." In *The Good News of the Body: Sexuality and Feminism*, edited by Lisa Isherwoord, 20–34. Sheffield: Sheffield Academic Press, 2000.

Ivarsson, Fredrik. "Vice Lists and Deviant Masculinity: The Rhetorical Function of 1 Corinthians 5:10–11 and 6:9–10." In *Mapping Gender in Ancient Religious Discourses*, edited by Todd Penner and Caroline Vander Stichele, 163–84. Leiden: Brill, 2007.

Jack, Alison. "Out of the Wilderness: Feminist Perspective on the Book of Revelation." In *Studies in the Book of Revelation*, edited by Steven Moyise, 149–62. New York: T. & T. Clark, 2001.

James, E. L. *Fifty Shades of Grey*. New York: Vintage, 2011.

Jennings, Theodore W. "Same-Sex Relations in the Biblical World." In *The Oxford Handbook of Theology, Sexuality, and Gender*, edited by Adrian Thatcher, 206–21. Oxford: Oxford University Press, 2017.

Jensen, David H. *God, Desire, and a Theology of Human Desire*. Louisville: Westminster, 2013.

Kamitsuka, Margaret D. *The Embrace of Eros: Bodies, Desires, and Sexuality in Christianity*. Minneapolis: Fortress, 2010.

Kaper, Esther. *Hot Issues: Eerlijk over seks*. Vaassen: Medema, 2011.

Karras, Ruth Mazo. *Common Women: Prostitution and Sexuality in Medieval England*. Oxford: Oxford University Press, 1996.

———. *Sexuality in Medieval Europe: Doing Unto Others*. London: Routledge, 2017.

Killermann, Sam. *A Guide to Gender: The Social Justice Advocate's Handbook*. Austin: Impetus, 2017.

King, Helen. *The One-Sex Body on Trial: The Classical and Early Modern Evidence*. London: Routledge, 2013.

King, Karen L. "Jesus." In *The Oxford Handbook of New Testament, Gender and Sexuality*, edited by Benjamin H. Dunning, 407–27. Oxford: Oxford University Press, 2019.

Knijff, Hans W. de. *Venus aan de leiband: Europa's erotische cultuur en christelijke sexuele ethiek*. Kampen: Kok, 1987.

Knust, Jennifer W. "Marriage, Adultery, and Divorce." In *The Oxford Handbook of New Testament, Gender and Sexuality*, edited by Benjamin H. Dunning, 521–38. Oxford: Oxford University Press, 2019.

Kovacs, Judith, and Christopher Rowland. *Revelation: The Apocalypse of Jesus Christ*. Oxford: Blackwell, 2004.

Kuefler, Matthew. *The Manly Eunuch: Masculinity, Gender Ambiguity, and Christian Ideology in Late Antiquity*. Chicago: University of Chicago Press, 2001.

LaCocque, André. *Romance, She Wrote: A Hermeneutical Essay On Song of Songs*. Eugene, OR: Wipf & Stock, 1998.

Ladin, Joy. *The Soul of the Stranger: Reading God and Torah from a Transgender Perspective*. Waltham: Brandeis University Press, 2019.

Lakeland, Paul. "Ecclesiology, Desire, and the Erotic." In *The Embrace of Eros: Bodies, Desires, and Sexuality in Christianity*, edited by Margaret D. Kamitsuka, 247–60. Minneapolis: Fortress, 2010.

Langton, Rae. *Sexual Solipsism: Philosophical Essays on Pornography and Objectification*. Oxford: Oxford University Press, 2009.

Laqueur, Thomas. *Making Sex: Body and Gender from the Greeks to Freud*. Cambridge: Harvard University Press, 1990.

Leene, Almatine. *Triniteit, antropologie en ecclesiologie: Een kritisch onderzoek naar de implicaties van de godsleer voor de positie van mannen en vrouwen in de kerk*. Amsterdam: Buijten & Schipperheijn, 2013.

Lehmiller, Justin J. *The Psychology of Human Sexuality*. Chichester: Wiley, 2014.

———. *The Psychology of Human Sexuality*. 2nd ed. Chichester: Wiley, 2018.

Leman, Kevin. *Tussen de lakens: Seksuele intimiteit in je huwelijk*. Haarlem: Arrowz, 2020.

Levavi-Feinstein, Eve. *Sexual Pollution in the Hebrew Bible*. Oxford: Oxford University Press, 2014.

Levine, Amy-Jill. "The Gospels and Acts." In *The Oxford Handbook of New Testament, Gender and Sexuality*, edited by Benjamin H. Dunning, 295–314. Oxford: Oxford University Press, 2019.

Lewis, Hannah. *Deaf Liberation Theology*. Burlington: Ashgate, 2007.

Liddiard, Kirsty. "Theorising Disabled People's Sexual, Intimate and Erotic Lives: Current Theories for Disability and Sexuality." In *The Routledge Handbook of Disability and Sexuality*, edited by Russell Shuttleworth and Linda R. Mona, 37–52. London: Routledge, 2021.

Lindsey, Linda L. *Gender Roles: A Sociological Perspective*. New York: Routledge, 2016.

Loader, William. *Sexuality in the New Testament: Understanding the Key Texts*. London: SPCK, 2010.

Long-Westfall, Cynthia. *Paul and Gender: Reclaiming the Apostle's Vision for Men and Women in Christ*. Grand Rapids: Baker, 2016.

Macapagal, Kathryn R., and Erick Janssen. "The Valence of Sex: Automatic Affective Associations in Erotophilia and Erotophobia." *Personality and Individual Differences* 51.6 (2011) 699–703.

Martin, Dale B. *The Corinthian Body*. New Haven: Yale University Press, 1995.

———. *Sex and the Single Savior: Gender and Sexuality in Biblical Interpretation*. Louisville: Westminster John Knox, 2006.

Mattebo, Magdalena. *Use of Pornography and Its Associations with Sexual Experiences, Lifestyles and Health among Adolescents*. Uppsala: Uppsala Universitet, 2014.

Maurer, Trent W., and David W. Robinson. "Effects of Attire, Alcohol, and Gender on Perceptions of Date Rape." *Sex Roles: A Journal of Research* 58.5–6 (2008) 423–34.

Mayhem, Robert. *The Female in Aristotle's Biology: Reason or Rationalization*. Chicago: University of Chicago Press, 2004.

McRuer, Robert. *Crip Theory: Cultural Signs of Queerness and Disability*. New York: New York University Press, 2006.

Medrano, Martha, et al. "Childhood Trauma and Adult Prostitution Behavior in a Multiethnic Heterosexual Drug-Using Population." *The American Journal of Drug and Alcohol Abuse* 29.2 (2003) 463–86.

Meeks, Wayne A. "The Image of the Androgyne: Some Uses of a Symbol in Earliest Christianity." *History of Religions* 13 (1974) 165–208.

Messer, Neil. "Contributions from Biology." In *The Oxford Handbook of Theology, Sexuality, and Gender*, edited by Adrian Thatcher, 69–87. Oxford: Oxford University Press, 2017.

Messerschmidt, James W., et al. *Gender Reckonings*. New York: New York University Press, 2018.

Mikkola, Mari, ed. *Beyond Speech: Pornography and Analytic Feminist Philosophy*. Oxford: Oxford University Press, 2017.

Mohler, R. Albert Jr., ed. *God and the Gay Christian? A Response to Matthew Vines*. Louisville: SBTS, 2014.

Moore, Stephen D. *Untold Tales from the Book of Revelation: Sex and Gender, Empire and Ecology*. Atlanta: SBL, 2014.

Myers, Alicia D. *Blessed among Women? Mothers and Motherhood in the New Testament*. Oxford: Oxford University Press, 2017.

Neutel, Karin B. *A Cosmopolitan Ideal: Paul's Declaration "Neither Jew Nor Greek, Neither Slave Nor Free, Nor Male and Female" in the Context of First-Century Thought*. The Library of New Testament Studies 513. London: Bloomsbury, 2015.

Okami, Paul, and Todd K. Schackelford. "Human Sex Differences in Sexual Psychology and Behavior." *Annual Review of Sex Research* 12 (2001) 186–241.

Økland, Jorunn. "Pauline Letters." In *The Oxford Handbook of New Testament, Gender and Sexuality*, edited by Benjamin H. Dunning, 315–32. Oxford: Oxford University Press, 2019.

Oosterhuis, Harry. *Stepchildren of Nature: Krafft-Ebing, Psychiatry, and the Making of Sexual Identity*. Chicago: University of Chicago Press, 2000.

O'Reggio, Trevor. "Martin Luther on Marriage and Family." In *History Research* 2.3 (2012) 195–218.

Osmer, Richard R. *Practical Theology: An Introduction*. Grand Rapids: Eerdmans, 2008.

Padte, Richa Kaul. *Cyber Sexy: Rethinking Pornography*. London: Penguin, 2018.

Pisan, Christine de. *Le Livre de la Cité des dames*. Paris: n.p., 1405.

Pleij, Herman. *Oefeningen in genot: Liefde en lust in de late Middeleeuwen*. Amsterdam: Prometheus, 2020.

Pol-Drent, Fina van de. *Puur! in balans—Je lust en je leven. Samen praten over seksualiteit*. Utrecht: Kok, 2016.

Rambukkana, Nathan. "Open Non-monogamies." In *The Palgrave Handbook of the Psychology of Sexuality and Gender*, edited by Christina Richards and Meg John Barker, 236–52. New York: Palgrave, 2015.

Regnerus, Mark D. *Forbidden Fruit: Sex and Religion in the Lives of American Teenagers*. Oxford: Oxford University Press, 2007.

Rich, Adrienne. "Compulsory Heterosexuality and Lesbian Existence." In *Powers of Desire: The Politics of Sexuality*, edited by Ann Snitow, Christine Stansell, and Sharon Thompson, 177–205. New York: Monthly Review, 1983.

Richards, Christina, and Meg John Barker, eds. *The Palgrave Handbook of the Psychology of Sexuality and Gender*. New York: Palgrave, 2015.

Richardson, Sarah S. *Sex Itself: The Search for Male and Female in the Human Genome*. Chicago: Chicago University Press, 2013.

Riggs, Damien W. "Gay Men." In *The Palgrave Handbook of the Psychology of Sexuality and Gender*, edited by Christina Richards and Meg John Barker, 77–91. New York: Palgrave, 2015.

Rippon, Gina. *The Gendered Brain: The New Neuroscience that Shatters the Myth of the Female Brain*. London: Penguin, 2019.

Romenesko, Kim, and Eleanor M. Miller. "The Second Step in Double Jeopardy: Appropriating the Labor of Female Street Hustlers." In *Crime and Delinquency* 35.1 (1989) 109–35.

Rosen, Robert. *Beaver Street. A History of Modern Pornography*. London: Headpress, 2011.

Rudy, Kathy. *Sex and the Church: Gender, Homosexuality and the Transformation of Christian Ethics*. Boston: Beacon, 1997.

Sands, Kathleen M. *God Forbid: Religion and Sex in American Public Life*. Oxford: Oxford University Press, 2000.

———. "Homosexuality, Religion, and the Law." In *Homosexuality and Religion: An Introduction*, edited by Jeffrey S. Siker, 3–18. London: Greenwood, 2007.

Sauerteig, Lutz D. H., and Roger Davidson, eds. *Shaping Sexual Knowledge: A Cultural History of Sex Education in Twentieth Century Europe*. New York: Routledge, 2009.

Schaik, Carel van, and Kai Michel. *De waarheid over Eva: Hoe de ongelijkheid tussen vrouwen en mannen ontstond*. Amsterdam: Balans, 2020.

Schippers, Mimi. *Beyond Monogamy: Polyamory and the Future of Polyqueer Sexualities*. New York: New York University Press, 2016.

Selvidge, Marla J. "Powerful and Powerless Women in the Apocalypse." *Neotestamentica* 26.1 (1992) 157–67.

Siker, Jeffrey S. *Homosexuality and Religion: An Introduction*. London: Greenwood, 2007.

Sinfield, Alan. *On Sexuality and Power*. New York: Columbia University Press, 2004.

Slavenburg, Jacob. *Vrijen met God: Over "heilige bruiloften," erotiek & religie*. Amsterdam: Amsterdam University Press, 2015.

Smit, Peter-Ben. "Jesus and the Ladies: Constructing and Deconstructing Johannine Macho-Christology." *The Bible and Critical Theory* 2.3 (2006). DOI: 10.2104/bc060031.

———. *Masculinity and the Bible*. Survey, Models, and Perspectives. Brill Research Perspectives in Biblical Interpretation. Leiden: Brill, 2017.

Smith, Clarissa, Feona Attwood, and Brian McNair, eds. *The Routledge Companion to Media, Sex and Sexuality*. London: Routledge, 2018.

Smulders, Beatrijs. *Bloed. Een vrouwengeschiedenis*. Amsterdam: Nijgh & van Ditmar, 2021.

Soh, Debra. *The End of Gender: Debunking The Myths of Sex and Identity in Our Society*. New York: Simon & Schuster, 2020.

Stewart, Anna, and Simon Coleman. "Contributions from Anthropology." In *The Oxford Handbook of Theology, Sexuality, and Gender*, edited by Adrian Thatcher, 105–19. Oxford: Oxford University Press, 2017.

Stone, Ken. "Marriage and Sexual Relations in the World of the Hebrew Bible." In *The Oxford Handbook of Theology, Sexuality, and Gender*, edited by Adrian Thatcher, 173–88. Oxford: Oxford University Press, 2017.

Storr, Merl M. *Bisexuality: A Critical Reader*. London: Routledge, 1999.

Stowers, Stanley K. *A Rereading of Romans: Justice, Jews, and Gentiles*. New Haven: Yale University Press, 1994.

Stuart, Elizabeth. "The Theological Study of Sexuality." In *The Oxford Handbook of Theology, Sexuality, and Gender*, edited by Adrian Thatcher, 18–31. Oxford: Oxford University Press, 2017.

Struckman-Johnson, Cindy, and David Struckman-Johnson. "Sexual Coercion Reported by Women in Three Midwestern Prisons." *Journal of Sex Research* 39.3 (2002) 217–27.

Swancutt, Diana. "The Disease of Effemination: The Charge of Effeminacy and the Verdict of God (Romans 1:18–26)." In *New Testament Masculinities*, edited by Stephen D. Moore and Janice Capel Anderson, 193–234. Atlanta: SBL, 2003.

Swinton, John. *Dementia: Living in the Memories of God*. Grand Rapids: Eerdmans, 2012.

Tanner, Paul. "Song of Songs." *Bibliotheca Sacra* 154 (1997) 23–46.

Tarrant, Shira. *The Pornography Industry: What Everyone Needs to Know*. Oxford: Oxford University Press, 2016.

Tennent, Timothy C. *For the Body: Recovering a Theology of Gender, Sexuality, and the Human Body*. Grand Rapids: Zondervan, 2020.

Thatcher, Adrian. *God, Sex, and Gender: An Introduction*. Malden, MA: Wiley-Blackwell, 2011.

———. *Marriage After Modernity: Christian Marriage in Postmodern Times*. Sheffield: Sheffield University Press, 1999.

———, ed. *The Oxford Handbook of Theology, Sexuality, and Gender*. Oxford: Oxford University Press, 2017.

———. *Redeeming Gender*. Oxford: Oxford University Press, 2016.

———. *Theology and Families*. Malden, MA: Blackwell, 2007.

Tonstad, Linn Marie. *God and Difference: The Trinity, Sexuality, and The Transformation of Finitude*. London: Routledge, 2016.

———. *Queer Theology*. Eugene, OR: Wipf & Stock, 2018.

Toulalan, Sarah, and Kate Fisher, eds. *The Routledge History of Sex and the Body: 1500 to the Present*. London: Routledge, 2013.

Townsley, Gillian. "Gender Trouble in Corinth: Que(e)rying Constructs of Gender in 1 Corinthians 11.2–16." *The Bible and Critical Theory* 2 (2006) 17.1–17.14.

Troost, Ari. *Exegetical Bodybuilding: Gender and Interpretation in Luke 1–2*. Gieten: Zwinderman, 2019.

Trumbach, Randolph. *Sex and the Gender Revolution*. Vol. 1, *Heterosexuality and the Third Gender in Enlightenment London*. Chicago: University of Chicago Press, 1999.

Turley, Emma L., and Trevor Butt. "BDSM—Bondage and Discipline; Dominance and Submission; Sadism and Masochism." In *The Palgrave Handbook of the Psychology of Sexuality and Gender*, edited by Christina Richards and Meg John Barker, 24–41. New York: Palgrave, 2015.

Valenti, Jessica. *The Purity Myth: How America's Obsession with Virginity Is Hurting Young Women*. Berkeley: Seal, 2009.

Vanwesenbeeck, Ine, Floor Bakker, and Susanne Gesell. "Sexual Health in the Netherlands: Main Results of a Population Survey Among Dutch Adults." *International Journal of Sexual Health* 22.2 (2010) 55–71.

Veen, Mirjam van. *Calvijn*. Kampen: Kok, 2006.

Warner, Michael. "Introduction: Fear of a Queer Planet." *Social Text* 29 (1991) 3–17.

Waterfield, Robin, ed. *Plato: Symposium*. Oxford: Oxford University Press, 2008.

Weeks, Jeffrey. *What is Sexual History?* Cambridge: Polity, 2016.

Weitzer, Ronald. "Interpreting the Data: Assessing Competing Claims in Pornography Resarch." In *New Views on Pornography: Sexuality, Politics, and the Law*, edited by Lynn Comella and Shira Tarrant, 257–76. London: Bloomsbury Academic, 2015.

———. *Sex for Sale: Prostitution, Pornography, and the Sex Industry*. New York: Routledge, 2010.

Wijn, Sophie de. *Verkering na je zestigste: Een gebruiksaanwijzing*. Amsterdam: SWP Scrivare, 2007.

Williams, Craig A. *Roman Homosexuality*. Oxford: Oxford University Press, 2010.

Williams, Rowan D. *Being Human: Bodies, Minds, Persons*. London: SPCK, 2018.

———. "The Body's Grace." In *Theology and Sexuality*, edited by Eugene F. Rogers Jr., 309–21. Classic and Contemporary Readings. Oxford: Blackwell, 2002.

Wilson, Gary. *Your Brain on Porn: Internet Pornography and the Emerging Science of Addiction*. Margate: Commonwealth, 2014.

Winkler, John J. *The Constraints of Desire: The Anthropology of Sex and Gender in Ancient Greece*. New York: Routledge, 1990.

Wotton, Rachel. "Paid Sexual Services for People with Disability: Exploring the Range of Modalities Offered throughout the World." In *The Routledge Handbook of Disability and Sexuality*, edited by Russell Shuttleworth and Linda R. Mona, 433–49. London: Routledge. 2021.

Zeichmann, Christopher B. "Rethinking the Gay Centurion: Sexual Exceptionalism, National Exceptionalism in Readings of Matt. 8:5–13/Luke 7:1–10." *The Bible and Critical Theory* 11 (2015) 35–54.

Zorgdrager, Heleen. *Tussen Hooglied en #MeToo: Een publiek-theologische bijdrage aan het debat over seksualiteit*. Dies-rede PThU. Amsterdam: PThU, 2019.

Websites and Other Media

"Artikel 248bis van het Wetboek van Strafrecht." Wikipedia, n.d. https://nl.wikipedia. org/wiki/Artikel_248bis_van_het_Wetboek_van_Strafrecht.

"Beleid voor een veilige en gezonde seksbranche." Rijksoverheid, n.d. https://www. rijksoverheid.nl/onderwerpen/prostitutie/veilige-en-gezonde-prostitutiebranche.

Bosman, Frank. "Waarom doen christenen altijd zo moeilijk over seks?" Universiteit van Nederland, April 11, 2018. https://universiteitvannederland.nl/college/ waarom-doen-christenen-altijd-zo-moeilijk-over-seks.

Borrel, Daan. "Jongeren beginnen later met seks." *NRC Next*, June 20, 2017. https://www.nrc.nl/nieuws/2017/06/19/jongeren-beginnen-later-met-seks-11168453-a1563651.

Brewington, Kelly. "Hopkins Pioneer in Gender Identity: Dr. John Money 1921–2006." *The Baltimore Sun*, July 9, 2006. https://www.baltimoresun.com/2006/07/09/ hopkins-pioneer-in-gender-identity/.

Bureau Beke/Ateno. "Voor de verandering: Een exploratief onderzoek naar pogingen tot het veranderen van de seksuele gerichtheid en genderidentiteit in Nederland." In opdracht van VWS, 2020.

Congregation for Catholic Education. "Male and Female He Created Them: Towards a Path of Dialogue on the Questions of Gender Theory in Education." Vatican, 2019. http://www.educatio.va/content/dam/cec/Documenti/19_0997_INGLESE.pdf.

"David Reimer." Wikipedia, n.d. https://en.wikipedia.org/wiki/David_Reimer.

"Diversity in Human Sexuality: Implications for Policy in Africa." Academy of Science of South Africa, 2014. https://research.assaf.org.za/bitstream/ handle/20.500.11911/38/2015_assaf_diversity_human_sexuality. pdf?sequence=1&isAllowed=y.

Evangelical Lutheran Church in America. "A Statement on Human Sexuality: God and Trust." Minneapolis, 2009. https://www.elca.org/faith/faith-and-society/social-statements/human-sexuality.

Hakkenes, Emiel. "Een vrouw in huis is handig." *Trouw*, February 4, 2009. https://www. trouw.nl/nieuws/een-vrouw-in-huis-is-handig~b8562bc0/.

Intimitijd. https://www.intimitijd.nl/.

Killermann, Sam. "The Genderbread Person." It's Pronounced Metrosexual, n.d. https:// www.itspronouncedmetrosexual.com/2018/10/the-genderbread-person-v4/.

"Kuisheidsbals nieuwe rage in VS." *Het Parool*, March 22, 2007. https://www.parool.nl/ voorpagina/kuisheidsbals-nieuwe-rage-in-vs~bd8562e0/.

Laan, Ellen. "De man heeft altijd zin en andere seksfabels op het hakblok." *NRC*, November 17, 2017. https://www.nrc.nl/nieuws/2017/11/17/benadruk-dat-jongens-en-meisjes-gelijk-zijn-ook-seksueel-14079075-a1582889.

Lorenzen, Emiliann. "A Radical Feminist Review of The End of Gender by Dr. Debra Soh." Women's Liberation Radio News, September 19, 2020. https:// womensliberationradionews.com/2020/09/19/a-radical-feminist-review-of-the-end-of-gender-by-dr-debra-soh/.

Lucas, Nicole. "Zo verschillend zijn mannen en vrouwen niet, betoogt Gina Rippon: 'Gender leren we onszelf aan.'" *Trouw*, March 30, 2019. https://www.trouw.nl/ nieuws/zo-verschillend-zijn-mannen-en-vrouwen-niet-betoogt-gina-rippon-gender-leren-we-onszelf-aan~b5d1d41f/.

"Luther was tot Freud de man met de meest realistische kijk op seks." *Trouw*, February 28, 1996. https://www.trouw.nl/home/luther-was-tot-freud-de-man-met-de-meest-realistische-kijk-op-seks~b3c3acfc/.

"Memorie van Toelichting Wet regulering sekswerk." Rijksoverheid, January 21, 2021. https://www.rijksoverheid.nl/documenten/rapporten/2021/01/21/mvt-mr-wet-regulering-sekswerk.

"My Life Inside the Purity Movement." *Truly*, YouTube, 16:31, October 10, 2018. https://youtu.be/covTn177UVg.

"Nashvilleverklaring: Een gezamenlijke verklaring over Bijbelse seksualiteit." https://nashvilleverklaring.nl/wp-content/uploads/2019/01/Nashville-Verklaring-Nederlands-definitieve-versie-met-naschrift.pdf.

"Paraphilic Disorders." American Psychiatric Association, 2013. https://www.psychiatry.org/File%20Library/Psychiatrists/Practice/DSM/APA_DSM-5-Paraphilic-Disorders.pdf.

"Purity Balls: Lifting the Veil on Special Ceremony." *ABC News*, YouTube, 9:57, March 26, 2014. https://www.youtube.com/watch?v=6CCSeOwiHnI.

Radio EenVandaag. "Feit of fictie: 1 op de 7 mannen betaalt weleens voor seks." *NPO Radio 1*, October 24, 2019. https://www.nporadio1.nl/nieuws/onderzoek/66b5c88d-2105-450f-9f2c-5d15c476aeee/feit-of-fictie-1-op-de-5-mannen-betaalt-weleens-voor-seks.

"Rechten van mensen met een beperking." Rijksoverheid, n.d. https://www.rijksoverheid.nl/onderwerpen/rechten-van-mensen-met-een-handicap.

"Report on LGBT Conversion Therapy Harms." La Trobe University, October 15, 2018. https://www.latrobe.edu.au/news/articles/2018/release/report-on-lgbt-conversion-therapy-harms.

Saarloos, Simone van. "Het monogame drama: Een pleidooi voor multi-intimiteit." *De Correspondent*, November 12, 2015. https://decorrespondent.nl/3612/het-monogame-drama-een-pleidooi-voor-multi-intimiteit/da19298a-503c-023f-2f95-fd2e50279a42.

Scharlaken koord. https://www.scharlakenkoord.nl.

Seumeren, Ineke van. "Maagdelijkheid is niet medisch aantoonbaar." *Trouw*, June 9, 2011. https://www.trouw.nl/nieuws/maagdelijkheid-is-niet-medisch-aantoonbaar~b9261a69/.

"Transgender, geloof en kerk: Praktische gids voor geloofgemeenschappen, pastores en andere naasten van trans*personen." Protestantse Theologische Universiteit, n.d. https://www.pthu.nl/over-pthu/organisatie/medewerkers/h.e.zorgdrager/downloads/brochure-transgender-geloof-en-kerk.pdf.

Universiteit van Nederland. "Waarom doen christenen altijd zo moeilijk over seks?" YouTube, 16:13, April 11, 2018. https://www.youtube.com/watch?v=k2nNCRyHgYY.

Van der Waal, Tineke. "Kinderen krijgen les in nieuwe genderideeën." *Reformatorisch Dagblad*, March 17, 2021. https://www.rd.nl/artikel/919020-kinderen-krijgen-les-in-nieuwe-genderideeen.

"The Virgin Daughters (Celibacy Documentary)." YouTube, 47:43, July 20, 2018. https://youtu.be/HGDoJbbjug4.

Zorgdrager, Heleen. "Terug naar de natuur? Een feministisch theologe op de rand van bekering." Liberaal Christendom (blog), n.d. https://liberaalchristendom.wordpress.com/terug-naar-de-natuur-een-feministisch-theologe-op-de-rand-van-bekering/.

Index